Anthropometric Standardization Reference Manual

Timothy G. Lohman, PhD
University of Arizona

Alex F. Roche, MD
Wright State University

Reynaldo Martorell, PhD
Stanford University

Human Kinetics Books
Champaign, Illinois

103202

Library of Congress Cataloging-in-Publication Data

Anthropometric standardization reference manual.

Includes bibliographies.
1. Anthropometry. I. Lohman, Timothy G., 1940–
II. Roche, Alex F., 1921– . III. Martorell,
Reynaldo, 1947– .
GN51.A58 1988 573'.6 87-8623
ISBN 0-87322-121-4

Senior Editor: Gwen Steigelman, PhD
Production Director: Ernie Noa
Projects Manager: Lezli Harris
Copy Editors: Janet Mullany and Laura E. Larson
Assistant Editors: Julie Anderson and Phaedra Hise
Proofreader: Jane Clapp
Typesetter: Theresa Bear
Text Design: Keith Blomberg
Text Layout: Denise Mueller
Cover Design: Keith Blomberg
Printed By: Braun-Brumfield, Inc.

ISBN: 0-87322-121-4

Copyright © 1988 by Timothy G. Lohman, Alex F. Roche, and
Reynaldo Martorell

All rights reserved. Except for use in a review, the reproduction or utilization of this work
in any form or by any electronic, mechanical, or other means, now known or hereafter
invented, including xerography, photocopying and recording, and in any information
retrieval system, is forbidden without the written permission of the publisher.

Printed in the United States of America

10 9 8 7 6 5 4 3 2 1

Human Kinetics Books
A Division of Human Kinetics Publishers, Inc.
Box 5076, Champaign, IL 61820

1-800-DIAL-HKP
1-800-334-3665 (in Illinois)

Contents

Preface

This reference manual is designed to serve as a comprehensive set of measurement procedures describing over 40 anthropometric dimensions. The purpose of the manual is to provide a standardized set of descriptions that can be used across disciplines, for example, epidemiology, exercise and sport science, human biology, human nutrition, medicine, physical anthropology, and physical education.

The major impetus for developing this manual was the diverse description of measurement procedures in current use and difficulty in comparing results among investigations employing different measurement procedures. Because of the wide use of anthropometry in many fields, it was considered important to develop a consensus among experts from various disciplines on a carefully developed set of procedures for future research and clinical applications of anthropometry. This project was funded by the National Institute of Child Health and Human Development; National Institute of Arthritis, Diabetes, Digestive and Kidney Diseases; National Cancer Institute; and Ross Laboratories, Columbus, Ohio.

With this background a proposal was written to the National Institute of Health by Tim Lohman, who subsequently planned the Conference and all the steps that led to it. Unique in the development of this reference manual is the process applied to each dimension before the final description was accepted. First, an expert was assigned by Tim Lohman to write each report giving the background literature and previous descriptions of the dimension under study. Then the expert formulated a recommended procedure for future measurements. The recommendations were sent to all members of the consensus committee who reviewed each report and rated the extent of their agreement with the proposed recommendation along with sugges-

tions for change. These critiques and ratings were summarized for each investigator and returned to the author for study and revisions. The revised reports were then sent to all participants prior to the Airlie Consensus Conference. The reports were then presented and discussed at the conference and final ratings and critiques were given by each participant. These ratings were again summarized and incorporated into final reports which were sent to Alex Roche who edited them into a common format. Photographs and illustrations were then completed at the University of Arizona and Wright State University under the supervision of Tim Lohman. Special thanks are due to Cheri Carswell and Matt Hall who were subjects for many of the photographic illustrations and for Michael Hewitt's photographic expertise.

This reference manual also includes a section on Special Issues including right vs. left side, measurement error, and equipment availability, and a section on Applications. The papers on applications were reviewed by outside experts and edited under the supervision of Reynaldo Martorell after presentation at the Airlie Conference. These papers show the many applications of anthropometry to research involving children, the elderly, handicapped or obese individuals, clinical nutrition, epidemiology, physical anthropology, sports medicine, and coronary heart disease.

The completion of this manual was dependent on many individuals playing roles in the formulation and development of this project. The editors are extremely grateful for their contributions to this effort. Finally, we all anticipate careful use of the recommended procedures so that the efforts to produce this manual will bear greater knowledge on anthropometry and its application to many fields of study.

Airlie Conference Committee Members

Planning Conference Committee

W. Callaway, MD
G. Harrison, PhD
F. Johnston, PhD
T. Lohman, PhD

R. Martorell, PhD
A. Roche, PhD, MD
J. Wilmore, PhD

Consensus Conference Committee

R. Andres, MD
B. Bistrian, MD
G. Blackburn, PhD,MD
C. Bouchard, PhD
G. Bray, MD
E. Buskirk, PhD
C. Callaway, MD
L. Carter, PhD
C. Chumlea, PhD
W. DeWys, PhD
D. Drinkwater, PhD
P. Eveleth, PhD
R. Frisancho, PhD
C. Gordon, PhD
G. Grave, MD
S. Guo, PhD
G. Harrison, PhD
K. Hendry, PhD
S. Heymsfield, MD
J. Himes, PhD, MPH
V. Hubbard, PhD, MD
A. Jackson, PhD
C. Johnson, MSPH
F. Johnston, PhD

T. Lohman, PhD
R. Malina, PhD
A. Martin, PhD
R. Martorell, PhD
M. Micozzi, MD, PhD
C. Mitchell, PhD, RD
W. Moore, MD
W. Mueller, PhD
R. Murphy, MSPH
G. Owen, MD
M. Pollock, PhD
A. Roche, PhD, MD, DSc
W. Ross, PhD
M. Rowland, PhD
V. Seefeldt, PhD
M. Steinbaugh, PhD, RD
F. Trowbridge, PhD
T. Van Itallie, MD
J. Wilmore, PhD
C. Woteki, PhD

Part I

MEASUREMENT DESCRIPTIONS AND TECHNIQUES

People unfamiliar with anthropometry who wish to measure human beings for research or clinical purposes should begin by reading this manual. The advice of a trained person can be very helpful. The first steps are to select the measurements to be made, to acquire the correct instruments, and to design a recording form. The recording form should be in a format that facilitates entry of the data into a computer. The form should provide for records of the date of birth and the dates of examinations so that ages in years can be calculated to two decimal places; these calculations are best done by a computer.

Practice is necessary. Reliability should be established (as described in chapter 6 by Mueller & Martorell in this manual), and the best order for recording the measurements selected for a particular study should be determined. An assistant is needed to record the values read aloud by the measurer from the scales, stadiometer, caliper, or tape. More sophisticated procedures are possible by which data are automatically entered into a computer from these instruments, but these procedures are not widely used.

The measurements should be made carefully, in a quiet room, without undue haste, and without the presence of unnecessary people. The measurer should note any bruising, swelling, edema, scarring, or muscle atrophy that might affect the measurements being made. The recommendations regarding quality control presented in chapter 11 of this manual should be followed.

Many of the descriptions of the techniques that follow state that the subject's head should be in the Frankfort Horizontal Plane. In this position, the most inferior point on the left orbital margin is at the same horizontal level as the left tragion. Tragion is the deepest point in the notch superior to the tragus of the auricle. When the head is in the Frankfort Horizontal Plane the line of vision ("look straight ahead") is approximately horizontal, and the sagittal plane of the head is vertical.

Full reference citations for Part I are located at the end of chapter 5. However, abbreviated references (author and date) relevant to each topic are provided throughout each of the chapters for the reader's convenience. Also four compendiums, listed among the literature cited, may be useful as source books for other techniques and sets of reference data. These are the publications of Garrett and Kennedy, 1971; *Anthropometric Source Book* (National Aeronautics and Space Administration, 1978); Malina and Roche, 1983; and Roche and Malina 1983.

1

Chapter 1

Stature, Recumbent Length, and Weight

Claire C. Gordon,
William Cameron Chumlea, and
Alex F. Roche

Stature

Recommended Technique

The measurement of stature requires a vertical board with an attached metric rule and a horizontal headboard that can be brought into contact with the most superior point on the head (see Figure 1). The combination of these elements is called a "stadiometer." Fixed and portable models are available, and plans to assist fabrication of a stadi-

ometer by an investigator are available from the Field Services Branch, Division of Nutrition, Centers for Disease Control, Atlanta, Georgia 30333.

The subject is barefoot or wears thin socks and wears little clothing so that the positioning of the body can be seen. The subject stands on a flat surface that is at a right angle to the vertical board of the stadiometer (see Figure 2). The weight of the subject is distributed evenly on both feet, and the head is positioned in the Frankfort Horizontal Plane. The arms hang freely by the sides of the

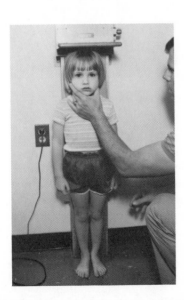

Figure 1 Measurement of stature using stadiometer (front view).

Figure 2 Measurement of stature using stadiometer (side view).

trunk, with the palms facing the thighs. The subject places the heels together, with both heels touching the base of the vertical board. The medial borders of the feet are at an angle of about 60°. If the subject has knock knees, the feet are separated so that the medial borders of the knees are in contact but not overlapping. The scapulae and buttocks are in contact with the vertical board. The heels, buttocks, scapulae, and the posterior aspect of the cranium of some subjects cannot be placed in one vertical plane while maintaining a reasonable natural stance. These subjects are positioned so that only the buttocks and the heels or the cranium are in contact with the vertical board.

The subject is asked to inhale deeply and maintain a fully erect position without altering the load on the heels. The movable headboard is brought onto the most superior point on the head with sufficient pressure to compress the hair. The measurement is recorded to the nearest 0.1 cm, and the time at which the measurement was made is noted.

Recumbent length is measured in place of stature until the age of two years. Between 2 and 3 years, recumbent length or stature can be measured, and the choice made between these variables must be noted because they differ systematically. Two measurers are needed to measure stature in children aged 2 to 3 years. One measurer places a hand on the child's feet to prevent lifting of the heels and to keep the heels against the vertical board and makes sure the knees are extended with the other hand. The second measurer lowers the headboard and observes its level.

When there is lower limb anisomelia (inequality of length), the shorter side is built up with graduated wooden boards until the pelvis is level, as judged from the iliac crests. The amount of the buildup is recorded because it can alter the interpretation of weight-stature relationships.

Purpose

Stature is a major indicator of general body size and of bone length. It is important in screening for disease or malnutrition and in the interpretation of weight. Variations from the normal range can have social consequences, in addition to their associations with disease.

When stature cannot be measured, recumbent length can be substituted and, depending on the purpose of the study, adjustments for the systematic differences between these highly correlated

measurements may be desirable (Roche & Davila, 1974). Arm span may be used in place of stature, when stature cannot be measured and it is not practical to measure recumbent length. The measurement of arm span is described in the section on segment lengths. Also, stature can be estimated from knee height as described in the section on recumbent anthropometry.

Literature

Stature can be measured using a fixed or movable anthropometer. An anthropometer consists of a vertical graduated rod and a movable rod that is brought onto the head. An anthropometer can be attached to a wall or used in a free-standing mode using a base plate to keep the vertical rod properly aligned (see Figures 3, 4, and 5; Hertzberg et al., 1963). Measurements of stature with a movable

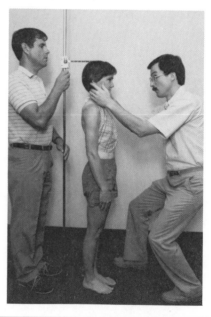

Figure 3 Measurement of stature using moveable anthropometer (side view).

anthropometer tend to be less than those with a stadiometer (Damon, 1964). It is not recommended that stature be measured against a wall, but if this must be done, a wall should be chosen that does not have a baseboard, and the subject should not stand on a carpet. An apparatus that allows stature to be measured while the subject stands on a platform scale is not recommended.

Some workers have not asked subjects to stretch to an unusual extent. This is likely to lead to less reproducible positioning and less reliability than

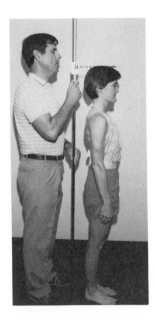

Figure 4 Measurement of stature using moveable anthropometer (side view).

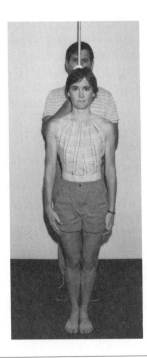

Figure 5 Measurement of stature using moveable anthropometer (front view).

the recommended procedure. Some workers ask the subjects to assume a position of military attention; this is inappropriate for young children and for the elderly. In one alternative technique, a measurer exerts upward force under the mastoid processes to keep the head at the maximum level to which it was raised when the subject inhaled

deeply. A second measurer lowers the headboard and observes its level, while a third person records the value (Weiner & Lourie, 1981). The need for three measurers reduces the practicality of this technique, but when it is applied the diurnal variation in stature is reduced (Whitehouse et al., 1974).

Some workers place the head in a "normal" position, with the eyes looking straight ahead; this is less precise than positioning in the Frankfort Horizontal Plane. Others tilt the head backwards and forwards and record stature when the head is positioned so that the maximum value is obtained. It is difficult to apply the latter procedure while the subject maintains a full inspiration.

It is general practice to place the subject's heels together but the angle between the medial borders has varied from study to study. If these borders are parallel, or nearly so, many young children and some obese adults are unable to stand erect.

Reliability

Intermeasurer differences for large samples in the Fels Longitudinal Study are as follows: $M = 2.4$ mm $(SD = 2.1$ mm$)$ at 5 to 10 years; $M = 2.0$ mm $(SD = 1.9$ mm$)$ at 10 to 15 years; $M = 2.3$ mm $(SD = 2.4$ mm$)$ at 15 to 20 years; $M = 1.4$ mm $(SD = 1.5$ mm$)$ at 20 to 55 years, and $M = 2.1$ mm $(SD = 2.1$ mm$)$ at 54 to 85 years (Chumlea & Roche, 1979).

Sources of Reference Data

Children

Demirjian, 1980
Demirjian et al., 1972
Hamill et al., 1977, 1979
Kondo & Eto, 1975
Wilson, 1979

Adults

Abraham et al., 1979
National Aeronautics and Space Administration, 1978

Recumbent Length

Recommended Technique

Two observers are required to measure recumbent length. The subject lies in a supine position upon a recumbent length table (see Figure 6). The crown of the head touches the stationary, vertical headboard, and the center line of the body coincides with the center line of the measuring table. The

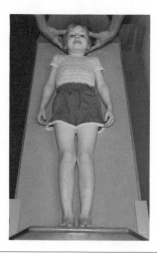

Figure 6   Subject in supine position for recumbent length.

subject's head is held with the Frankfort Plane aligned perpendicular to the plane of the measuring table. The shoulders and buttocks are flat against the tabletop, with the shoulders and hips aligned at right angles to the long axis of the body. The legs are extended at the hips and knees and lie flat against the tabletop, with the arms resting against the sides of the trunk. The measurer positioning the head stands behind the end of the table to ensure that the subject does not change position and to check the alignment of the body with the long axis of the table. The second measurer places one hand on the knees to ensure that the legs remain flat on the table. He or she applies firm pressure with the other hand to shift the movable board against the heels (see Figure 7). The length is recorded to the nearest 0.1 cm.

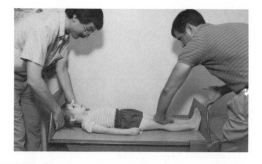

Figure 7   Measurement of recumbent length.

Purpose

Recumbent length is usually measured in those who are unable to stand erect or for whom stature would be spurious. It is an important measure of total skeletal length in infants and small children. Recumbent length is required for comparison with the National Center for Health Statistics reference data from birth to 3 years.

Literature

Recumbent length is measured commonly in infants but not at older ages. As a result, it is frequently omitted from texts on anthropometry (Olivier, 1969). Recumbent length should be measured on a table that has a fixed headboard and a movable footboard that are each perpendicular to the suface of the table. A measuring tape is needed along one or both sides of the table, with the zero end at the junction of the headboard and table surface (Moore & Roche, 1983).

There are only small differences among reported techniques of measurement (Cameron, 1984; Moore & Roche, 1983; Snyder et al., 1975; Snyder et al., 1977; Weiner & Lourie, 1981). For the accurate measurement of recumbent length, the head must be in firm contact with the headboard, the body positioned straight along the table, and the legs extended with the soles vertical. For an uncooperative child or very young infant, it may be necessary to apply gentle restraint to ensure adequate positioning. The more a child or infant deviates from the standard positioning, the poorer the reliability and validity of the measurement.

Reliability

Reliability for recumbent length should be good. Nevertheless, because recumbent length is commonly measured in infants and small children, some of whom are uncooperative, reliability is less than that for stature at older ages. Measurer variability is affected by the amount of pressure applied to the sliding footboard. Pressure should be sufficient to compress the soft tissues of the foot but not enough to alter the length of the vertebral column (Cameron, 1984). In the Fels Longitudinal Study, the mean absolute intermeasurer error for children, birth to 6 years of age, was 0.28 cm (Chumlea & Roche, 1979).

Sources of Reference Data

Children
Roche & Malina, 1983
Snyder et al., 1975, 1977

Adults
Roche & Malina, 1983
Hamill et al., 1977, 1979
Snyder et al., 1977

Weight

Recommended Technique

During infancy, a leveled pan scale with a beam and movable weights is used. The pan must be at least 100 cm long so that it can support a 2-year-old infant at the 95th percentile for recumbent length. A quilt is left on the scale at all times and the scale calibrated to zero and across the range of expected weights, when only a quilt is on it, using test objects of known weights. Calibration is performed monthly and whenever the scales are moved. Similar procedures are used to calibrate the scales used for older individuals. When the scales are not in use, the beam should be locked in place or the weights shifted from zero to reduce wear.

The infant, with or without a diaper, is placed on the scales so that the weight is distributed equally on each side of the center of the pan (see Figure 8). Weight is recorded, to the nearest 10 g,

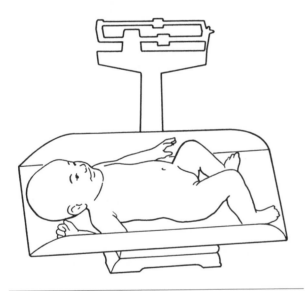

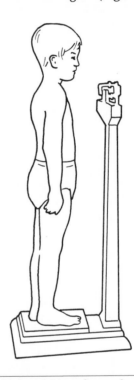

Figure 9 Subject positioned on a leveled platform scale for the measurement of weight.

Figure 8 Infant positioned on a pan scale for the measurement of weight.

with the infant lying quietly, which may require patience. When an infant is restless, it is possible to weigh the mother when holding the infant and then weigh the mother without the infant, but this procedure is unreliable, partly because the mother's weight will be recorded to the nearest 100 g. It is better to postpone the measurement and try later. The measurement is repeated three times and the average recorded after excluding any clearly erroneous value. If a diaper is worn, the weight of the diaper is subtracted from the ob-

served weight because most reference data for infants are based on nude weights.

In a clinic, the measured weight is recorded in tabular form, in addition to being plotted. This plotting is done while the subject is present. Irregularities may be noted in the serial data for a subject or there may be major discrepancies between the percentile levels for highly correlated variables. When this occurs, the measurer checks the accuracy of the plotting and remeasures the subject if the plotting is correct.

A subject able to stand without support is weighed using a leveled platform scale with a beam and moveable weights (Figure 9). The beam

on the scale must be graduated so that it can be read from both sides and the scale positioned so that the measurer can stand behind the beam, facing the subject, and can move the beam weights without reaching around the subject. The movable tare is arranged so that a screwdriver is needed to shift it. The subject stands still over the center of the platform with the body weight evenly distributed between both feet. Light indoor clothing can be worn, excluding shoes, long trousers, and sweater. It is better to standardize the clothing, for example, a disposable paper gown. The weight of this clothing is not subtracted from the observed weight when the recommended reference data are used. Weight is recorded to he nearest 100 g.

Handicapped subjects, other than infants, who cannot stand unsupported can be weighed using a beam chair scale or bed scale. If an adult weighs more than the upper limit on the beam, a weight can be suspended from the left-hand end of the beam after which the measurer must determine how much weight must be placed on the platform for the scale to record zero when there is no weight on the platform. This weight is added to the measured value when a scale modified in this fashion is used. In studies to assess short-term changes, weights must be recorded at times standardized in relation to ingestion, micturition, and defecation; generally this is not necessary.

Purpose

Weight is the most commonly recorded anthropometric variable, and generally it is measured with sufficient accuracy. Accuracy can be improved, however, by attention to details of the measurement technique. Strictly, this measurement is of mass rather than weight, but the latter term is too well established to be replaced easily. Weight is a composite measure of total body size. It is important in screening for unusual growth, obesity, and undernutrition.

Literature

There is general agreement that weight should be measured using a beam scale with movable weights and that a pan scale is needed for measurements made during infancy. The use of a spring scale is not recommended, despite its greater mobility, except in field conditions where there may be no practical alternative. Accurate electronic scales are available that are lighter than beam scales. These are expected to replace beam scales. Automatic scales that print the weight directly onto a permanent record are available but expensive. The scale should be placed with the platform level and in a position where the measurer can see the back of the beam without leaning around the subject. Scales with wheels to facilitate movement from one location to another are not recommended, because they need calibration every time they are moved.

Weight is best measured with the subject nude, which is practical during infancy (Moore & Roche, 1983). At older ages, nude measurements may not be possible (Tuddenham & Snyder, 1954). If not, standardized light clothing, for example, a disposable paper gown, should be worn (Hamill et al., 1970) in preference to "light indoor clothing" (Van Wieringen et al., 1971).

There are diurnal variations in weight of about 1 kg in children and 2 kg in adults. Therefore, recording the time of day at which measurements are made is necessary (Krogman, 1950; Sumner & Whitacre, 1931). Usually it is not practical to measure at a fixed time, but a narrow range may be achievable.

Reliability

Intermeasurer differences in the Fels Longitudinal Study are as follows: $M = 1.2$ g ($SD = 3.2$ g) at 5 to 10 years; $M = 1.5$ g ($SD = 3.6$ g) at 10 to 15 years; 1.7 g ($SD = 3.8$ g) at 15 to 20 years; and $M = 1.5$ g ($SD = 3.6$ g) for adults (Chumlea & Roche, 1979). In the Health Examination Survey by the National Center for Health Statistics, the intermeasurer and intrameasurer technical errors were about 1.2 kg, when pairs of measurements were made 2 weeks apart (Hamill et al., 1973a). About 10% of the observed error would have been due to growth.

Sources of Reference Data

Children
Hamill et al., 1977, 1979

Adults
Abraham et al., 1979

Chapter 2

Segment Lengths

Alan D. Martin,
J.E. Lindsay Carter,
Keith C. Hendy, and
Robert M. Malina

Lengths of Segments

Purpose

Stature is a composite measurement, including the lower extremities, trunk, neck, and head. Thus, stature can be viewed as comprising several segments. The same is true of the total lower and upper extremity lengths, that is, each consists of several segments. In addition to providing information on the differential contribution of specific segments to overall body size and to understanding differential growth and human variation in size and proportions, segment lengths are of clinical and occupational utility. In the former, many syndromes that involve dysmorphology are characterized by disproportionate limb or segment-length growth. As such, specific segment lengths, and more important, the ratios between segment lengths, are of diagnostic utility in studies of dysmorphology (Robinow & Chumlea, 1982; Smith, 1976). In the occupational context—for example, work space and equipment design, clothing and furniture manufacture, and safe toy design—information on specific segment lengths and other anthropometric dimensions are central. Applied anthropometry, also labeled human factors or ergonomics, uses a more comprehensive set of anthropometric dimensions, including both static and functional (dynamic) measurements, that are beyond the scope of this manual (Damon et al., 1966; Garrett & Kennedy, 1971; Hertzberg et al., 1963; Malina et al., 1973; Martin, 1954; Roche & Malina, 1983; Snyder et al., 1977).

This statement considers several aspects of the measurement and application of segment lengths. Details of the techniques of measurement of selected segments are given in subsequent sections.

Segment lengths are most commonly measured between specific bony landmarks and as vertical distances between a flat surface and a bony landmark. They should not be measured from joint creases.

Projected Versus Direct Measurements

Segments can be measured as heights or lengths. The former are vertical distances from the surface upon which the subject stands or sits to the particular landmark. The difference between the heights of two landmarks gives an estimate of a segment length. For example, acromiale height minus radiale height gives an estimate of upper arm length (acromiale is the most superior point on the lateral border of the acromial process; radiale is the most proximal point on the head of the radius); or, standing height minus suprasternale height gives an estimate of the height of the "neck plus head" (suprasternale is the most superior point on the manubrium in the midline). Lengths can be measured in the long axis of the segment as the distances between specific landmarks. As a rule, segment lengths measured directly between landmarks are greater than those derived as the differences between pairs of heights.

Estimates of segment lengths from specific pairs of heights are called *projected measurements*. Height measurements are perpendicular distances between pairs of landmarks, although the specific bone represented by the bony landmarks commonly has a slightly oblique orientation (Wilder, 1920).

Other problems with projected measurements relate to subject positioning and measurement errors. Most subjects have difficulty holding the standard erect posture (see the following section) for the time necessary to take a series of height measurements. This is particularly true in children and the elderly. And because two measurements are involved in deriving any projected segment length, there are two sources of measurement variability.

Subject Positioning

Most segment-length measurements are made with the subject standing in a position called *the standard erect posture,* that is, erect with the heels together and the upper limbs hanging at the sides. There is some variation in head position, some calling for the Frankfort Horizontal Plane (Cameron, 1978; Krogman, 1950), others calling for the head erect, looking straight ahead, so that the visual axis is parallel to the surface of the floor (Hrdlička, 1939; Montagu, 1960), or the head poised so that the visual axis is horizontal. The latter two descriptions essentially approximate the Frankfort Plane. Some describe the standard erect position as the "military position" (Montagu, 1960; Wilder, 1920), which generally implies the position of attention, with the shoulders drawn back, the chest projected forward, and the palms facing anteriorly. Positioning of the upper extremities is important in the measurement of segment lengths. In the standard position, the upper extremities are pendant at the sides, with the palms facing medially.

Some segment lengths are measured with the subject in the seated position, for example, sitting height. The subject sits erect with the head in the Frankfort Horizontal Plane and the thighs horizontal. In most directives, the legs hang freely over the edge of the sitting surface, although some special measuring tables have a built-in adjustable foot rest (see Sitting Height section for specific details).

Issues and Suggestions

Obviously, the measurements selected depend on the purpose of the study; that is, each measurement is designed to provide specific information within the context of the study. Hence, no single battery of segment measurements will meet the needs of every study. Where possible, directly measured segment lengths are preferred over projected lengths.

Although landmarks are specifically defined anatomically, some are difficult to locate. Some of the landmarks are not ossified at young ages; they are present in cartilage but are difficult to palpate. Hence, radiographic methods may be more appropriate to study extremity segment lengths in children younger than 10 years, but there are limitations to radiography that include irradiation, correction for distortion and magnification, consistent positioning, and cost.

Upper Extremity.   Measurement of upper extremity segment lengths should be made directly from landmark to landmark, with the subject in the standard erect position:

- Total length—acromiale to dactylion.
- Upper arm—acromiale to the olecranon.
- Forearm—radiale to stylion.
- Total arm—acromiale to stylion.
- Hand—stylion to dactylion.

Dactylion is the most distal point on the middle finger, excluding the nail; *stylion* is the most distal point on the lateral margin of the styloid process of the radius.

Valk (1971, 1972) has described an apparatus to measure ulnar length, which permits the study of segment growth during intervals of 1 to 3 weeks. This is of clinical relevance in situations where it may be essential to monitor short-term growth, as during hormonal therapy. The forearm and hand are fixed in the apparatus, and the measurement is made from the olecranon to the "dividing line" between the triquetral and the ulnar styloid process.

Lower Extremity.   The measurement of the length of the lower extremity and its specific segments is not as straightforward as for the upper extremity. Thigh length is measured from the inguinal ligament to the patella. Calf length is measured directly from tibiale to sphyrion, with the subject seated and the ankle resting on the opposite knee (Cameron, 1978). (*Tibiale* is the most superior point on the medial border of the medial condyle of the tibia; *sphyrion* is the most inferior point on the medial malleolus.) Foot length is measured directly as the maximum distance from the most posterior point on the heel (*acropodion*) to the tip of the most anteriorly projecting toe (*pternion*; Montagu, 1960; Wilder, 1920). Foot length can be measured with weight bearing (Montagu, 1960; Olivier, 1969;

Wilder, 1920) or without weight bearing (Cameron, 1978).

Stature minus sitting height is often used to provide an estimate of lower extremity *(subischial)* height. Other estimates of lower extremity length are symphysion, iliospinale, and trochanterion heights. *Symphysion* is the most superior point on the pubic arch in the midline, *iliospinale* is the most anterior point on the anterior superior iliac spine, and *trochanterion* is the most superior point on the greater trochanter. These three landmarks are difficult to locate, and none aligns with the head of the femur. The average of symphyseal height and iliospinal height is occasionally used to define inguinale, "which (corroborated by dissection) is at, or a bit above, the top of the femoral head" (Krogman, 1970, p. 9). Thigh length is ordinarily projected as the difference between iliospinale and tibiale heights, although it has been projected as the difference between inguinale and tibiale height (Krogman, 1970).

Valk et al. (1983a, 1983b) have described an apparatus for the measurement of lower leg length, which, as in the case for the apparatus for ulnar length, is designed to permit the study of segment growth during short intervals. Lower leg length is measured as the greatest distance between the measurement surface and the footstool. The measurement requires an adjustable chair that positions the thigh and calf of the subject at an angle less than 90° and permits medio lateral and antero posterior movements of the leg. The former is necessary so that the measurement surface touches the knee instead of the upper leg, whereas the latter permits movement of the leg to obtain the greatest distance.

Sitting height is a composite of trunk, neck, and head heights (see Sitting Height). It is often used as a measure of the length of the upper segment of the body. Specific segments of sitting height can be estimated. *Cervicale height sitting* and *suprasternale height sitting* are occasionally used to estimate trunk length excluding the neck and head, whereas *tragion height sitting* is used to estimate trunk length including the neck (Wilder, 1920). (*Tragion* is the deepest point in the notch just superior to the tragus of the auricle.) Sitting height minus *suprasternale height sitting* is used to estimate the height of the head plus neck (Montagu, 1960). In the standing position, the difference between suprasternale and symphysion heights is occasionally used to project anterior trunk length (Krogman, 1970; Olivier, 1969).

Some literature indicates the clinical utility of up-

per and lower segment heights, in contrast to sitting height (Engelbach, 1932; Smith, 1976). Symphyseal height is the usual clinical measure of lower segment height, whereas stature minus symphyseal height is the usual clinical measure of upper segment height. The two heights are ordinarily used to obtain a ratio.

Difficulties in measuring symphyseal height have been indicated earlier. Engelbach (1932) recommends that both upper and lower segment lengths be measured directly with the subject supine.

Although not a segment length per se, arm span is another composite measurement that includes both upper extremities and the breadth across the shoulders. It may have clinical relevance in cases in which stature or recumbent length cannot be measured (see Arm Span section later in this chapter).

Many segment lengths are used in the form of ratios, the most common being the ratio of sitting height to stature. As with specific segment lengths, the ratio of choice depends on the problem under study.

Sitting Height

Recommended Technique

The measurement of sitting height requires a table, an anthropometer, and a base for the anthropometer. The table should be sufficiently high so that the subject's legs hang freely. The subject sits on the table with the legs hanging unsupported over the edge of the table and with the hands resting on the thighs in a cross-handed position (see Figure 1). The knees are directed straight ahead. The backs of the knees are near the edge of the table but not in contact with it. The subject sits as erect as possible, with the head in the Frankfort Horizontal Plane. In positioning, it is useful to approach the subject from the left side and to apply gentle pressure simultaneously with the right hand over the lumbar area and with the left hand on the superior part of the sternum. This reinforces the erect position. Gentle upward traction on the mastoid processes ensures the fully erect seated posture.

The lower half of the anthropometer is set in its base, and it is positioned vertically in the midline behind the subject so that it nearly touches the sacral and interscapular regions. When almost ready to make the measurement, the measurer ap-

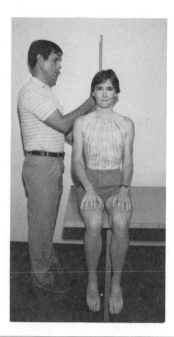

Figure 1   Measurement of sitting height (front view).

proaches from the subject's left side. The measurer's left hand is placed under the subject's chin to assist in holding the proper position, and the right hand moves the blade of the anthropometer onto the vertex (the most superior point on the head in the sagittal plane (see Figure 2). When the subject and measurer are so positioned, the subject is instructed to take a deep breath, and the measurement is made just before the subject

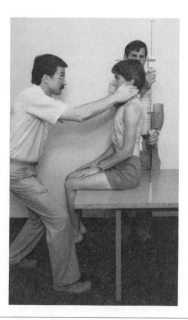

Figure 2   Side view of sitting height measurement illustrating proper positioning of subject.

exhales. Firm pressure is applied to compress the hair. The measurer should observe the level of the anthropometer blade without parallax; hence, a small stool may be required. The measurement is recorded to the nearest 0.1 cm.

It is important that the recorder observe both the position of the subject to avoid slouching and also the position of the anthropometer to ensure that it is vertical and that the blade is brought down in the midline of the head. If too much pressure is applied to the anthropometer blade, it may slide to one side off the vertex. It is important that the subject's arms rest relaxed on the thighs. The subjects should not place their hands on the side of the table and push themselves erect. This procedure may elevate the subjects, ever so slightly, off the table surface.

Purpose

Sitting height is a measure of the distance from the seating surface to the vertex. It is a composite measurement that includes the trunk, neck, and head. When the subject is seated, the body weight is supported by the ischia, therefore, the lower extremities contribute little to the measurement. Thus, ''stature minus sitting height'' provides an estimate of lower extremity or subischial height (see general statement on segment lengths). Sitting height should not be measured with the subject sitting on the floor or other flat surface with the legs extended. Crown-rump length (discussed in more detail in the following section) corresponds to sitting height and is measured in the first 2 to 3 years of life.

The ratio of sitting height to stature (Cormic Index), or crown-rump length to recumbent length in the first 2 to 3 years of life, is highest in infancy and decreases during childhood. Generally the lower value occurs early in pubescence due to the early growth of the lower extremities relative to the trunk. The ratio also shows ethnic/racial variation. It tends to be lowest in black populations, intermediate in white populations, and highest in Asiatic populations.

Literature

Sitting height can be measured with special equipment or with a modification of the procedures used for measuring stature. A special sitting-height measuring table is available (Cameron, 1978) that is equipped with an adjustable footrest so that the subject's legs do not hang unsupported and with a movable back piece that is moved toward the subject's buttocks. The back piece has a movable, horizontal headboard that can be brought in contact with the subject's head. Subject positioning is the same as in the recommended technique, except that the legs are supported by the footrest so that the thighs are horizontal. The use of the special measuring table or the recommended technique gives results that are in close agreement, but the latter is used more commonly.

The technique applied at the Fels Research Institute (Hrdlička, 1939; Roche & Chumlea, personal communication, 1985) uses a rectangular box (50 × 40 × 30 cm) as the sitting surface. The box is placed in front of a stadiometer. Subject position is as described above, except that the legs may or may not hang unsupported depending on the size of the subject. The subject is seated so that the buttocks are in contact with the backboard of the stadiometer. Depending on the size of the subject, the box may have to be rotated so that the subject's buttocks are in contact with the backboard. When the subject is seated properly, the headboard of the stadiometer is brought down onto the head as in the measurement of stature, and the reading is taken. Subsequently, 50 cm (the height of the box or sitting surface) is subtracted from the recorded reading to estimate sitting height. The box should not be so low that the thighs are not horizontal (Hrdlička, 1939).

Sitting height in the supine position has also been reported. A special table is used so that the measurement procedures are identical with those for sitting height in the erect position (Snyder et al., 1977). As expected, the supine measurement is longer than the seated measurement, but it closely approximates crown-rump length.

Reliability

The technical errors of measurement for sitting height in the U.S. Health Examination Survey of youth 12 through 17 years of age were 0.5 (intrameasurer) and 0.7 cm (intermeasurer), whereas the median intra- and intermeasurer differences were 0.4 cm and 0.7 cm, respectively (Malina et al., 1974). Intrameasurer technical errors of measurement for five studies of school-aged children from several ethnic groups at the University of Texas at Austin ranged between 0.1 cm and 0.7 cm, whereas the intermeasurer technical error of measurement in one study was 0.4 cm (Malina, 1986). Larger technical errors of measurement occurred in studies in which the replicate measurements were done about 1 month apart (0.6 and 0.7 cm), the smaller error estimates occurred in studies

in which the replicates were done the same day (0.1 to 0.3 cm).

Sources of Reference Data

Children
Hamill et al., 1973b
Johnson et al., 1981
Kondo & Eto, 1975
Malina et al., 1974
Snyder et al., 1977

Adults
Johnson et al., 1981

Crown-Rump Length

Recommended Technique

Two observers are required to measure crown-rump length. The subject lies in a supine position upon a recumbent-length board. The crown of the head touches the stationary, vertical headboard, with the long axis of the body coinciding with the long axis of the board. The subject's head is held with the Frankfort Plane perpendicular to the plane of the board (see Figure 3). The shoulders

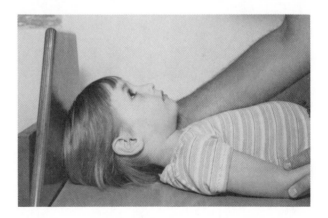

Figure 3 Positioning of head for crown-rump length.

and hips should be flat against the board and aligned at right angles to the long axis of the body (see Figure 4). The observer positioning the head stands behind the end of the board to ensure that the long axis of the subject coincides with the long axis of the board. The second observer raises the legs so that the thighs are at an angle of 90° to the surface of the board and, with the other hand, moves the sliding board against the buttocks with

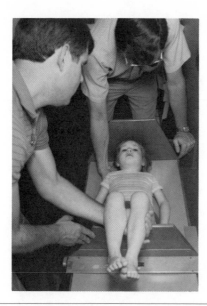

Figure 4 Positioning of truck and legs for crown-rump length.

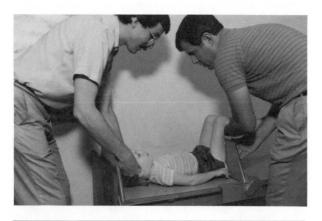

Figure 5 Measurement of crown-rump length.

firm pressure (see Figure 5). The measurement is recorded to the nearest 0.1 cm.

Purpose

Crown-rump length corresponds to sitting height in older children and adults. It is a measure of trunk length. It must be measured in place of sitting height when a measurement of trunk length is required and when the subject is unable to sit with the positioning recommended for sitting height.

Literature

The recommended methodology corresponds to that used in many studies (Cameron, 1984; Moore

& Roche, 1983; Snyder et al., 1975, 1977). The equipment needed is the same as for recumbent length, but during infancy, when the measurement is most common, a recumbent-length board can be used in place of a recumbent-length table.

Reliability

This measurement is slightly more reliable than sitting height at corresponding ages, but the differences are small. In the Fels Longitudinal Study, the mean absolute intermeasurer error for 40 boys and 25 girls, birth to 6 years of age, was 0.18 cm (Chumlea & Roche, 1979). In the Oakland Growth Study, the mean absolute intermeasurer error for stem length in adolescent boys was 1.3 cm (Stolz & Stolz, 1951). Stem length is closely similar to crown-rump length.

Sources of Reference Data

Children
McCammon, 1970
Snyder et al., 1975, 1977

Adults
None reported

Lower Extremity Length (Subischial Height)

Recommended Technique

Lower extremity length is the distance between the hip joint and the floor when the subject stands erect. In the living it can only be approximated because of the difficulty of precisely locating the hip joint. Functionally it is often defined as the difference between stature and sitting height. In those unable to stand or sit in the recommended manner, the difference between recumbent length and crown-rump length is used. These are the recommended measures; the techniques for determining them are described elsewhere.

Purpose

Lower extremity length is useful in studies of proportion, performance, and human engineering.

Literature

Literature is described under the separate measurements (stature, recumbent length, sitting height, crown-rump length).

Differences in landmark location among studies relate mainly to the proximal terminus. The *distal site* is defined as the floor (stature) or the soles of the feet (recumbent length). If sitting height or crown-rump length is used, lower extremity length is the distance between the inferior aspect of the ischial tuberosity and any compressed soft tissues to the distal landmark. Clearly this is an underestimate of the true length and is more correctly called subischial height.

The possible alternatives to sitting height are discussed in the Sitting Height section. Martin and Saller (1959) provide corrections that can be applied to some of these projected heights to estimate the center of the hip joint, but these corrections are sample specific. The landmarks that best approximate the level of the hip joint are symphysion (De Garay et al., 1974), gluteal arch, or trochanteric height (Ross et al., 1978), providing the pelvis is not tilted too far forward or backward, but it is difficult to identify these landmarks in all subjects (see Figure 6).

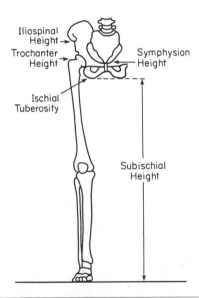

Figure 6 Illustration of subischial height.

The choice of measures depends on the objective. When stature and sitting height have been measured, lower extremity length is not always analyzed as a separate "measure" because it does not provide independent information.

Reliability

This is described in the statements for the separate measures.

Sources of Reference Data

Children

Roche & Malina, 1983
Zavaleta, 1976

Adults

Churchill et al., 1977
Clauser et al., 1972
McConville et al., 1977

Thigh Length

Recommended Technique

Thigh length is defined anatomically as hip-knee length; its measurement in the living is approximate because it is difficult to locate these joints. In the living, its measurement is either "direct" or "projected." Direct thigh length is measured from the midpoint of the inguinal ligament to the proximal edge of the patella (see Figure 7). The location of these points is described in the section on thigh skinfold. A nonstretchable tape measure is used. Projected thigh length is the difference between sitting height and tibial height. To obtain projected thigh length, the recommended technique for measuring sitting height is applied and tibial height is measured also. A table or special chair and an anthropometer are needed. The more desirable measure is direct thigh length.

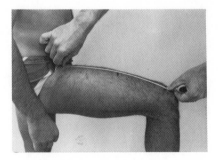

Figure 7 Measurement of direct thigh length.

Purpose

Thigh length is useful in studies of body proportions and in human engineering.

Literature

The literature relating to the proximal landmark is covered under thigh skinfold; the distal point is covered under calf length.

Sitting height is recommended as the proximal reference for the indirect measurement because of its common inclusion in anthropometric surveys (Clauser et al., 1972; Eveleth & Tanner, 1976; Hertzberg et al., 1963). Projected thigh length can be obtained also by subtracting tibiale height from symphysial, crotch, iliospinal, trochanteric, buttock, gluteal furrow, or gluteal arch height. These procedures are not recommened, partly because the set of recorded measurements would be increased. The symphysial and crotch landmarks will not be accepted by many subjects. The iliospinal and gluteal furrow levels do not provide good approximations to the location of the hip joint, and the trochanteric, buttock, and gluteal arch points cannot be located reliably. Buttock-knee or buttock-popliteal length are other indices of thigh length (Clauser et al., 1972; Weiner & Lourie, 1981). Crown-rump length is substituted for sitting height in those unable to sit in the recommended position (Cameron, 1984).

The choice of measures depends, in part, on the objectives. If lower extremity segments are to be summed, it is best to select a thigh-length measure that will not overlap with other segment lengths. This also serves as an error check if the sum of the segments is matched with another measure. For example, stature is equivalent to sitting height plus thigh length plus tibiale height; lower extremity length is equivalent to thigh length plus tibial height.

Reliability

Reliability data for direct thigh length are available for the elderly only (intermeasurer technical error: men 1.24 cm, women 0.88 cm; Chumlea, 1983). The reliability of projected thigh length depends on the reliability of sitting height and of tibial height. The reliability of sitting height is described separately; the reliability of tibial height has not been reported.

Sources of Reference Data

Children
Roche & Malina, 1983

Adults
Clauser et al., 1972
Stoudt et al., 1965

Calf Length

Recommended Technique

Calf length is measured as either (a) the direct length between the knee joint line and the tip of the medial malleolus (see Figure 8) or (b) the projected length, which is the vertical distance from the proximal surface of the tibia to the sole of the foot. An anthropometer is needed to make these measurements.

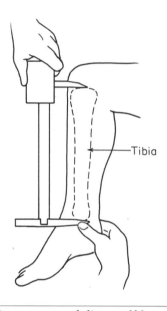

Figure 8 Measurement of direct calf length.

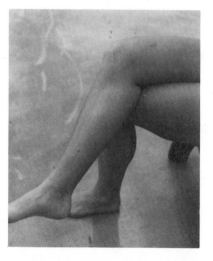

Figure 9 Subject position for direct calf length measurement.

Direct Length.   The subject sits and crosses the leg over the opposite knee (see Figure 9). The measurer marks the proximal end of the medial border of the tibia and the distal tip of the medial malleolus (see Figures 10 and 11). The measurer sits or crouches in front of the subject and applies the blades of the anthropometer, fitted as a sliding caliper, so that one is on each landmark. The shaft of the anthropometer is maintained parallel to the long axis of the tibia (Figure 12).

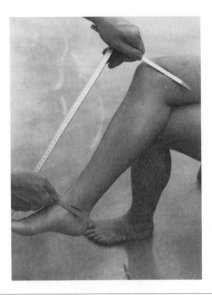

Figure 12   Anthropometer in position for direct calf length measurement.

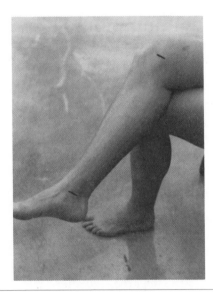

Figure 10   Landmarks for calf length measurement.

Projected length.   To locate the horizontal lateral border of the proximal end of the tibia, the measurer asks the subject to flex the knee. Then he or she finds the depression bounded by the epicondyle of the femur, the anterolateral portion of the proximal end of the tibia, and the head of the fibula. From this depression, the measurer presses medially, locating the border of the tibia, and then palpates posteriorly along the border to locate the most superior point. This point is at least one third of the distance from the anterior to the posterior surface of the knee joint on its lateral aspect (see Figure 13). The site is on the lateral aspect of the knee joint at the level of the superior surface of the

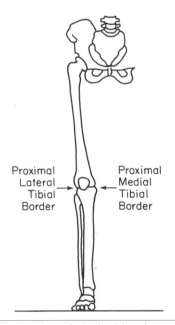

Proximal
Lateral
Tibial
Border

Proximal
Medial
Tibial
Border

Figure 11   Proximal medial tibial border.

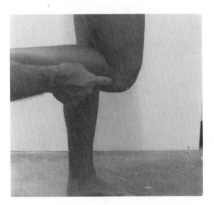

Figure 13   Location of lateral border of the proximal end of tibia for projected calf length measurement.

tibia but is not superficial to the tibia. When the landmark has been identified, the subject stands erect, and a mark is made at the site (see Figure 14). Standing at the side of the subject, the measurer holds the anthropometer shaft vertically, with its base on the floor, and slides the blade down until it touches the marked site (see Figure 15). The caliper is read to the nearest 0.1 cm.

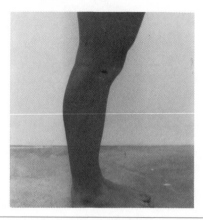

Figure 14 Landmark for lateral border of the proximal end of the tibia is marked.

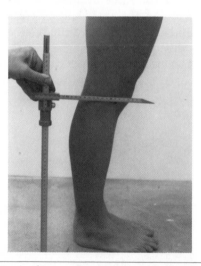

Figure 15 Anthropometer in position for direct calf length measurement.

Purpose

Calf length is one of the lower extremity segment lengths. It is useful in studies of body proportions and of human engineering.

Literature

Projected calf length can best be measured using a Martin (GPM) type anthropometer, preferably equipped with a base plate to help keep it vertical (Carter et al., 1982; Ross & Marfell-Jones, 1983). Direct calf length is measured using a Harpenden or Martin anthropometer assembled as a large sliding caliper (Cameron, 1984). Special calipers may be used (Behnke & Wilmore, 1974; Chumlea, 1985). The recently developed Mediform caliper is slightly more accurate than the Harpenden caliper (Chumlea, 1985).

Projected calf length is usually measured as part of a sequence of measures of bony landmark heights from superior to inferior while the subject holds a static, erect posture (Martin & Saller, 1959; Ross & Marfell-Jones, 1983). In this sequence, the lateral location of the site facilitates the measurement because the anthropometer is to the outside of the subject; otherwise the sagittal outline of some subjects would interfere with the vertical alignment of the instrument. A site on the medial aspect of the knee has been described (Clauser, 1972; Martin & Saller, 1959; Weiner & Lourie, 1981). Hertzberg et al. (1963) commented that they planned to mark the level of the proximal end of the tibia on the medial aspect of the knee, but their subjects were so "sinewy" that this was abandoned as too difficult to locate with certainty. If the tibial plateau is horizontal, there will be no difference between the levels of the medial and lateral sites in this area, but there will be differences in the presence of knock knees or bow legs.

Knee height (Chumlea et al., 1984a; Hertzberg et al., 1963), inferior patellar height, and popliteal height (Clauser et al., 1972; Hertzberg et al., 1963) are examples of measures similar to, but not identical with, calf length. Calf length can be derived also as the difference between tibial height and medial malleolus height. The recommended positioning for the direct measurement of calf length is based on the description by Cameron (1983).

Reliability

In elderly persons, the intermeasurer technical errors were 0.39 cm (men) and 0.68 cm (women) in an unpublished study by Chumlea (1983).

Sources of Reference Data

Children
Ross & Marfell-Jones, 1983
Adults
Clauser et al., 1972

Arm Span

Recommended Technique

The method requires a tape at least 2 m long, a flat surface (usually a wall), and an adjustable block that is fixed to the wall. The spool of the tape is fixed to the adjustable block. The block serves as the contact point for the middle (longest) finger of the right hand, which is in contact with it when the subject is positioned. The block must be movable so that it can be adjusted vertically to accomodate individuals of varying statures. The block is adjusted to bring the tape to the shoulder level for the subject, and then the tape is pulled horizontally along the wall. The subject stands with the feet together and so that his or her back is against the wall. The arms are outstretched laterally and maximally at the level of the shoulders, in contact with the wall, and with the palms facing forwards. The tip of the middle (longest) finger (excluding the fingernail) of the right hand is kept in contact with the block, while the zero end of the tape is set at the tip of the middle (longest) finger (excluding the fingernail) of the left hand (see Figures 16 and 17). Two measurers are necessary, one at the

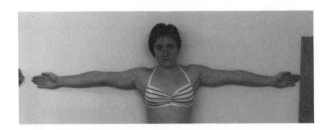

Figure 16 Subject positioning for arm span measurement.

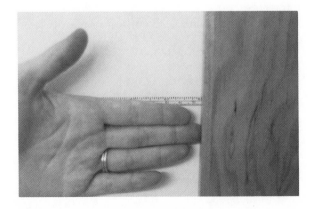

Figure 17 Measurement of arm span showing tip of longest fingers in contact with block.

zero end of the tape and the other at the block end to make the reading. The measurement is recorded to the nearest 0.1 cm. Occasionally a small stool may be required to make this measurement in tall subjects.

When making this measurement, it is imperative that the subject's arms be outstretched maximally and that they are held in this position until the reading is taken. Young children and older individuals tend to lower the arms.

Purpose

Arm span is the distance between the tips of the middle (longest) fingers of each hand (excluding the fingernails) when both arms are extended laterally and maximally to the level of the shoulders. This composite measurement includes both upper extremities and the breadth across the shoulders. Arm span is highly correlated with stature and, thus, may have clinical relevance when stature or recumbent length cannot be measured. Arm span is occasionally used to estimate stature at maturity in the elderly, that is, stature in young adulthood before age-associated stature loss has occurred (Rossman, 1979). In addition, there is considerable kyphosis in some elderly individuals and, as a result, an accurate measure of stature is not possible. Arm span-stature differences may be altered in some clinical syndromes (Engstrom et al., 1981). Hence, arm span in conjunction with stature may be useful in clinical diagnosis.

The relation between arm span and stature varies between American blacks and whites. The differences between means of arm span and stature are larger in black than in white adults (Davenport, 1921; McPherson et al., 1978). Similar differences are evident for projected arm length and stature in American black and white children and youth (Krogman, 1970). This is indirect evidence for corresponding racial differences in the arm span-stature relation during growth.

Data for changes in arm span and for arm span-stature relation during growth are not extensive. Serial data for Australian children of British ancestry indicate greater mean differences between arm span and stature in boys than in girls at all ages between 8 and 15 years (Engstrom et al., 1981). Arm span is, on the average, greater than stature at all ages in boys. In girls, however, stature is slightly greater than arm span before 11.5 years, whereas the reverse is true at older ages (Engstrom et al., 1981).

It is often assumed that arm span and stature are approximately equal in young adulthood. This appears to be so, on the average, in young white women, but not in young black women (Steele & Mattox, unpublished data), and in a small sample of Belgian women in their 30s and 40s (Dequeker et al., 1969). At older ages, arm span is, on the average, greater than recumbent length in white women, and the difference between the two measurements increases progressively with age (Brown & Wigzell, 1964; Dequeker et al., 1969). Among American black men and women, however arm span is, on the average, greater than recumbent length in all age groups between 50 and 90+ years (McPherson et al., 1978). Corresponding data for small samples of American white men and women in the study by McPherson et al. (1978) are not consistent with observations on elderly whites in the same study, or with data for hospital patients (Brown & Wigzell, 1964), and Belgian women (Dequeker et al., 1969).

Literature

The recommended procedure is based on that used by Engstrom et al. (1981). An alternative is to have the zero point of the tape in a corner, where two walls come together. The measurement is then taken from the side wall to the tip of the middle (longest) finger of the other hand after the subject is positioned as described above. An important feature of the arm-span measurement is the need to adjust the height of the tape to the subject's shoulder height. This is especially necessary when measuring children, among whom stature varies considerably. Thus, a vertically adjustable system is essential.

With adults, the range of shoulder heights can be estimated, and a millimeter scale can be affixed to the wall. In a Norwegian study, for example, "A piece of millimeter paper, 40 cm. in breadth, [was] fastened on the wall in such a position that it [formed] a tape measure on the wall with 'zero' in the corner at the cross-wall" (Udjus, 1964, cited in Garrett & Kennedy, 1971). With the subject properly positioned, the reading can be taken directly off the paper. The paper, of course, would be subject to wear and tear, and would probably be influenced by humidity. A plastic cover over properly affixed or laminated millimeter paper would reduce wear-and-tear effects.

Arm span can be measured with the subject supine, and the available data for adults have been collected in this manner (Brown & Wigzell, 1964; Dequeker et al., 1969; McPherson et al., 1978; Steele & Mattox, unpublished data). Each subject was supine on a flat surface with the feet together and the arms extended maximally and horizontally at the level of the shoulders. The measurement was made with a type of anthropometer (the cited studies refer to a "measuring stick" and do not indicate whether the palms faced upward). If arm span is to be measured supine, the fixed end of an anthropometer is placed at the tip of the middle (longest) finger of one hand, while the movable arm is set on the tip of the middle (longest) finger of the other hand, excluding the fingernails. The anthropometer is positioned so that it passes just over the clavicles. Two measurers are necessary to make the reading, one at the fixed end of the anthropometer and the other at the movable end. Measurements of arm span must be made with the subjects supine between birth and 2 or 3 years of age.

Deformity of an extremity or the presence of a contracture limits the validity of the measurement of arm span. Several investigators measure the distance from the "sternal notch" to the tip of the longest finger of the unaffected extremity and double this value to estimate arm span (Brown & Wigzell, 1964; Dequeker et al., 1969; Engelbach, 1932; McPherson et al., 1978). The sternal notch is not defined by these authors, but presumably it is the most superior point on the sternum in the midline (Hrdlička, 1939), or the deepest point in the suprasternal notch (Olivier, 1969). This procedure provides an estimate that does not take individual asymmetry into consideration.

Reliability

In the elderly the intermeasurer technical errors are 0.56 cm for men and 0.38 cm for women (Chumlea, 1983).

Sources of Reference Data

Children
Engstrom et al., 1981
Wolański et al., 1975

Adults
Dequeker et al., 1969
Gleń et al., 1982
McPherson et al., 1978
Wolański et al., 1975

Shoulder-Elbow Length

Recommended Technique

This measurement is made using an anthropometer configured as a sliding-beam caliper. The subject wears clothes that allow the body position to be seen. The shoulders and arms are bare. The subject stands erect on a flat surface with his or her weight distributed evenly on both feet, the head positioned in the Frankfort Plane and the line of sight horizontal.

The shoulders and upper arms are relaxed, with the shoulders drawn back and the upper arms hanging loosely at the subject's sides. Weight is distributed equally between the feet. Both elbows are flexed to place the ulnar surfaces of the forearms and the hands in the horizontal plane and parallel to each other (see Figure 18). The subject breathes normally.

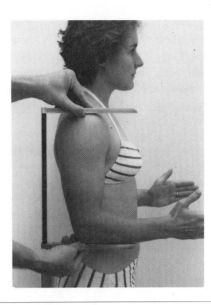

Figure 19 Anthropometer in position for shoulder-elbow length measurement.

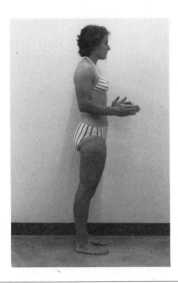

Figure 18 Subject position for shoulder-elbow length measurement.

The beam of the anthropometer is positioned parallel to the posterior aspect of the arm. While maintaining the fixed blade of the anthropometer in firm contact with the superolateral aspect of the acromion, the measurer moves the sliding blade of the anthropometer into firm contact with the posterior surface of the olecranon process of the ulna (see Figure 19). The measurement, which is the distance between the landmarks projected parallel to the longitudinal axis of the upper arm, is recorded to the nearest 0.1 cm

Purpose

Shoulder–elbow length is applied in human engineering studies of workspace design (e.g., location of hand controls), and in biomechanical analyses of human motion (e.g., composition and resolution of forces acting within or on the body, during movement or at rest). It is used also to generate limb-segment models of man. Functionally, the axes of rotation of the shoulder are not located at the junction of the humerus and scapula, but lie within the head of the humerus, and the joint axis shifts as the arm moves in space. In contrast, the axis of rotation of the elbow joint is proximal to its articular surfaces. Therefore, the relationships of surface anthropometric landmarks to the shoulder and elbow joint centers must be predetermined for functional analyses employing this measure.

Literature

Shoulder–elbow length should be measured with a portable anthropometer configured as a sliding-beam caliper, having a metric rule, a fixed blade, and a sliding blade. This instrument allows measurement of the distance from the acromion to the olecranon, with minimal effect of adipose and muscular tissue. Measurements using this equipment have been reported in most anthropometric studies (Garrett & Kennedy, 1971; Hertzberg et al., 1963; Roebuck et al., 1975).

One source (MacDonald et al., 1978) cites the use of two walls, at 90° to each other, to measure upper arm length. Using this technique, the subject stands with the scapulae touching the rear wall. The measured arm is extended so that the forearm is horizontal and parallel to the side wall. The recorded measure spans the horizontal distance from the olecranon process to the rear wall. This measure may be a good functional descriptor of arm length, but it restricts use of the data to human engineering applications such as hand–control placement. The data obtained are not equivalent to those obtained with an anthropometer.

The recommended positioning follows the method favored by most workers (Garrett & Kennedy, 1971). The elderly and the young may require assistance to maintain this position.

There is disparity in the definitions of the acromion landmark. In many instances, it has not been described at all (Garrett & Kennedy, 1971). In other reports, it is referred to as the lateral protrusion of the lateral edge of the acromial spine, the lateral point on the superior surface of the acromion process, the highest point on the lateral edge of the acromial spine, the top of the acromion process, or the outer point of the shoulder (Garrett & Kennedy, 1971; Stewart, 1985). To standardize this landmark, it is recommended that the most lateral point on the superior surface of the acromion process, as determined by palpation, be used.

Measurement of shoulder–elbow length can be made with the subject sitting or standing. However, if other arm measurements are to be made in addition to shoulder–elbow length (e.g., elbow–wrist length, hand length), a standing posture is recommended for all of these related measurements. A vertical mirror, placed directly in front of the subject, aids to establish a horizontal line of sight and can assist the subject's maintenance of a stable upright posture, either standing or sitting.

Reliability

Test-retest data from the 1985 survey of 530 Canadian Forces aircrew resulted in estimates for the intrameasurer and intermeasurer variance of 2.7 and 8.4 mm², respectively (Stewart, 1985).

Sources of Reference Data

Children
Krogman, 1970

Malina et al., 1973
Snyder et al., 1975

Adults
National Aeronautics and Space Administration, 1978
Hertzberg et al., 1963
Stewart, 1985

Elbow-Wrist Length

Recommended Technique

Elbow-wrist length is measured with a sliding caliper. The subject wears clothing that permits body positioning to be observed. The arms and shoulders are bare. The subject, unsupported by a wall or similar structure, stands erect on a flat horizontal surface with heels together, weight equally distributed between both feet, and the shoulders drawn back. The subject breathes normally with the head in the Frankfort Plane.

The subject's arms hang by the sides. The elbows are flexed to 90°, and the palms face medially, with the fingers extended in the direction of the long axes of the forearms. The very young and the elderly may need assistance to maintain this position.

The fixed arm of the caliper is positioned to make firm contact with the most posterior point overlying the olecranon, while the sliding arm of the caliper is aligned with the most distal palpable point of the styloid process of the radius (see Figures 20 and 21). During this measurement, the arms of the sliding caliper are held perpendicular to the long axis of the forearm. The measurement is recorded to the nearest 0.1 cm.

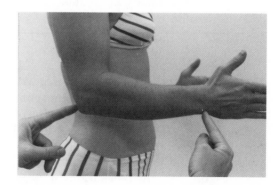

Figure 20 Landmarks for elbow-wrist length measurement.

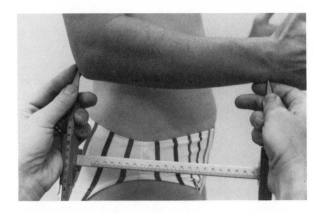

Figure 21 Sliding caliper in position for elbow-wrist length measurement.

Purpose

Limb and limb-segment lengths are important in human biomechanics and in the application of anthropometric data to workspace design, including the construction of anthropometric human-form models. Elbow-wrist length, in conjunction with hand length, is used in human-engineering studies of hand-control location.

Literature

Elbow–wrist length has been measured with the elbow flexed at 90° and the posterior surface of the arm in contact with a plane vertical surface, such as is found in anthropometric measuring rigs based on Morant's apparatus (Bolton et al., 1973; MacDonald et al., 1978; Roebuck et al., 1975). Because the measurement is likely to be affected by local adipose and muscular tissues, this method is not considered equivalent to the recommended technique. Also an instrument that makes a point-to-point measurement, such as a spreading caliper, is not equivalent to a sliding caliper for this measurement.

The recommended positioning follows the method favored by most anthropometrists, as reported in Garrett and Kennedy's collation (1971). However, some anthropometrists have measured forearm length, with the arm and forearm hanging vertically (Garrett & Kennedy, 1971). This is not a functional measurement in engineering anthropometry and has no known advantage for other applications over the recommended technique. Methods that measure from a vertical datum plane in contact with the posterior surface of

the arm, although arguably more "functional," confound long-bone measurement with soft-tissue measurement. This tends to restrict use of the data to situations where the functional aspect of the dimension is of prime importance, for example, in placing hand controls in relation to a seat back.

This measurement can be made with the subject sitting, but if both shoulder-elbow length and elbow-wrist length are to be measured, a standing posture is recommended. A vertical mirror, placed directly in front of the subject, aids in establishing a horizontal line of sight and, in conjunction with other devices (e.g., a movable sight line; Hendy, 1979), can help the subject maintain a stable upright posture.

Reliability

Test-retest data from the 1985 anthropometric survey of Canadian Forces aircrew resulted in estimates for the intrameasurer and intermeasurer variances of 2.9 and 9.8 mm², respectively (Stewart, 1985). In the elderly, the intermeasurer technical errors were 0.34 cm for men and 0.31 cm for women (Chumlea, 1983).

Sources of Reference Data

Children

Martin, 1955

Adults

National Aeronautics and Space Administration, 1978
Stewart, 1985

Hand Length

Recommended Technique

This measurement is made with a small sliding caliper from the styloid process of the radius to the tip of the middle finger. The subject sits or stands with arms hanging relaxed and the forearms extended horizontally. The subject's hand and fingers, palm up, are extended in the direction of the longitudinal axis of the forearm (see Figure 22). In this position the fingers are together and extended but not hyperextended.

With the bar of the sliding caliper held parallel to the longtidunal axis of the hand, the fixed arm of the caliper is aligned with the most distal palpable point of the styloid process of the radius. The sliding arm of the caliper is placed so that it makes light contact with the fleshy tip of the third (middle) digit (see Figure 22). The measurement is recorded to the nearest 0.1 cm.

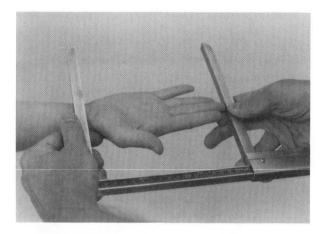

Figure 22 Sliding caliper in place for hand length measurement.

Purpose

Hand length is one of a suite of measurements that can be made on the hand for use in the design of personal clothing items (e.g., gloves) and for workspace layout. In conjunction with forearm-hand length, it may be used to generate a limb-segment anthropometric model of human beings.

Literature

There is a widespread acceptance of the sliding caliper as a measuring device for this dimension. Of the surveys cited in Garrett and Kennedy's collation (1971), in which the measuring instrument for hand length is mentioned, the sliding caliper is universally favored.

The main variation in site location for hand-length measurements concerns the wrist landmark. This has been located at the wrist crease at the base of the hypothenar eminence, the midpoint of a line joining the styloid processes, the midpoint of a line joining the proximal limits of the thenar and hypothenar eminences, and the proximal end of the scaphoid (Garrett & Kennedy, 1971). Garrett (1971) investigated the relation between wrist marks at the distal end of the styloid process of the radius, the proximal edge of the scaphoid, and the major wrist crease. He reported that for 79% of his subjects, the wrist crease lay between the

scaphoid (most proximal) landmark and the styloid (most distal) landmark. Garrett advises the use of wrist-crease landmark because of this central tendency and because of possible difficulties in palpating bony edges in some subjects. However, some patterns of wrist creases make the unequivocal identification of the appropriate landmark extremely difficult. Therefore, despite the difficulty of location by palpation, a skeletal landmark has been selected for the recommended technique rather than a skin crease. The styloid landmark is marginally easier to locate than the scaphoid and is already firmly entrenched as a landmark for elbow-wrist length (Garrett & Kennedy, 1971).

Reliability

Inter- and intrameasurer variability data are not available.

Sources of Reference Data

Children
Pieper & Jürgens, 1977
Simmons, 1944
Snyder et al., 1975

Adults
National Aeronautics and Space Administration, 1978

Forearm-Hand Length

Recommended Technique

This measurement is made with a sliding-beam caliper between the olecranon and the tip of the middle finger. The subject wears clothing that permits the positioning to be observed. The arms and shoulders are bare. The subject, unsupported by a wall or similar structure, stands erect on a flat horizontal surface with heels together (or as close as is possible), weight equally distributed on both feet, shoulders back, breathing normally, and with the head positioned in the Frankfort Horizontal Plane but not rigidly to attention.

The subject's arms are vertical, with the elbows resting lightly against the sides of the body. The elbows are flexed to about 90° so that the forearms and the supinated hands are extended forwards horizontally. The fingers are together and extended in the direction of the longitudinal axes of the forearms (see Figure 23).

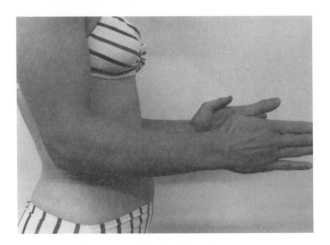

Figure 23 Subject position for forearm-hand length measurement.

The fixed arm of the beam caliper is placed to make firm contact with the most posterior surface overlying the olecranon, while the sliding arm of the caliper is shifted to make contact with the fleshy tip of the third digit (middle finger) of the extended hand (see Figure 24). During this measurement, the arms of the sliding caliper are perpendicular to the longitudinal axis of the forearm. The measurement is recorded to the nearest 0.1 cm.

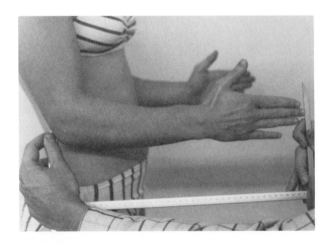

Figure 24 Sliding caliper in place for forearm-hand length measurement.

Purpose

Limb and limb-segment lengths are important to those concerned with human biomechanics and the application of anthropometric data to workspace design and analysis. Forearm-hand length is used in human-engineering studies of hand-control location and, in conjunction with hand length, can generate a limb-segment anthropometric model of human beings.

Literature

Forearm-hand length has been measured with the elbow flexed at 90° and the posterior surface of the arm in contact with a plane vertical surface (Bolton et al., 1973; McDonald et al., 1978), as is found in anthropometric measuring rigs based on Morant's apparatus (Roebuck et al., 1975). Because this measurement is likely to be affected by the amount of local adipose and muscular tissue, this method is not equivalent to the recommended technique. Also an instrument that makes a point-to-point measurement, such as a spreading caliper, is not equivalent to the beam caliper for the measurement of this dimension.

The recommended positioning generally follows that favored by most anthropometrists (Garrett & Kennedy, 1971). However, supination of the hand is a variation intended to avoid complications that may be introduced if the subject has long fingernails. Some anthropometrists have made a forearm-length measurement with the arm and forearm hanging vertically (Garrett & Kennedy, 1971). This is not a functional measurement in engineering anthropometry and has no advantage for other applications over the recommended technique. Methods that measure from a vertical datum plane that is in contact with the posterior surface of the arm, although arguably more "functional," confound long-bone measurement with tissue measurement. This tends to restrict the use of the data to those situations where the functional aspect of the dimension is of prime importance, for example, in placing hand controls in relation to a seat back.

Forearm–hand length can be measured with the subject sitting. However, if both forearm–hand length and shoulder-elbow length are to be measured, a standing posture is recommended for both measurements. A vertical mirror, placed directly in front of the subject, helps establish a horizontal line of sight and, in conjunction with other devices (e.g., a movable sight line; Hendy, 1979), can assist the subject to maintain a stable upright sitting or standing posture.

Reliability

Intrameasurer and intermeasurer variability data are not available.

Sources of Reference Data

Children

Verghese et al., 1969

Adults

National Aeronautics and Space Administration,
  1978
Stewart, 1985

Chapter 3

Body Breadth Equipment and Measurement Techniques

Jack H. Wilmore,

Roberto A. Frisancho,

Claire C. Gordon,

John H. Himes,

Alan D. Martin,

Reynaldo Martorell, and

Vernon D. Seefeldt

Body breadth measurements are used for several research and clinical purposes. Body breadths are used in the determination of body types, for example, the Heath-Carter somatotyping technique (1967); in determining frame size for estimating desirable weight from standard stature-weight charts, and in estimating the potential for lean weight gains in various populations, for example, athletes and anorexics.

Body breadths are typically measured by special calipers that vary according to the body segment being measured. Generally, narrow or broad blade anthropometers are used to measure the breadth of large segments, for example, biacromial or bitrochanteric breadths. Smaller sliding calipers are preferred to measure the breadth of small segments, for example, elbow and wrist, but spreading calipers can be used effectively if care is taken to keep the line between the tips oriented as recommended for the particular measure. Special spreading calipers may be used to measure chest depth, for which the standard anthropometer is awkward.

From a review of the research literature over the past 20 years, the Siber-Hegner (#101) anthropometer appears to be the instrument used most fre-quently. This Martin-type anthropometer consists of a rod comprised of four sections and two blades. One blade is fixed, and the other moves along the rod, which is calibrated in centimeters and millimeters. For most breadths, a single section, as opposed to all four sections, can be used. The minimum measurement obtainable is 0.4 cm, the maximum is 210 cm, with an accuracy of 0.5 cm (Chumlea, 1985). The Holtain anthropometer has a minimum measurement of 5 cm and a maximum measurement of 57 cm, with an accuracy of 0.1 cm (Chumlea, 1985). The Mediform anthropometer has a minimum measurement of 0 cm, a maximum measurement of 80 cm, and an accuracy of 0.05 cm (Chumlea, 1985).

The small sliding caliper (Siber-Hegner #104 or the Fisher precision caliper) consists of a flat metal bar upon which a slide moves. It is calibrated in centimeters and millimeters, and one blade is fixed while the other moves. Spreading calipers (Siber-Hegner #106) are configured to allow measurements between landmarks that would be difficult with standard anthropometers. Figure 1 illustrates a standard anthropometer, Figure 2 shows a small sliding caliper, and Figure 3 displays a spreading caliper. All calipers should be maintained careful-

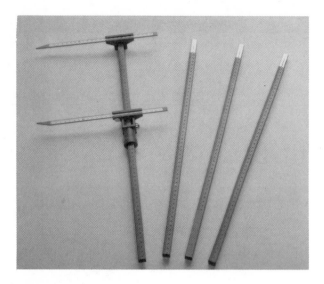

Figure 1   A standard anthropometer with extension rods.

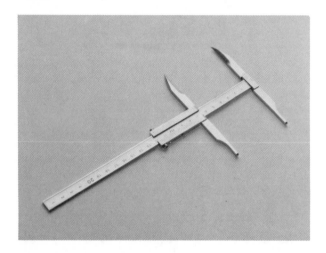

Figure 2   A small sliding caliper.

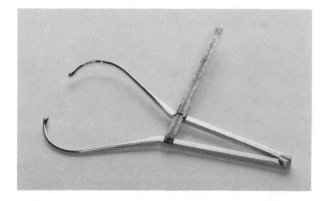

Figure 3   A spreading caliper.

ly to assure smooth sliding of the caliper arms, and their calibration should be checked regularly. Calibration is particularly important with spreading calipers, which are made of soft metal that is easily distorted.

Body breadth sites are typically defined by bony landmarks. It is important to select landmarks that are palpable not only in lean but also in obese individuals. The anthropometer or caliper is held so that the tips of the index fingers are adjacent to the tips of the projections of the anthropometer/caliper. The landmarks are first identified by the tips of the index fingers and then the projections of the anthropometer/caliper are positioned at those points. Sufficient pressure should be applied to assure that the blades of the anthropometer/caliper are measuring bony breadths and that the underlying muscle, fat, and skin make minimal contributions to the obtained dimensions. For most sites, firm pressure to the point where the measurement is stable (that is, it does not continue to decrease as pressure is applied) is mandatory. A minimum of three measurements should be obtained for each site, but the second and third measurements should be obtained sequentially, not consecutively, to avoid experimenter bias.

Biacromial Breadth

Recommended Technique

Biacromial breadth is measured from the rear of the subject, because this allows the measurer to locate the acromial processes with ease. The subject stands, because sitting interferes with the posture required for measurement. The heels of the subject are together as in the measurement of stature, and the arms hang by the sides. The shoulder region should be free of clothes. The position of the shoulders is of great importance. The objective is to have the subject relaxed with the shoulders downward and slightly forward so that the reading is maximal. For tall subjects, a measurer should use a stool to allow accurate reading of the anthropometer.

Standing directly behind the subject, the measurer runs his or her hands from the base of the neck outwards to the tips of the shoulders, relaxing any tension. The most lateral borders of the acromial processes (see Figure 4) are palpated and, holding the anthropometer so that its blades are between the index and middle fingers and resting on the base of the thumb, the blades are applied firmly to the most lateral borders of the acromial

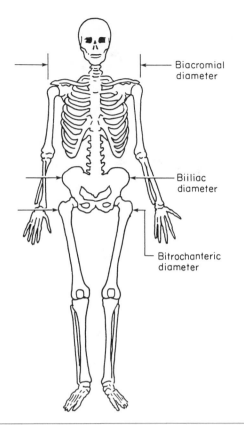

Figure 4 Illustration of locations of biacromial, biiliac and bitrochanteric diameters.

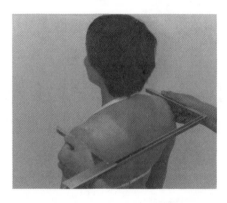

Figure 5 Anthropometer in place for biacromial breadth measurement.

processes (see Figure 5). The width is read to the nearest 0.1 cm.

Purpose

Biacromial breadth is often measured as an index of body frame. It is also useful in somatotyping and in the evaluation of sex-associated differences in physique. This measurement is relevant to the design of clothing and work spaces.

Literature

Although the lateral projections of the acromial processes are easily palpable, the measurement has large errors if the shoulders are not positioned properly. If the shoulders are braced back, the measurement is reduced by 2 to 3 cm (Cameron, 1978; Harrison et al., 1964). Faulhaber (1970), noted large interobserver error variances due to marked differences in "the observers' ability to get the subjects to square their shoulders."

There is agreement that biacromial breadth should be measured from the rear (Cameron, 1978; Tuddenham & Snyder, 1954; Weiner & Lourie, 1981), but Behnke and Wilmore (1974) include a photograph showing the measurement being taken from the front. Cameron (1978) states that the measurer should sit or stand directly behind the subject.

An aspect of considerable importance is the amount of pressure applied in making the measurement. The recommendation of Behnke and Wilmore (1974), Cameron (1978), Weiner and Lourie (1981), and Ross and Marfell-Jones (1983) is to apply firm pressure so as to compress the soft tissues.

Reliability

The intrameasurer and intermeasurer technical errors for biacromial diameter in children are about 0.1 to 0.7 cm (Buschang, 1980; Malina, 1968; Meleski, 1980; Zavaleta, 1976).

In college-aged males the test-retest correlation for measurements made the same day was 0.92 (Wilmore & Behnke, 1969). In adults measured 5 years apart, the test-restest correlation for biacromial breadth was 0.83 (Friedlander et al., 1977). Chumlea et al. (1984b) reported a technical error of measurement of 0.48 cm for male senior citizens, 1.15 cm for female senior citizens, and 0.29 cm for younger adult subjects. The population standard deviation is about 2.2 cm (Friedlander et al., 1977); hence, the ratio of the technical error variance to the population variance, an indicator of the relative magnitude of the error variance (Martorell et al., 1975), is low for male senior citizens and for adult subjects (0.05 and 0.02 respectively) but high for female senior citizens (0.27). Other than for the anomalously high error variances for the subsample of female senior citizens, the measurement of biacromial width appears to have high reliability.

Sources of Reference Data

Children

McCammon, 1970
Roche & Malina, 1983
Snyder et al., 1975

Adults

Clauser et al., 1972
Stoudt et al., 1970

Chest Breadth and Depth

Recommended Techniques

Chest Breadth. The measurement of chest breadth requires a large spreading caliper. The subject stands erect, with the feet at shoulder width and the arms slightly abducted to allow easy access to the measurement site. The measurer stands directly in front of the subject (see Figure 6). The measurement is made with the tips of the caliper on the sixth ribs, in the midaxillary line.

Upon palpation of each sixth rib, the measurer places the caliper tips directly on the ribs, with his or her fingers just beneath the caliper tips to prevent them from slipping into intercostal spaces. Very light pressure is applied. The sixth ribs in the

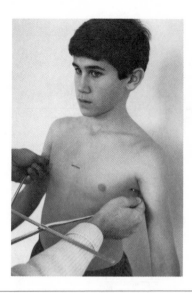

Figure 7   Location of chest breadth landmarks at level of the sixth rib.

midaxillary line correspond, anteriorly, to the fourth costo-sternal joints (see Figure 7). Location of the fourth costo-sternal joints is described in the section on chest circumference. A line is then drawn on the sternum between these junctions.

Chest breadth is measured with the caliper tips in a horizontal plane, at the end of a normal expiration to the nearest 0.1 cm.

Chest Depth. The measurement of chest depth requires a large spreading caliper. The measurement is made with the subject in a natural standing position, arms at the sides. The measurer locates the fourth costo-sternal joints by using the two-handed palpation method described in the section on chest circumference. A line is then drawn horizontally on the sternum between these junctions (see Figure 8).

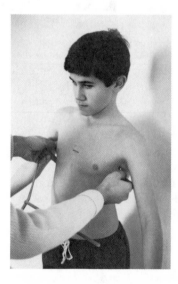

Figure 6   Subject position for measurement of chest breadth.

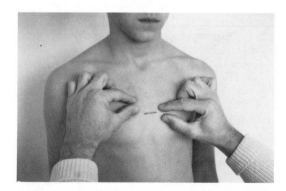

Figure 8   Line drawn on sternum at level of fourth costo-sternal joints.

The measurer stands at the right side of the subject. One tip of the caliper is placed on the sternum in the midline at the level of the fourth costo-sternal junctions. The other tip is placed on the spinous process of the vertebra that is in the same horizontal plane. The measurement is made at the end of the normal expiration to the nearest 0.1 cm (see Figure 9).

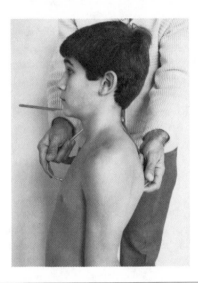

Figure 9 Spreading caliper in place for chest depth measurement.

Purpose

Chest breadth and chest depth are used as indices of growth in children and adolescents, as measures of body size in human engineering to determine appropriate sizes of workspaces, clothing and implements, and as measures of functional capacity in physical performance and in screening tests for respiratory function.

Literature

Many investigators use the anthropometer as a sliding caliper for both breadth and depth measures (Behnke & Wilmore, 1974; De Garay et al., 1974; Malina et al., 1973). Nevertheless, Bailey (1967) and Ross and Marfell-Jones (1982) used a spreading caliper for depth, whereas Montagu (1960) recommended a spreading caliper for both measures.

The techniques used in measuring chest breadth have varied considerably. Orientation of the anthropometer has usually been horizontal for both breadth and depth measures, but some have an-

gled the caliper arms postero-inferiorly for chest breadth, presumably to avoid unusually large latissimus dorsi muscles (Garrett & Kennedy, 1971). It is assumed, and sometimes explicitly stated (Weiner & Lourie, 1981), that the arms of the anthropometer or caliper should rest over the rib surfaces, not the intercostal spaces.

Another source of variation is the pressure with which the anthropometer is applied. Many prefer light contact without soft tissue compression (Olivier, 1969; Weiner & Lourie, 1981). The alternative approach, firm rib contact with soft tissue compression, is frequently termed *chest breadth/depth—bone* (Garrett & Kennedy, 1971).

Chest breadth and depth are most frequently measured at the level of the nipple, with the inferior angles of the scapulae used as posterior landmarks (Garrett & Kennedy, 1971). Variation in the location of the nipples in women, relative to skeletal landmarks, renders this location unreliable. Instead, the superior border of the fourth chondro-sternal joint is frequently substituted for the nipple landmark in women, or in both genders (Comas, 1960; Hertzberg, 1968; Hrdlička, 1920; Olivier, 1969; Weiner & Lourie, 1981). Other observers have measured the chest at the xiphoid level, high in the axilla, or where a maximum reading was obtained (Frisancho & Baker, 1970; Garrett & Kennedy, 1971; Montagu, 1960; Olivier, 1969).

Intraindividual variation in chest size during inspiration and expiration further complicates the measuring techniques used for chest breath or depth. Some measure at maximum expiration and maximum inspiration and calculate a mean of the two values (Frisancho, 1976; Montagu, 1960). Others measure only once at either maximum expiration (Olivier, 1969; Weiner & Lourie, 1981) or maximum inspiration (Laubach et al., 1977).

Reliability

Cameron (1978) placed the measurement of chest depth in the category of "medium consistency," with a coefficient of variation of 1.9%.

Sources of Reference Data

Children

Malina et al., 1973
Morris et al., 1980
Snyder et al., 1975

Adults

Borkan et al., 1981

Biiliac Breadth

Recommended Technique

Synonyms for this measure are *bicristal* or *biilocristal breadth, transverse pelvic breadth,* and *pelvic breadth*. An anthropometer with straight blades is needed to make the measurement. The measurement is made from the rear; this allows easy palpation of landmarks. The subject stands with the feet about 5 cm apart to prevent swaying. The arms need to be away from the area of measurement, preferably folded across the chest (see Figure 10). The anthropometer blades are brought into contact with the iliac crests so that the maximum breadth is recorded. The anthropometer is applied at a downward angle of 45° with firm pressure. The measurement is recorded to the nearest 0.1 cm (Figure 10). During infancy, this measurement must be made with the subject supine.

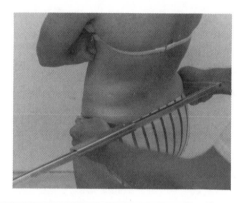

Figure 10   Anthropometer in place for biiliac breadth measurement.

Purpose

Biiliac breadth is frequently included as an index of frame size, and it is a widely used measure of pelvic size.

Literature

It is generally recommended that the subject stand with heels together and with arms folded or abducted (Cameron, 1978). Children too young to stand in the recommended position are measured when supine.

There is considerable difference of opinion in the literature regarding the amount of pressure to be exerted with the blades of the anthropometer on the landmarks (Cameron, 1978). Most authors state that the measurement of the biiliac width requires the application of more pressure than does biacromial width because of the greater deposition of fat over the pelvic area, particularly in females (Behnke & Wilmore, 1974; Cameron, 1978; Harrison et al., 1964; Weiner & Lourie, 1981). The measurement is difficult in obese subjects. Olivier (1969) states that very light pressure should be applied so that there is no compression, but this is inappropriate for a skeletal dimension.

The caliper is best applied at a downward angle of 45° to separate and compress the tissues (Cameron, 1978; Ross & Marfell-Jones, 1983; Weiner & Lourie, 1981). Most prefer the measurement to be made from the rear (Cameron, 1978; Weiner & Lourie, 1981), but Ross and Marfell-Jones (1983) measure from the front, which they consider preferable, particularly in the obese.

Reliability

In children, the intrameasurer and intermeasurer technical errors vary from 0.1 to 0.6 cm. (Buschang, 1980; Malina, 1968; Meleski, 1980; Zavaleta, 1976). In adults measured 5 years apart, the test-retest correlation was .85 for biiliac breadth (Friedlander et al., 1977). A test-retest correlation of .97 was reported by Wilmore and Behnke (1969) for measurements made the same day in college age males. Chumlea et al. (1984b) reported a technical error of measurement of 0.39 cm for male senior citizens, 0.29 cm for female senior citizens, and 0.38 cm for adult subjects. The population standard deviation is 1.6 to 1.7 cm (Friedlander et al., 1977). Hence, the ratio of the technical error variance to the population variance, an indicator of the relative magnitude of the error variance (Martorell et al., 1975), is low. It appears that biiliac breadth has a high level of reproducibility when measured carefully.

Meredith and Spurgeon (1980) specify a "pre-set limit" of 0.3 cm between two measures by different observers. If the difference exceeds this limit, more measurements are made. Chumlea et al. (1984b) have used a more liberal limit of 1.0 cm.

Sources of Reference Data

Children

Demirjian & Jeniček, 1972
Roche & Malina, 1983
Simmons, 1944

Adults

National Aeronautics and Space Administration, 1978

Snow et al., 1975

Bitrochanteric Breadth

Recommended Technique

Bitrochanteric breadth is the distance between the most lateral projections of the greater trochanters (see Figure 11). An anthropometer with straight blades is used. The subject stands with the heels together and the arms folded over the chest; the measurer stands behind the subject. The maximum distance between the trochanters is measured (see Figure 11). If an index of frame size is required, considerable pressure must be applied with the anthropometer blades to compress the soft tissues. If the measurement is required to design seating, the subject sits, and gentle pressure is applied. The distance is recorded to the nearest 0.1 cm.

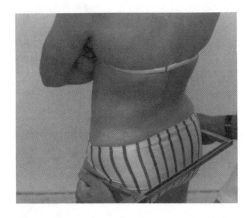

Figure 11 Anthropometer in place for bitrochanteric breadth measurement.

Purpose

The measurent of bitrochanteric breadth is less common than the measurement of biiliac or biacromial breadth as an index of frame size and of fat-free mass. The anthropometric battery proposed by the International Biological Program did not include bitrochanteric breadth (Weiner & Lourie, 1981). If the intent is to obtain a skeletal dimension, as in a study of frame size, firm pressure needs to be exerted. For the design of seating, the objective is to measure the maximum dimension, including soft tissues. The latter requires that the subject be sitting and that the blades of the anthropometer be applied with minimal pressure.

Literature

Some measure this dimension from the front; others from the back. The only other difference noted in the literature concerns the pressure to be exerted.

Reliability

In children, the intrameasurer and intermeasurer technical errors are 0.1 to 0.3 cm. (Buschang, 1980; Malina, 1968; Meleski, 1980). The test-retest correlation between paired measurements on the same day was .97 for college-aged males (Wilmore & Behnke, 1969). Behnke and Wilmore (1974) state that biacromial, biiliac, and bitrochanteric breadths can be measured with a high degree of reliability because the measurements approximate a bone-to-bone contact, if the soft tissues are compressed. This reduces the variability of repeated measurements and increases accuracy. Less accuracy would be expected in obese subjects and when minimal pressure is applied.

Sources of Reference Data

Children

Roche & Malina, 1983

Adults

National Aeronautics and Space Administration, 1978

Knee Breadth

Recommended Technique

This measurement is defined as the distance between the most medial and most lateral aspects of the femoral condyles (see Figure 12). These points are known as the medial and lateral epicondyles. The leg is flexed 90° at the knee with the subject sitting (see Figure 13). Alternatively, with the subject standing, the leg is flexed 90° at the hip and 90° at the knee, with the foot resting on a suitable raised surface (see Figure 12). The measurer stands facing the subject.

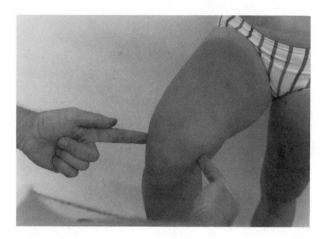

Figure 12 Location of lateral aspects of femoral condyles.

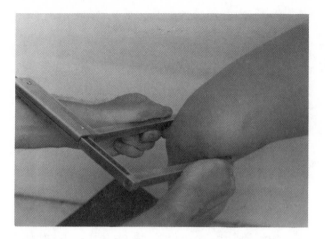

Figure 14 Caliper in place for knee breadth measurement.

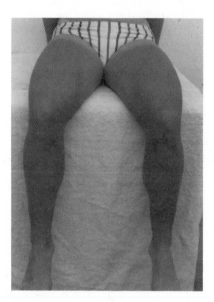

Figure 13 Subject positioning (sitting) for knee breadth measurement.

Using either a sliding or a spreading caliper, the measurer guides the caliper blades or tips with the thumb and index finger of each hand, applying the caliper diagonally downward and towards the subject. The most lateral aspect of the lateral femoral epicondyle is palpated with the index or middle finger of the left hand while the corresponding fingers of the right hand palpate the most medial aspect of the medial epicondyle. The caliper blades or tips are then placed on these points, firm pressure is applied, and the breadth is recorded to the nearest 0.1 cm (see Figure 14). This measurement is not necessarily made in a horizontal plane.

Purpose

Knee breadth is commonly used as an indicator of frame size or skeletal mass (Matiegka, 1921; von Döbeln, 1964). Knee breadth is less useful than elbow or wrist breadth in the prediction of skeletal mass probably because of a greater amount of intervening soft tissue at this site (Martin, 1984). Also, it is included in somatotyping based on anthropometry, specifically for the musculoskeletal, or mesomorphic, component (Heath & Carter, 1967; Parnell, 1954).

Literature

The literature shows general agreement regarding the technique to be used. Flexing the leg at the knee minimizes the intrusion of soft tissues into the measurement.

Reliability

The intra- and intermeasurer technical errors in children are 0.1 to 0.2 cm (Buschang, 1980; Malina, 1968; Meleski, 1980; Zavaleta, 1976). Intraobserver reliability on a small sample ($n = 21$) was very high ($r = .99$; Martin, 1986). Wilmore and Behnke (1969) reported a test-retest correlation of .97 for measurements made the same day in college-aged males.

Sources of Reference Data

Children
Roche & Malina, 1983
Zavaleta, 1976

Adults

National Aeronautics and Space Administration, 1978

Clauser et al., 1972

Ankle (Bimalleolar) Breadth

Recommended Technique

The measurement of ankle breadth requires a sliding caliper or a spreading caliper. The barefoot subject stands on a flat surface, with the feet separated about 6 cm and weight evenly distributed on both feet. The subject should stand on an elevated surface to facilitate making the measurement and reading the caliper scale accurately (see Figure 15). The measurer stands behind the subject. Ankle (bi-

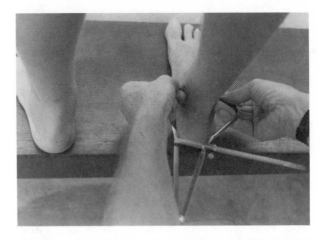

Figure 16 Spreading caliper in place for ankle breadth measurement.

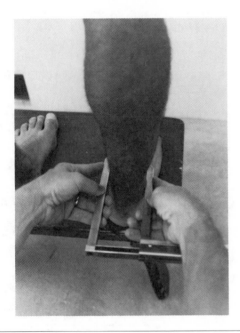

Figure 15 Sliding caliper in place for ankle breadth measurement.

malleolar) breadth should be measured from the posterior aspect of the ankle if there is sufficient "space" for the caliper. When the space is insufficient, the measurement can be made from the anterior aspect. The measurement recorded is the maximum distance between the most medial extension of the medial malleolus and the most lateral extension of the lateral malleolus in the same horizontal plane (see Figure 16). A horizontal distance is measured, but the plane between the most medial and most lateral points in this area is ob-

lique, because the lateral malleolus is posteroinferior to the medial malleolus.

Ankle (bimalleolar) breadth is measured with the bar of a sliding caliper perpendicular to the long axis of the foot and near the standing surface, and with the caliper blades slanting upward at an angle of 45° to meet both malleoli at the appropriate measurement points (see Figure 15). If a spreading caliper is used, the line between the tips must be perpendicular to the long axis of the foot (see Figure 16). Sufficient pressure must be applied to compress the tissues overlying the malleoli because the measurement is considered a "skeletal" one. Ankle (bimalleolar) breadth is recorded to the nearest 0.1 cm.

When measuring infants and other subjects unable to stand in the appropriate position, the subject should be supine with knees flexed and the soles of the feet flat on the supporting surface.

Purpose

Ankle (bimalleolar) breadth has been proposed as a measure of frame size. It is a weight-bearing joint diameter and is important for interpreting weight-stature relationships because it is correlated with fat-free mass but not with body fat (Himes & Bouchard, 1985).

Literature

Ankle (bimalleolar) breadth can be measured using a sliding caliper or an anthropometer. Spreading calipers are not recommended because they are difficult to position on the malleoli.

Some early workers recommended that the subject stand erect, with heels together. This positioning makes it difficult to measure the dimension. Others have measured ankle (bimalleolar) breadth with the subject sitting on a table (Weiner & Lourie, 1981). Ankle breadth has been reported as the minimum breadth proximal to the malleoli, but this dimension has considerable independence from that measured by the recommended procedure.

Reliability

The intrameasurer technical error for ankle (bimalleolar) breadth in Cycle III of the U.S. Health Examination Survey was 0.92 mm, with a mean difference between replicates of 0.97 mm; corresponding values for the intermeasurer errors were 1.71 mm and 1.86 mm, respectively (Malina et al., 1973). An intraclass reliability coefficient of .94 for replicate measurements has been reported (Himes & Bouchard, 1985).

Sources of Reference Data

Children

Roche & Malina, 1983
Schutte, 1979

Adults

National Aeronautics and Space Administration, 1978
Clauser et al., 1972
Hertzberg et al., 1963

Elbow Breadth

Recommended Technique

The measurement of elbow breadth requires a broad-faced sliding caliper or a small spreading caliper to measure the distance between the epicondyles of the humerus (see Figure 17). The subject raises the right arm to the horizontal, and the elbow is flexed to 90°. The dorsum (back) of the subject's hand faces the measurer. The measurer stands in front of the subject and palpates the lateral and medial epicondyles of the humerus (see Figure 18). If a sliding caliper is used it is then applied pointing the blades upwards to bisect the right angle formed at the elbow. The caliper is held at a slight angle to the epicondyles rather than parallel to them, because the medial epicondyle is

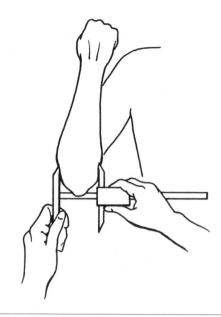

Figure 17 Elbow breadth measurement at the epicondyles of the humerus.

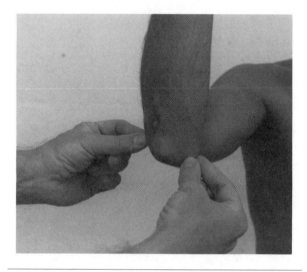

Figure 18 Location of epicondyles of the humerus.

distal to the lateral epicondyle. If a spreading caliper is used, the tips are placed on the medial and lateral epicondyles. The measurer exerts firm pressure to decrease the influence of soft tissue (see Figure 19). The measurement is recorded to the nearest 0.1 cm.

Purpose

Elbow breadth is an index of skeletal mass and has been used as a measure of frame size (Frisancho, 1984).

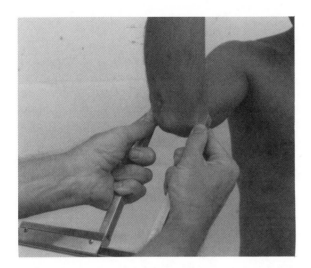

Figure 19 Sliding caliper in place for elbow breadth measurement.

Literature

Firm pressure is exerted so that a skeletal measure will be approximated. Flat-bladed sliding calipers are preferred to spreading calipers because the tips of the latter tend to slip off the bony landmarks. Frisancho (1986) has developed an instrument that consists of a fixed baseboard and a mobile board to measure elbow breadth (see Figure 20).

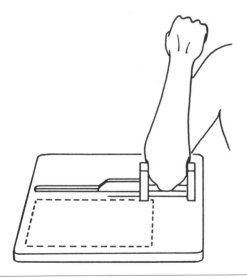

Figure 20 Elbow breadth measures on a fixed baseboard.

Reliability

In children, the intra- and intermeasurer technical errors are about 0.1 cm (Buschang, 1980; Malina

et al., 1972; Malina, 1968; Meleski, 1980; Zavaleta, 1976).

Sources of Reference Data

Children
Johnson et al., 1981
Frisancho, 1986

Adults
Frisancho & Flegel, 1983
Frisancho, 1984

Wrist Breadth

Recommended Technique

The standing subject flexes the forearm 90° at the elbow, keeping the upper arm vertical and near the side of the chest. The measurer stands facing the subject. Guiding the tips of a spreading caliper with the thumb and first finger of each hand, the measurer palpates the most medial aspect of the ulnar styloid with the middle or index finger of the right hand and slides the right tip of the caliper onto this landmark (see Figure 21). Alternate ulnar and radial deviation of the hand at the wrist assists identification of the ulnar and radial styloid processes because they do not move. The most lateral aspect of the radial styloid is located with the middle or index finger of the left hand moving proximally from the space between the extensor pollicis longus and the abductor pollicis longus

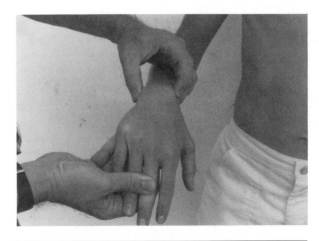

Figure 21 Location of medial aspect of ulna styloid and lateral aspect of radial styloid for the measurement of wrist breadth.

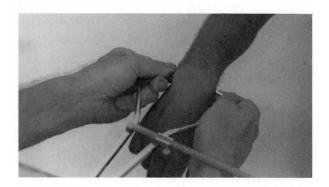

Figure 22 Spreading caliper in place for wrist breadth measurement.

(the anatomical snuff-box; see Figure 22). Alternatively, a sliding caliper can be used to measure the distance between the bony landmarks described above. Firm pressure is applied, and the breadth is recorded to the nearest 0.1 cm.

Purpose

Wrist breadth is used as an index of skeletal mass and of frame size. It has been included in equations for the prediction of skeletal mass (Matiegka, 1921; von Döbeln, 1964). In the Brussels Cadaver Study, wrist breadth was the skeletal measure most highly correlated with skeletal mass $(r = .88;$ Clarys et al., 1984). The value of wrist breadth for this purpose has been confirmed by studies showing it to have low correlations with body fat (Himes & Bouchard, 1985).

Literature

The small contact area of the classical spreading caliper makes positioning on the landmarks difficult. The large flat blades of an adapted engineer's caliper (Carter, 1980) enable accurate placement, and these blades do not shift readily when the necessary pressure is applied, but the scale is difficult to read. A prototype has proved satisfactory, but is expensive and has not been produced in significant quantity (Ross & Marfell-Jones, 1983).

Standardizing wrist positioning is of particular importance because wrist breadth encompasses two bones. The forearm should be midway between pronation and supination, with the dorsum of the hand towards the measurer. Otherwise, there is potential for relative movement of the radial and ulnar styloid processes.

Reliability

Limited data show wrist breadth to be a highly reliable measure with an intrameasurer correlation coefficient of $r = .994; n = 16$ (Martin, 1986). A test-retest correlation of .96 between paired measurements the same day has been reported for college-aged males (Wilmore & Behnke, 1969).

Sources of Reference Data

Children
Huenemann et al., 1974

Adults
National Aeronautics and Space Administration, 1978
Hertzberg et al., 1963

Chapter 4

Circumferences

C. Wayne Callaway,

William Cameron Chumlea,

Claude Bouchard,

John H. Himes,

Timothy G. Lohman,

Alan D. Martin,

Carol D. Mitchell,

William H. Mueller,

Alex F. Roche, and

Vernon D. Seefeldt

Circumferences are important measurements that record the size of cross-sectional and circumferential dimensions of the body. Circumferences used alone, in combination with skinfold measurements taken at the same location or in combination with other circumferences, are measures of growth and can provide indices of nutritional status and levels of fat patterning. For children younger than 6 years of age, head circumference is an index of brain growth, and the ratio of head circumference to chest circumference is an indirect measure of nutritional status. During later childhood and into adulthood, circumferences of the limbs, together with skinfold measures of subcutaneous adipose tissue thicknesses at corresponding levels, can provide cross-sectional areas of adipose tissue or the areas of the underlying "muscle plus bone." When computed from the appropriate formulae, these areas can be used to monitor levels and changes in amounts of adipose tissue and muscle during nutritional therapy or physical rehabilitation. Ratios between selected circumferences of the trunk and of the limbs can provide indices of the patterning of subcutaneous adipose tissue. These uses of circumferences are detailed in other parts of this manual.

Specific techniques for measuring the circumference of the head, neck, chest, waist, abdomen, hips or buttocks, thigh, calf, ankle, arm, forearm, and wrist are described in the pages that follow. There are several important points common to these techniques. All require the use of a tape measure. The tape measure selected should be flexible but inelastic (nonstretchable), should preferably have only one ruling on a side, (i.e., metric or English), and be about 0.7 cm wide. For the measurement of wrist circumference, the tape must be narrow enough to fit into the depression between the styloid processes of the radius and ulna and the carpals.

Many tapes have a spring-retractable mechanism that is activated by pressing a button. In measuring a circumference with such a tape, the tape should be held so that the retraction spring tension on the tape does not affect the measurement. Some other tapes are designed so that the tension of a spring necessarily affects the measurement; these tapes are not recommended for the measurement of circumferences for which tension should be minimal. Circumferences should be recorded with the zero end of the tape held in the left hand above the remaining part of the tape held by the right hand. Differences within and between observers in this positioning of the zero end of a tape can affect reliability for a measurement.

The positioning of the tape for each specific circumference is important because inconsistent positioning reduces validity and reliability. For each circumference, except those of the head and neck, the plane of the tape around the body is perpendicular to the long axis of that part of the body. For those circumferences typically measured with the subject erect (chest, waist, abdomen, hip, thigh, calf, ankle, arm, and forearm), the plane of the tape is also parallel to the floor. Head circumference is measured as a maximum dimension, whereas neck circumference is measured as a minimum dimension. Techniques for measuring circumferences from subjects in recumbent positions are described in another section of this manual.

The tension applied to the tape by the measurer affects the validity and reliability of the measurements. For head circumference, the tape is pulled tightly to compress the hair and soft tissue of the scalp. For all other circumferences, the tape is held snugly around the body part, but not tight enough to compress the subcutaneous adipose tissue. For these circumferences, the measurer and the recorder should check to ensure that the tape is not indenting the skin. For circumferences of the chest, calf, and arm, there may be gaps between the tape and the skin in some individuals. If the gap is large, a note should be made in the subject's record, but in most instances, this gap is small and of little concern. Attempting to reduce the gap by increasing the tension of the tape is not recommended.

Circumferences appear to be relatively easy measures, but control of intra- and intermeasurer reliability can be difficult. The primary causes of poor reliability are the improper positioning of the tape and differences between measurers in the tension applied. Some error in measures of the trunk may be due to their being made at various phases of respiration. Limits for accepted differences between repeated measures for normal subjects are presented in Table 1. If the limit is exceeded for a pair of intra- or intermeasurer values, an additional pair of measurements should be recorded. Different limits may be needed when individuals who have specific diseases or other abnormal conditions are measured.

Head Circumference

Recommended Technique

An infant is measured when seated on the lap of the mother or caretaker. At older ages, head circumference is measured with the subject standing, but few children less than 36 months old will stand still for this purpose. A nonstretching tape about 0.6 cm wide is used. Added objects, for example, pins, are removed from the hair. The measurer stands facing the left side of the infant and positions the tape so that the zero end is on the lateral aspect of the head (see Figure 1). This involves passing the tape around the head and then transferring the ends of the tape from one hand to the other so that the zero mark on the tape is inferior

Table 1   Intra- and Intermeasurer Limits for Circumferences

Circumference	Limit (cm)
Head	0.2
Neck	0.3
Chest	1.0
Waist	1.0
Abdomen	1.0
Buttocks	1.0
Thigh	0.5
Calf	0.2
Ankle	0.2
Arm	0.2
Forearm	0.2
Wrist	0.2

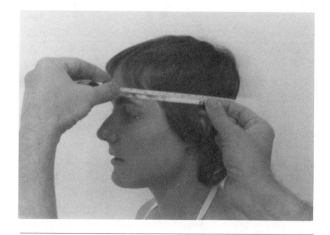

Figure 1   Measurement of head circumference.

to the value to be recorded. The tape is positioned so that large amounts of cranial hair (braids) are excluded. Anteriorly, the tape is placed just superior to the eyebrows and posteriorly it is placed so that the maximum circumference is measured. The tape need not be in the Frankfort Horizontal Plane, but the plane of the tape must be the same on both sides of the head. The tape is pulled tightly to compress hair and obtain a measure that "approximates" cranial circumference. The measurement is recorded to the nearest 0.1 cm.

Purpose

Head circumference is a standard component of infant anthropometry because it is closely related to brain size (Cooke et al., 1977). After 36 months, growth in head circumference is slow although brain weight increases by about 30% after this age. Head circumference should be measured also in the parents of infants whose head circumferences are abnormal because head circumferences of parents and their offspring are closely associated and adjustment equations are available (Illingworth & Eid, 1971).

Literature

There is widespread agreement regarding the technique to be used except that gentle pressure is used by some Dutch workers and in Swedish Infant Welfare Clinics. In addition, a wide tape (2 cm) is used in Swedish Infant Welfare Clinics. Measurements made with a tape 0.6 cm wide are about 0.5 cm smaller than those made with a tape 2 cm wide (Karlberg et al., 1976).

Reliability

In the Fels Longitudinal Study the intermeasurer differences were small and independent of age, with technical errors of 0.09 mm and coefficients of variation of .02 (Roche et al., 1987). Wilmore and Behnke (1969) reported a test-retest correlation of .96 for measurements of young men 1 day apart.

Sources of Reference Data

Children
Nellhaus, 1968
Roche & Himes, 1980
Roche et al., 1987

Adults
Churchill et al., 1977
White & Churchill, 1971

Minimal Neck Circumference

Recommended Technique

The subject does not wear any clothes around the neck and sits or stands erect with the head in the Frankfort Horizontal Plane (see Figure 2). The measurer stands facing the left side of the subject. A self-retracting inelastic tape is applied around the neck just inferior to the laryngeal prominence (Adam's Apple; see Figure 2). The minimal circumference is measured to the nearest 0.1 cm, with the tape perpendicular to the long axis of the neck. The tape will not necessarily be horizontal. The zero mark on the tape should be inferior to the value that will be recorded. The pressure of the tape on the skin should be minimal while maintaining complete contact. The measurement should be made in less than 5 s to avoid discomfort.

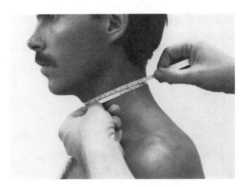

Figure 2 Measurement of minimal neck circumference.

Purpose

Minimal neck circumference can be used in the study of growth, motor and athletic performance, obesity, and aging. The measurement can have useful medical and engineering applications.

Literature

The general concensus is that neck circumference should be measured with the head in the Frankfort Horizontal Plane and should be performed similarly in children and in adults. It has been recommended that neck circumference be measured with the subject standing (Behnke & Wilmore, 1974), but others have recommended a sitting position (Anthropology Research Project, 1978).

In the 1978 Anthropology Research Project "Anthropometric Source Book," the measurement is defined as "the maximum circumference of the neck at a point just inferior to the bulge of the thyroid cartilage" (Volume I: *Anthropometry for Designers)* and later as "the maximum circumference of the neck, including the Adam's Apple" (Volume II: *A Handbook of Anthropometric Data).* Wilmore and Behnke (1969) suggested that this circumference be measured "just inferior to the larynx."

Most have measured at right angles to the long axis of the neck, as is recommended, but some have described the measurement as "taken in the horizontal plane, just below the level of the thyroid cartilage" (Weiner & Lourie, 1981).

Reliability

There are few reliability data. Wilmore and Behnke (1969), from test-retest data for college-aged males, reported that neck circumference was a reliable measurement with an interclass correlation of .95. Gavan (1950) concluded that neck circumference was a measurement of medium reliability.

Sources of Reference Data

Children
Pieper & Jürgens, 1977
Snyder et al., 1975

Adults
Clauser et al., 1972
White & Churchill, 1971

Shoulder Circumference

Recommended Technique

The measurement of shoulder circumference requires that the subject be dressed so that the appropriate landmarks can be located. The subject stands, head erect and looking ahead with weight evenly distributed between both feet, which are about 5 cm apart, and with shoulders back and the arms by the sides (see Figure 3). The measurement

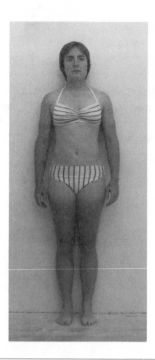

Figure 3 Subject position for shoulder circumference measurement.

is made at the end of a normal expiration. This can be accomplished easily by engaging the subject in light conversation, or by asking that the subject count to 10 during the measurement. The tape is positioned over the maximum muscular bulges (deltoid muscles) inferior to each acromion (see Figure 4). A mirror, or assistant, helps to ensure that the tape is horizontal. The tape is held snug, in contact with the skin, without compressing the tissue. The measurement is recorded to the nearest 0.1 cm.

Purpose

Shoulder circumference reflects muscular development of the shoulder regions and upper thorax.

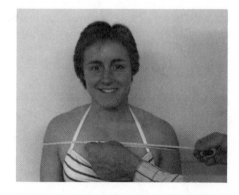

Figure 4 Measurement of shoulder circumference.

Because the deltoid musculature is proportional to lean body mass, shoulder circumferences may indicate changes due to strength training. It is important in human engineering and physical education research.

Literature

Some investigators have defined bony landmarks rather than the maximal protrusion of the deltoid muscles. Circumference measurements are made to estimate the quantity of soft tissue, unlike skeletal breadths and lengths, which estimate frame size. Consequently, the choice of a muscular landmark is appropriate. Also, unlike skeletal measurements, shoulder circumference is measured with little pressure and without compressing the skin (Behnke & Wilmore, 1974). Anteriorly, the tape passes approximately over the junction between the sternum and the second costal cartilage when the recommended technique is followed.

Timing a measurement at the end of a normal expiration is easier to achieve than other timing within the respiratory cycle. It produces less variability between measurements than the choice of other phases of respiration.

Reliability

Reports are not available.

Sources of Reference Data

Children
Huenemann et al., 1974
Adults
National Aeronautics and Space Administration, 1978

Chest Circumference

Recommended Technique

The measurement of chest circumference requires a highly flexible inelastic tape measure that is no more than 0.7 cm wide. During the measurement, the subject stands erect, in a natural manner, with the feet at shoulder width. The arms are abducted slightly to permit passage of the tape around the chest. When the tape is snugly in place, the arms are lowered to their natural postition at the sides of the trunk. The chest should be bare except that women may wear a strapless bra. Chest circumference is measured at the level of the fourth costo-

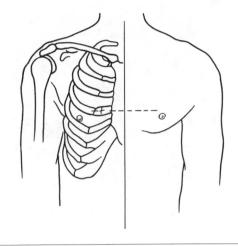

Figure 5 The level of the fourth-sternal joints for chest circumference measurement.

sternal joints (see Figure 5). Laterally, this corresponds to the levels of the sixth ribs. The measurement is made in a horizontal plane, at the end of a normal expiration.

The fourth costo-sternal joints are located by a two-handed palpation method whereby the measurer places both index fingers on the superior surfaces of the clavicles, while the thumbs locate the first intercostal spaces. The index fingers then replace the thumbs, which are lowered to the second intercostal spaces. This procedure is repeated until the fourth ribs are located. The fourth ribs and their costal cartilages are followed medially to their articulations with the sternum. The level of the fourth costo-sternal joints is marked. An alternative procedure is to locate the manubrio-sternal joint, which projects markedly and is at the level of the second costal cartilages. The third and fourth costo-sternal junctions can then be located sequentially.

The measurer stands in front of the subject but slightly to one side. The tape housing is held in the right hand while the free end of the tape is passed in front of the subject and retrieved by the measurer's left hand as it passes around the subject's back. The free end of the tape is then positioned between the right axilla and the sternum. At this time, the measurer ensures that the tape is at the correct horizontal position, first at the back and then at the front. The reserve end of the tape is then placed near the zero end (see Figure 6).

The tape should be in light contact with the skin, without indenting it, but the tape may be away from the skin near the vertebral column. The skin should be free of perspiration, because this may increase friction between the skin and the tape.

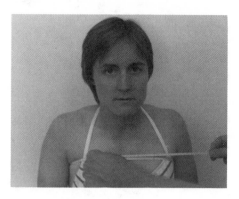

Figure 6 Measurement of chest circumference.

Purpose

In infants and children, chest circumference serves as a screening variable for malnutrition. In children and adults, it can be used as an index of frame size.

Literature

The tape measure should be divided to metric units with unequivocal identification of millimeters and centimeters. There should be a free space between the end of the tape and the zero line to facilitate handling. Spring-loaded tapes are not recommended because they may indent the soft tissues.

Chest circumference has been measured at various sites and at various phases of the respiratory cycle (Behnke & Wilmore, 1974; De Garay et al., 1974; Hrdlička, 1920; Simmons, 1944; Weiner & Lourie, 1981). Consideration was given to the possibility of measuring chest circumference at maximum inspiration and at maximum expiration, which would provide an index of respiratory functional capacity. This is not recommended for general use because it is not applicable to the very young and the elderly, and it does not match the recommended techniques for other thoracic and abdominal dimensions. If all these dimensions were measured at both maximum inspiration and at maximum expiration, many additional measurements would be necessary.

The most frequently mentioned anatomical landmark on the anterior aspect of the thorax is the nipple, which corresponds approximately to the fourth intercostal space (Bailey, 1967; Behnke & Wilmore, 1974; De Garay et al., 1974; Osborne & De George, 1959; Ross & Marfell-Jones, 1982; Singh & Bhasin, 1968). Weiner and Lourie (1981) suggested that the tape be placed at the level of the third and fourth sternebrae, whereas Olivier (1960) recommended a level superior to the nipples.

The position of the tape on the posterior aspect of the thorax is described generally as either crossing the lower angles of the scapulae or passing just distal to them (Bailey, 1967; De Garay et al., 1974; Singh & Bhasin, 1968). Note that when a tape is placed anteriorly at or superior to the nipples and distal to the inferior angles of the scapulae posteriorly, the plane of measurement slopes postero-inferiorly. Alternative levels described in the literature include the xiphoid process (Hrdlička, 1920; Osborne & De George, 1959; Simmons, 1944) and the axilla (Snyder et al., 1975). Ross et al. (1982) recommended that measurements of the chest be made at a midsternal level in a horizontal plane without reference to anatomical landmarks on the posterior aspect of the thorax.

The time of measurement within the respiratory cycle ranges from maximum inspiration and expiration (De Garay et al., 1974; Hrdlička, 1920; Simmons, 1944) to normal or quiet inspiration and expiration (Weiner & Lourie, 1981) and to mid-respiration (Behnke & Wilmore, 1974).

Reliability

Intermeasurer and intertrial reliability coefficients are generally slightly lower than those for limb measures but are well within acceptable ranges. Weltman and Katch (1975) reported intertrial and intermeasurer correlations between .94 and .99. Slaughter, Lohman, and Boileau (1978) reported intertrial correlations greater than .90 for chest circumferences of children from 7 to 12 years of age.

Sources of Reference Data

Children
Meredith, 1970
Malina et al., 1973
Slaughter et al., 1978

Adults
Stoudt et al., 1970
Weltman & Katch, 1975

Waist Circumference

Recommended Technique

The subject wears little clothing so that the tape may be correctly positioned. The measurement should not be made over clothing. If clothing must be worn, subjects should undress to light underwear and wear only a cloth or paper smock during the measurement. The subject stands erect with the abdomen relaxed, the arms at the sides and the feet together. The measurer faces the subject and places an inelastic tape around the subject, in a horizontal plane, at the level of the natural waist, which is the narrowest part of the torso, as seen from the anterior aspect (see Figure 7). An assistant is needed to help position the tape in a horizontal plane. In some obese subjects, it may be difficult to identify a waist narrowing. In such cases, the smallest horizontal circumference should be measured in the area between the ribs and iliac crest. The measurement should be taken at the end of a normal expiration, without the tape compressing the skin. It is recorded to the nearest 0.1 cm.

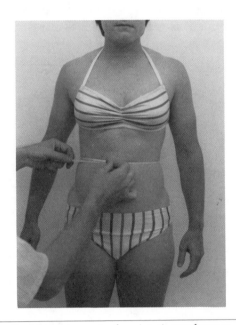

Figure 7 Measurement of waist circumference.

Purpose

Waist circumference is an index of deep adipose tissue (Borkan et al., 1983), and it is related to fat-free mass (Jackson & Pollock, 1976). When used in a ratio with the thigh or buttock (hip) circumference, waist circumference is an indicator of the degree of masculine distribution of adipose tissue: The higher the waist to the thigh or buttock (hip) ratio, the more masculine the pattern of adipose tissue distribution and the greater risk of diseases such as noninsulin-dependent diabetes mellitus (Hartz et al., 1984; Krotkiewski et al., 1983. Waist circumference is highly correlated with weight/stature² (Kannel & Gordon, 1980), which is an index of general obesity. Waist circumference has important applications in human engineering.

Literature

Waist circumference has usually been measured at the smallest circumference of the torso, which is at the level of the natural waist (Garrett & Kennedy, 1971). Some measure "waist circumference" at the level of the umbilicus, but this leads to recording larger values.

Reliability

The technical error of measurement in adolescents is 1.31 cm for intrameasurer errors and 1.56 cm for intermeasurer errors (Malina et al., 1973). The technical error of measurement in the elderly is 0.48 cm in men and 1.15 cm in women (Chumlea et al., 1984b). Thus, the "true" measurement of an individual would typically be within ± 1 cm of the measured value in most cases.

Sources of Reference Data

Children

Huenemann et al., 1974
Roche & Malina, 1983

Adults

National Aeronautics and Space Administration, 1978
Stoudt et al., 1970

Abdominal Circumference

Recommended Technique

If clothing must be worn, subjects should undress to light underwear and wear only a cloth or paper smock during the measurement. The measurer faces the subject. The subject stands with the arms by the sides and the feet together. The procedures are the same as those to be followed for the waist circumference, except that the tape is placed around the subject at the level of the greatest anterior extension of the abdomen in a horizontal plane. This level is usually, but not always, at the level of the umbilicus (see Figure 8). An assistant is needed to position the tape behind the subject. The tape is held snug against the skin without compressing the tissues and with its zero end below the value to be recorded. The measurement is made at the end of a normal expiration to the nearest 0.1 cm.

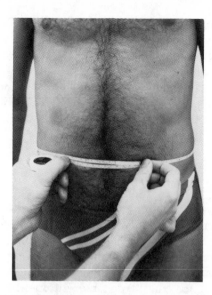

Figure 8   Measurement of abdominal circumference.

Purpose

The abdominal circumference, like the waist circumference, is an anthropometric indicator of subcutaneous and deep adipose tissue. It differs from the waist circumference in being the maximum circumference of the abdomen and, therefore, may be a better indicator of adipose tissue. It is probable that the waist and abdominal circumferences are highly correlated, although the extent is unknown because in most studies one or the other measurement is recorded.

Literature

The recommended procedure is the one used commonly (Behnke, 1963; Hertzbert et al., 1963; Huenemann et al., 1974; Wilmore & Behnke, 1969).

Reliability

Wilmore and Behnke (1969) reported a test-retest correlation of .99 in young men measured 1 day apart.

Sources of Reference Data

Children

Huenemann et al., 1974

Adults

National Aeronautics and Space Administration, 1978
Clauser et al., 1972
Hertzberg et al., 1963

Buttocks (Hip) Circumference

Recommended Technique

The subject should wear only nonrestrictive briefs or underwear, or light smock over underwear. The subject stands erect with arms at the sides and feet together. The measurer squats at the side of the subject so that the level of maximum extension of the buttocks can be seen. An inelastic tape is placed around the buttocks in a horizontal plane at this level without compressing the skin (see Figure 9). An assistant is needed to help position the tape on the opposite side of the subject's body. The zero end of the tape should be below the measurement value. The tape is in contact with the skin but does not indent the soft tissues. The measurement is recorded to the nearest 0.1 cm.

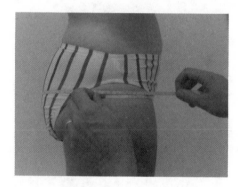

Figure 9   Measurement of buttocks (hip) circumference.

Purpose

Buttocks (hip) circumference is a measurement of external pelvic size that reflects the amount of adipose tissue in the region. As defined, it is more properly called "buttocks circumference" than "hip circumference." Adipose tissue in this region is largely sucutaneous and relates to the lower segment of the body. Hence, buttocks circumference is an indicator of lower body fatness. Used in conjunction with waist circumference, in the waist-to-hip (buttocks) circumference ratio, it is an indicator of the pattern of subcutaneous adipose tissue distribution, with low values being characteristic of women. This type of adipose tissue distribution is associated with a decreased risk of diabetes mellitus in men and in women (Krotkiewski et al., 1983; Hartz et al., 1984). In addition, the buttocks circumference has important applications in human engineering.

Literature

There are many ways in which a circumference around the hip region has been measured (Garrett & Kennedy, 1971). These can be reduced to two basic methods, plus a combination of the two. In the first, usually called "buttocks circumference," the measurement is made horizontally at the level of maximum extension of the buttocks posteriorly, as recommended. In the second, the circumference is measured horizontally at the level of the greatest lateral extension of the hips, the usual landmark being the greater trochanter. The buttocks level is recommended because it is easier to locate than the trochanteric level, because buttocks adipose tissue is related to lower limb adipose tissue (Mueller & Wohlleb, 1981), and because the buttocks circumference is generally the maximum circumference of the hip area in a horizontal plane.

Usually the trochanteric level is inferior to the level of the maximum extension of the buttocks posteriorly. Hence, when a circumference is measured at the trochanteric level, the tape tends to slip down over the buttocks. In very obese subjects, the anterior abdominal wall may sag and be included in the measurement. This is a potential problem with either of the two main methods for measurement.

Some pass the tape around both the trochanteric and buttock areas (Montagu, 1960). With this technique, the circumference is measured in an oblique plane leading to a less well-defined circumference and larger measurement errors. In the epidemiological literature, the method for the measurement of buttocks circumference is often omitted (Kalkhoff et al., 1983), or it deviates considerably from usual procedures. Some have measured this circumference at the level of the iliac crest, which is virtually the same as waist circumference (Ohlson et al., 1985).

Reliability

Little is known about the reliability of buttock circumference measurements. In a U.S. National Survey of adolescents, the technical error of measurement was 1.23 cm for intrameasurer errors and 1.38 cm for intermeasurer errors (Malina et al., 1973). Thus, the true value for an individual will be within approximately 1 cm of that recorded in most determinations. Using a slightly different measurement technique, Behnke and Wilmore (1969) found a correlation of .99 between measurements 1 day apart in young men.

Sources of Reference Data

Children

Huenemann et al., 1974
Roche & Malina, 1983

Adults

National Aeronautics and Space Administration, 1978
Clauser et al., 1970
White & Churchill, 1971

Thigh Circumference

Recommended Technique

The subject wears a bathing suit or other minimal clothing so that the appropriate landmarks can be located. Measurement of the proximal and distal thigh circumferences requires only a measuring tape. Measurement of midthigh circumference requires a grease pencil and a bench. The subject places the left foot flat on the top of the bench so that the knee is flexed to about 90°. An alternative positioning for the measurement of midthigh circumference is for the subject to sit erect with the knees flexed to about 90°. Each of the measurements is made with the subject standing, with the heels about 10 cm apart and the weight evenly distributed between both feet. The three locations are illustrated in Figures 10 and 11.

Proximal Thigh Circumference. A tape is passed horizontally around the thigh, immediately distal

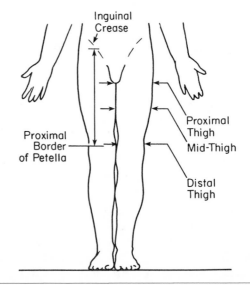

Figure 10 Anterior view of locations for thigh circumferences.

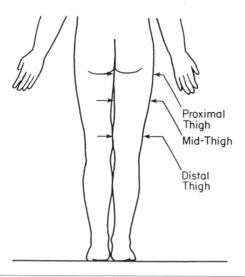

Figure 11 Posterior view of locations for thigh circumferences.

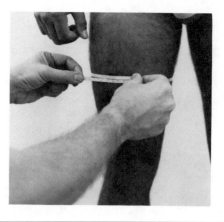

Figure 13 Measurement of midthigh circumference.

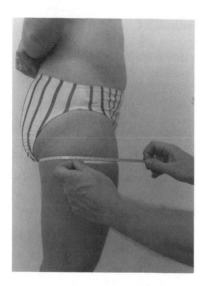

Figure 12 Measurement of proximal thigh circumference.

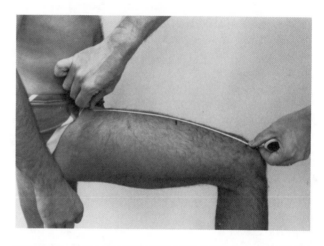

Figure 14 Locating the level for the measurement of midthigh circumference.

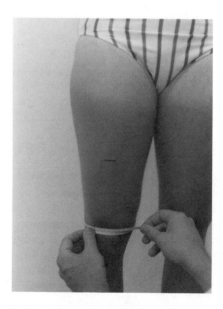

Figure 15 Measurement of distal thigh circumference.

to the gluteal furrow. This may not be the maximum circumference of the thigh (see Figure 12).

Midthigh Circumference. The measuring tape is placed horizontally around the thigh at the level of the thigh skinfold measurement, that is, midway between the midpoint of the inguinal crease and the proximal border of the patella (see Figure 13). The proximal border of the patella is marked while the subject extends the knee. The midpoint of the inguinal crease is easily located if the hips are slightly flexed. An insertion tape can be used to locate the midpoint between these points (see Figure 14).

Distal Thigh Circumference. The measuring tape is placed around the thigh just proximal to the femoral epicondyles (see Figure 15). These circumferences are recorded to the nearest 0.1 cm. Each is measured with the tape in complete contact with the skin but without compression of the soft tissues. In infants and in the elderly, these measurements can be made with the subject supine.

Purpose

The three thigh circumferences might facilitate the estimation of body density and be useful indicators of adiposity or lean body mass. Thigh circumferences, especially distal thigh circumference, are important indicators of muscle atrophy due to disease or injury, and they have applications in human engineering. It is expected that, in most studies, a selection will be made from among these measurements.

Literature

The recommended technique for the proximal thigh circumference is essentially that of Mac-Dougall et al. (1981). Some consider that this circumference should be measured with the muscles of the thigh maximally contracted. This may decrease reliability, especially in children and the elderly. This measurement is unacceptable to some cultural groups.

Midthigh circumference has been measured midway between the greater trochanter and the proximal border of the patella. The inguinal crease has been chosen instead of the trochanter as a proximal landmark because it can be located more precisely. The recommended technique for distal thigh circumference matches that of Cameron (1978).

Rationale

The choice of technique for each of these circumferences is based on the accurate recognition of landmarks. In addition, the level recommended for the midthigh circumference matches that for the anterior thigh skinfold and thereby allows estimation of tissue areas.

Reliability

Wilmore and Behnke (1969) in a study of young men found a correlation of .99 between proximal thigh circumferences measured on two occasions, 1 day apart.

Sources of Reference Data

Children

Huenemann et al., 1974 (proximal)
Matheny & Meredith, 1947 (proximal)

Adults

National Aeronautics and Space Administration, 1978 (proximal, distal)
Clauser et al., 1972 (proximal, distal)
Hertzberg et al., 1963 (proximal, distal)

Calf Circumference

Recommended Technique

The subject sits on a table so that the leg to be measured hangs freely, or the subject stands with the feet about 20 cm apart and weight distributed equally on both feet. An inelastic tape measure is positioned horizontally around the calf and moved up and down to locate the maximum circumference in a plane perpendicular to the long axis of the calf. The zero end of the tape is placed below the measurement value. The level is marked so that a calf skinfold can be measured at the same level (see Figure 16). The maximum circumference is recorded to the nearest 0.1 cm, with the tape in contact with the whole circumference but not indenting the skin. During infancy and in the elderly, calf circumference can be measured with the subject supine and the left knee flexed to 90°.

Purpose

Calf circumference is a common measurement that can be used alone or in combination with lateral

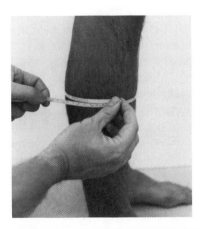

Figure 16 Measurement of calf circumference.

and/or medial calf skinfolds to provide estimates of cross-sectional muscle and adipose tissue areas of the calf. Calf circumference is important as a predictor of body composition in adults (Chumlea et al., 1984; Guo et al., 1987), and to predict body weight in the elderly (Chumlea et al., unpublished data, 1983).

Literature

Calf circumference is included in the "basic list" of anthropometric variables of Weiner and Lourie (1981). The recommended technique does not differ greatly from those reported in the literature. Calf circumference can be measured with the subject sitting on a table so that the leg hangs freely off the edge, or with the leg extended from the table, or with the subject standing with the feet separated about 20 cm and body weight distributed equally on both feet (Cameron, 1978; Malina et al., 1974; Snyder et al., 1975, 1977; Weiner & Lourie, 1981). In addition, calf circumference can be measured with the subject supine and the left knee flexed to a 90° angle (Chumlea et al., 1985); this is appropriate for infants and those who are bedfast. Comparisons have not been reported between measurements made with the subject standing and those made with the subject seated, but the differences between measurements with subjects standing and supine are very small.

Reliability

The intrameasurer technical error from Cycle III of the Health Examination Survey (6 to 11 years) was 0.87 cm, and the intermeasurer technical error was 0.34 cm (Malina et al., 1974). For children of similar age and for adults in the Fels Longitudinal Study, the intermeasurer technical error was about 0.08 cm (Chumlea & Roche, 1979). The intermeasurer technical error for elderly men and women is about 0.08 cm (Chumlea et al., 1984b). Wilmore and Behnke (1969) reported a test-retest correlation of .98 for young men measured one day apart. Intrameasurer technical errors of 0.1 to 0.5 mm and an intermeasurer technical error of 0.2 mm have been reported (Brown, 1984; Buschang, 1980; Malina, 1968; Malina & Buschang, 1984; Meleski, 1980; Zavaleta & Malina, 1982).

Sources of Reference Data

Children

Roche & Malina, 1983

Adults

Chumlea et al., 1985
Churchill et al., 1977
White & Churchill, 1971

Ankle Circumference

Recommended Technique

The subject stands barefoot on a flat elevated surface, with feet separated slightly and the weight evenly distributed between the feet. The measurer faces the side of the subject. An inelastic tape is placed around the minimum circumference of the calf, perpendicular to its long axis, just proximal to the malleoli (see Figure 17). The zero end of the tape is held below the measurement value. The tape is pulled so that it fits the ankle snugly but does not compress the underlying tissues (see Figure 18). The measurement is recorded to the nearest 0.1 cm.

Two measurers are required to measure infants and other subjects unable to stand in the appropri-

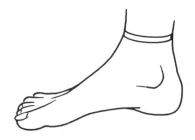

Figure 17   Level of ankle circumference measurement.

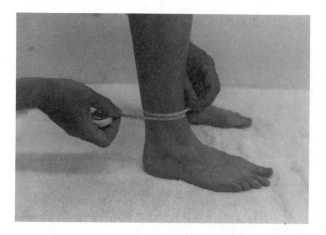

Figure 18   Measurement of ankle circumference.

ate position. The subject lies supine while one measurer elevates the leg and dorsally flexes the foot to approximately a right angle. The minimum ankle circumference is then measured as described above.

Purpose

Ankle circumference is a measure of frame size and is useful in the design of clothing, especially footwear.

Literature

Ankle circumference is measured using a tape that is sufficiently flexible to conform to the irregular shape at the level of measurement. It has been measured with the subject sitting on a table, with the feet placed in a chair high enough to form a right angle at the knee (O'Brien & Shelton, 1941). Others have measured children sitting on a table with the leg extended and relaxed (Snyder et al., 1975). The degree of dorsiflexion of the foot and support of weight by the foot are important considerations. Dorsiflexion to more than 90° is accompanied by marked contraction of the tibialis anterior and the anterior extensor muscles of the lower leg. The associated elevation of the tendons of these muscles from the surface of the ankle distorts the cross-sectional shape of the ankle and increases its circumference at the level of measurement.

Ankle circumference has been measured so that the superior border of the tape passes over the tip of the medial malleolus (O'Brien & Shelton, 1941; Randall & Baer, 1951). Ankle circumference measured in this way is not highly correlated ($r = .69$) with that measured by the recommended method (O'Brien & Shelton, 1941). The minimum circumference is recommended because reliability is known to be high, and it is the technique that has been used in studies of body composition (Wilmore & Behnke, 1969).

Reliability

Huenemann and co-workers (1974) measured ankle circumference in 2 subjects 20 times during a 4-week period. The standard deviations of replicate measurements for the 2 subjects were 0.11 and 0.12 cm for the right side and 0.12 and 0.13 cm for the left side. Wilmore and Behnke (1969) reported a test-retest correlation of .99 in young men measured on successive days.

Sources of Reference Data

Children
Huenemann et al., 1974
McCammon, 1970
Snyder et al., 1975

Adults
National Aeronautics and Space Administration, 1978
Clauser et al., 1972
White & Churchill, 1971

Arm Circumference

Recommended Technique

For this measurement the subject stands erect, with the arms hanging freely at the sides of the trunk and with the palms facing the thighs. The subject wears loose clothing without sleeves to allow total exposure of the shoulder area. If the midpoint of the upper arm has been marked for the measurement of triceps or biceps skinfolds, this should be used as the level for the measurement of arm circumference. To locate the midpoint, the subject's elbow is flexed to 90° with the palm facing superiorly. The measurer stands behind the subject and locates the lateral tip of the acromion by palpating laterally along the superior surface of the spinous process of the scapula. A small mark is made at the identified point. The most distal point on the acromial process is located and marked. A tape is placed so that is passes over these two marks, and the midpoint between them is marked (see Figure 19).

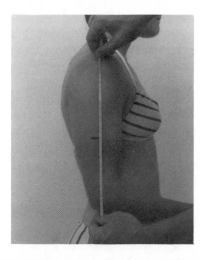

Figure 19 Location of the midpoint of the upper arm.

With the arm relaxed and the elbow extended and hanging just away from the side of the trunk and the palm facing the thigh, place the tape around the arm so that it is touching the skin, but not compressing the soft tissues. The tape is positioned perpendicular to the long axis of the arm at the marked midpoint, and the circumference is recorded to the nearest 0.1 cm (see Figure 20).

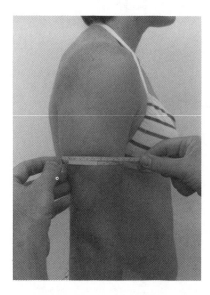

Figure 20 Measurement of arm circumference.

Purpose

Arm circumference provides an index of body energy stores and protein mass. Although it can be used as an independent measure, it is often combined with skinfold thicknesses to calculate arm-muscle circumference and the areas of arm muscle and adipose tissue (Gurney & Jelliffe, 1973; Heymsfield et al., 1984). Low values are interpreted as evidence of protein-energy malnutrition (Blackburn et al., 1977).

The recommended measurement is made with muscles relaxed. Arm circumference can be measured with the elbow flexed and the biceps contracted when there is particular interest in muscle development. This measurement is called *arm circumference-flexed*.

Literature

If possible, the subject should stand, but the arm circumference can be measured with the subject sitting erect with the back straight and the head in the Frankfort Plane.

Reliability

Bray et al. (1978) reported intermeasurer errors of selected circumferences and skinfold thicknesses in lean and obese patients. They found less variability with the circumference measurements than with skinfold thicknesses. The intermeasurer variation in obese patients after a 2-week interval was 2.1% ($\pm$ 0.10 *SEM*) for arm circumference. Hall et al. (1980) calculated the measurer error for arm circumference as 1.54 cm². Martorell et al. (1975) reported that in preschool children, arm circumference had a total measurement standard deviation of 0.24 cm; 56% of the total variance was due to intrameasurer variance. Intrameasurer technical errors of 0.1 to 0.4 mm and an intermeasurer technical error of 0.3 mm have been reported (Brown, 1984; Buschang, 1980; Malina, 1968; Malina & Buschang, 1984; Meleski, 1980; Zavaleta & Malina, 1982).

Sources of Reference Data

Children
Frisancho, 1974, 1981
McCammon, 1970

Adults
National Aeronautics and Space Administration, 1978
Frisancho, 1974, 1981
Bishop et al., 1981

Forearm Circumference

Recommended Technique

For the measurement of forearm circumference, the subject stands with the arms hanging downward but slightly away from the trunk, with the palms facing anteriorly (see Figure 21). The tape is placed loosely around the proximal part of the forearm, perpendicular to its long axis, and moved up and down until the level of the maximum circumference is located (see Figure 22). At this level the measurement is recorded to the nearest 0.1 cm, with the tape in contact with the skin but not compressing the soft tissues.

Purpose

Forearm circumference is used with other body measurements in some equations to predict body density from anthropometric data (Boileau et al., 1981; Jackson & Pollock, 1978; Katch & McArdle,

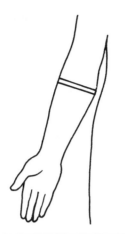

Figure 21 Diagram to illustrate the location of forearm circumference.

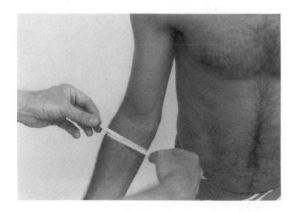

Figure 22 Measurement of forearm circumference.

1973; Pollock et al., 1975, 1976). If a forearm skinfold is measured at the same level, the cross-sectional areas of adipose tissue and of "muscle plus bone" can be estimated.

Literature

A flexible inelastic tape should be used. An insertion tape is also acceptable for this measurement. The procedures described in the literature match the recommended technique.

Reliability

Behnke and Wilmore (1969) reported a correlation of .99 between measurements 1 day apart in young men. An intrameasurer technical error of 0.2 mm was reported by Malina (1968).

Sources of Reference Data

Children

Huenemann et al., 1974

Roche & Malina, 1983

Adults

National Aeronautics and Space Administration, 1978

Wilmore & Behnke, 1969, 1980

Wrist Circumference

Recommended Technique

The measurer faces the subject who stands and flexes the arm at the elbow so that the palm is uppermost and the hand muscles relaxed (see Figure 23). An inelastic tape is placed just distal to the styloid processes of the radius and ulna, which are located by palpating with the index or middle fingers of each hand. The tape is positioned perpendicular to the long axis of the forearm and in the same plane on the anterior and posterior aspects of the wrist (see Figure 24). The tape must

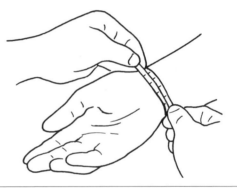

Figure 23 Positioning for the measurement of wrist circumference.

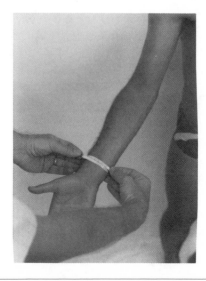

Figure 24 Measurement of wrist circumference.

be no more than 0.7 cm wide, so that it can fit into the medial and lateral depressions at this level. The measurement is made with the tape touching the skin around the whole circumference but not compressing the soft tissues. The wrist circumference is recorded to the nearest 0.1 cm.

When wrist circumference is included in a series of measurements, it is likely to be measured after another upper limb circumference, such as maximum forearm circumference. In this case, the measuring tape, still encircling the limb, is moved to the wrist region.

Purpose

Wrist circumference is a useful index of frame size because this region is relatively free from adipose tissue and muscle (Martin, 1984). Also, wrist circumference is useful as an indicator of growth, in genetic syndromology and in the modeling of body segments.

Literature

There is ambiguity in the literature over the location of the wrist circumference; hence, caution should be exercised in using reported data. In their collation of anthropometry, Garrett and Kennedy (1971) list many studies in which wrist circumfer-

ence was defined as the circumference proximal to the styloid processes of the ulna and radius. For clarity, the latter measurement should be called ''minimum forearm circumference.''

In adults, the measurement of wrist circumference is easy because a narrow tape fits readily into the depressions present at the level of measurement. In infants, however, obtaining a satisfactory wrist circumference is impossible because the landmarks are indeterminable and the tape is generally too wide.

Reliability

Limb circumferences are highly reliable measurements; intraobserver correlations exceed .99 (Wilmore & Behnke, 1969).

Sources of Reference Data

Children

Huenemann et al., 1974
McCammon, 1970
Michael & Katch, 1968
Pieper & Jürgens, 1977

Adults

National Aeronautics and Space Administration, 1978
Clauser et al., 1972
Hertzberg et al., 1963

Chapter 5

Skinfold Thicknesses and Measurement Technique

Gail G. Harrison,

Elsworth R. Buskirk,

J.E. Lindsay Carter,

Francis E. Johnston,

Timothy G. Lohman,

Michael L. Pollock,

Alex F. Roche, and

Jack Wilmore

Skinfold thicknesses, sometimes called "fatfold" thicknesses, are actually the thicknesses of double folds of skin and subcutaneous adipose tissue at specific sites on the body. Spring-loaded or other calipers exerting standardized pressure per unit of caliper jaw surface are used, of which several types are available (see section on Equipment for details).

The utility of skinfold thicknesses is twofold. First, they provide a relatively simple and non-invasive method of estimating general fatness. The extent to which the subcutaneous adipose tissue compartment reflects total body fat varies with age as well as among individuals and populations. The predictive value of skinfold thicknesses for total body fat also varies by site, with some sites closely related to overall body composition and others relatively independent of it. Numerous equations for the prediction of body composition from anthropometric measurements have been developed (Durnin & Womersley, 1974; Jackson & Pollock, 1978; Lohman, 1981; Sloan, 1967) that make use of skinfold thicknesses as essential components.

The second major use of skinfold thicknesses is in the characterization of the distribution of sub-cutaneous adipose tissue. There is mounting evidence that not all subcutaneous adipose tissue depots are alike in terms of lability or of contribution to the health risks associated with obesity. It is particularly important to standardize site selection and location, because small differences in location can make significant differences in measurement. Because skinfold thicknesses are soft-tissue measurements, standardization of site is difficult and should always involve location in relation to unambiguous landmarks. The compressibility of both skin and adipose tissue varies with state of hydration, age, size, and individual. In general, younger individuals have more compressible skinfolds due to greater hydration of tissue. Extremes of hydration, as in edema, also effect compressibility.

The ease with which the adipose layer is separated from underlying muscle varies by site and among individuals. Very lean and very obese individuals pose special measurement problems. In general, the thicker the skinfold the more difficult it is to achieve a reproducible measure. Reliability data for skinfold measures in some populations are available for those sites that have been measured frequently, especially for those that have been included in large surveys. For some of the less commonly used sites, little or no information has been published on their inter- and intrameasurer replicability. After much deliberation, the cheek and chin were excluded from the sites for which recommended measurement techniques are described. Those interested in these sites will find details in Allen et al. (1956) and Pařižková (1977).

Skinfold Measurement Technique—General

The sites at which skinfolds are to be measured need not, in general, be marked on the subject, but this can be done, if desired. The sites must be marked in studies of intercaliper differences and when measurements of the midthigh skinfold, the triceps skinfold (at the midpoint of the upper arm), or the medial or lateral calf skinfolds (at the level of the maximum circumference of the calf) are to be combined with circumferences at the same levels to obtain estimates of cross-sectional areas.

The following description is independent of the type of caliper used and is based on the assumption that the measurer is right-handed. Palpation of the site prior to measurement helps familiarize the subject with contact in the area. The thumb and index finger of the left hand are used to elevate a double fold of skin and subcutaneous adipose tissue about 1 cm proximal to the site at which the skinfold is to be measured (Pett & Ogilvie, 1957). This separation between the fingers and the site of measurement is necessary so that pressure from the fingers does not affect the measured value. A skinfold is elevated by placing the thumb and index finger on the skin about 8 cm apart, on a line perpendicular to the long axis of the future skinfold. The thumb and index finger are drawn towards each other, and a fold is grasped firmly between them (see Figure 1).

The amount of tissue elevated must be sufficient to form a fold with approximately parallel sides. Care must be exercised so that only skin and adipose tissue are elevated. The amount of skin and adipose tissue to be elevated depends on the thickness of the subcutaneous adipose tissue at the site. The thicker the adipose tissue layer, the more separation is needed between the thumb and index finger when the measurer begins to elevate the skinfold. The errors of measurement are larger for thicker skinfolds.

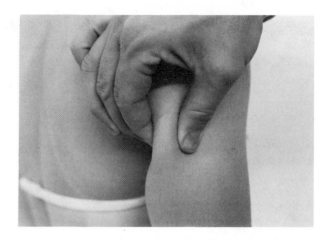

Figure 1   Position of thumb and index finger prior to grasping the fold.

The fold is raised perpendicular to the surface of the body at the measurement site (see Figure 1). The long axis of the fold is aligned as described in the instructions for each skinfold. The basic principle is that the long axis be parallel to the natural cleavage lines of the skin (Langer's lines) in the region of the measurement. The fold is kept elevated until the measurement has been completed.

The caliper is held in the right hand while a skinfold is elevated with the left hand. To make a skinfold measurement, with all except some plastic calipers, pressure is exerted to separate the caliper jaws, and the caliper is slipped over the skinfold so that the fixed arm of the caliper is positioned on one side of the skinfold. The measurement is made where the sides of the skinfold are approximately parallel (Brožek, 1961). This is approximately midway between the general surface of the body near the site and the crest of the skinfold (see Figure 2). The jaws of the caliper are placed so that the thickness of the skinfold is measured perpendicular to its long axis when the pressure on the caliper is released and the caliper jaws come towards each other. The release of pressure should be gradual to avoid discomfort.

The measurement is made about 4 seconds after the pressure is released, with the caliper and measurer positioned so that errors due to parallax are avoided (Becque et al., 1986; Ross & Marfell-Jones, 1983). If the caliper exerts force for longer than 4 seconds, a smaller measurement will be obtained because fluids will be forced out of the tissues. Timing in seconds is preferable to judgments based on the end of the rapid decrease in the measurement. A procedure has been described by Brans et al. (1974), in which skinfold thicknesses

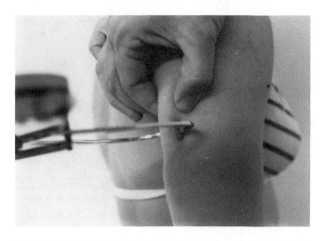

Figure 2 Measurement of skinfold thickness with caliper.

are measured at various times after application of the caliper. The changes with length of application are said to differ between premature and full-term infants.

With some plastic calipers, the jaws are apart when the calipers are not in use. When they are used, the open jaws are slipped over the skinfold and pressure is exerted, to the extent described by the manufacturer, to record a skinfold thickness. With either type of caliper, the measurement is repeated several times and the mean recorded.

With young children, it is helpful to demonstrate the caliper on the hand of the measurer and on the hand of the child, measuring total palm thickness, before beginning to measure skinfold thicknesses. The measurer must be alert to the possibility that a young child may pull away suddenly when a skinfold is being measured. If the caliper pressure is not released quickly, bruising or laceration may result.

The error due to variations in skin thickness is small, but there may be large errors due to subcutaneous edema (Keys & Brožek, 1953; Newman, 1952). In the obese, it may be impossible to elevate a skinfold with parallel sides, particularly over the abdomen. In these circumstances, a measurement is not made, unless a two-handed technique produces a satisfactory skinfold. In the two-handed technique, one measurer lifts the skinfold using two hands and another measures its thickness. This procedure gives slightly larger values (Damon, 1965). This is not recommended for general use, because of the need for a second measurer and because the reference data were not obtained in this way. In those who have lost a lot of weight, the skin is loose, and the subcutaneous

adipose tissue is soft and mobile (McCloy, 1936). Consequently, repeated measurements yield progressively lower values.

Some statistical analyses require that the data be normally distributed. Commonly the distributions of skinfold thicknesses are skewed to the right (Jackson & Pollock, 1978; Patton, 1979; Welham & Behnke, 1942). The transformation suggested by Edwards et al. (1955) usually normalize these distributions.

Subscapular Skinfold

Recommended Technique

The subscapular skinfold is picked up on a diagonal, inclined infero-laterally approximately 45° to the horizontal plane in the natural cleavage lines of the skin. The site is just inferior to the inferior angle of the scapula (see Figure 3). The sub-

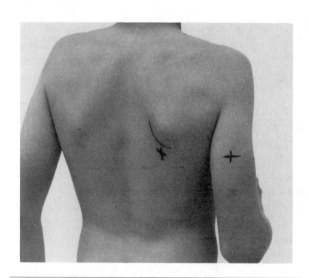

Figure 3 Landmarks for subscapular and triceps skinfolds.

ject stands comfortably erect, with the upper extremities relaxed at the sides of the body. To locate the site, the measurer palpates the scapula, running the fingers inferiorly and laterally, along its vertebral border until the inferior angle is identified. For some subjects, especially the obese, gentle placement of the subject's arm behind the back aids in identifying the site. The caliper jaws are applied 1 cm infero-lateral to the thumb and finger raising the fold, and the thickness is recorded to the nearest 0.1 cm (see Figure 4).

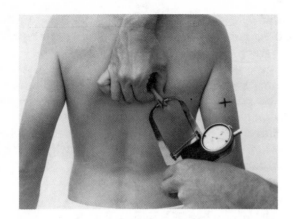

Figure 4 Measurement of subscapular skinfold.

Purpose

Subscapular skinfold thickness is a measure of subcutaneous adipose tissue and skin thickness on the posterior aspect of the torso. It is an important measure of nutritional status and, in combination with other skinfold measurements, is a useful predictor of total body fat, blood pressure, and blood lipids.

Literature

The International Biological Programme recommended the subscapular skinfold thickness as one of 21 basic measurements to be included in survey studies of growth and physique (Weiner & Lourie, 1981). Cameron (1978), citing the work of Durnin and associates (Durnin & Rahaman, 1967; Durnin & Womersley, 1974) recommended the subscapular skinfold thickness, in combination with the triceps, biceps, and suprailiac skinfold thicknesses, as the smallest number of skinfolds representative of body fat. Together with the triceps skinfold thickness, this site is used in health-related fitness tests for children.

There has been general agreement on the location of the subscapular skinfold site, although some authors recommend measuring a verticular skinfold (Cameron, 1978). A diagonal fold, in the natural cleavage of the skin, at the inferior angle of the scapula, is recommended because this makes it easier to raise a fold.

Reliability

The reproducibility of the subscapular skinfold measurement is good. Intrameasurer errors range from 0.88 (Lohman, 1981) to 1.16 mm (Wilmore & Behnke, 1969). Intermeasurer errors range from

0.88 (Sloan & Shapiro, 1972) to 1.53 mm (Johnston et al., 1972).

Sources of Reference Data

Children
Johnston et al., 1972, 1974

Adults
Durnin & Womersley, 1974
Stoudt et al., 1970

Midaxillary Skinfold

Recommended Technique

Midaxillary skinfold thickness is measured at the level of the xiphi-sternal junction, in the midaxillary line, with the skinfold horizontal (see Figure 5). The subject stands erect, except that young in-

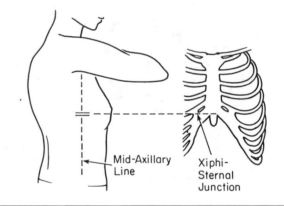

Figure 5 Illustration of the level of the xiphi-sternal junction at which the midaxillary skinfold is measured.

fants sit on the lap of the mother or caretaker. Care is taken to ensure that the subject does not flex the trunk towards the side being measured. The left arm is slightly abducted and flexed at the shoulder joint (see Figure 6). A bra can be worn while the measurement is made, but the strap may have to be undone. The measurer stands facing the side of the subject to be measured, elevates a horizontal skinfold with the left hand, and measures its thickness to the nearest 0.1 cm (see Figure 7).

Purpose

Midaxillary skinfold thickness is a guide to the total amount and the distribution of trunk subcutaneous adipose tissue. It is less highly associated than

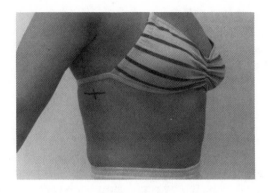

Figure 6 Subject position for midaxillary skinfold measurement.

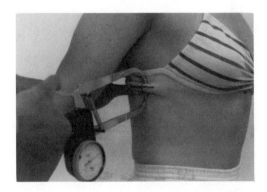

Figure 7 Measurement of midaxillary skinfold.

the subscapular skinfold thickness with the total trunk adipose tissue. It is easier to measure the midaxillary skinfold than the subscapular skinfold in bedfast individuals, and the former skinfold is less likely to be affected by edema. Also, the midaxillary skinfold is easier to measure than most other trunk skinfolds in the obese because it tends to be thinner (Johnston et al., 1974).

Literature

The literature includes few descriptions of the positioning of a subject for the measurement of the midaxillary skinfold, but the positioning in the recommended technique is in agreement with the usual practice.

Most have related the level of measurement to a bony landmark, most often the xiphoid process (Oberman et al., 1965; Pascale et al., 1956; Young, 1964). Less commonly, the measurement has been made at the level of the fifth rib (Slaughter et al., 1978; Wilmore & Behnke, 1969), or the ninth or tenth rib (Lohman et al., 1975). It has been measured midway between the nipples and the umbilicus (Johnston et al., 1974), and at the level of the nipples (Johnston et al., 1972). The latter

level usually corresponds to the fifth rib in the midaxillary line except in women.

The midaxillary skinfold, as the name implies, is measured in the midaxillary line (Johnston et al., 1974; Pascale et al., 1956; Young, 1964), but Pařiźková (1961) measured in the anterior axillary line.

The fold should be parallel to the cleavage lines of the skin at the site. These lines are nearly horizontal in the midaxillary line at the level of the xiphoid process. Nevertheless, this measurement was made across a vertical fold by Wilmore and Behnke (1969). Pascale et al. (1956) measured a vertical fold unless "the lines of Langer resulted in tension of the skinfold. Then the skinfold was taken along these lines." A fold at 45° to the horizontal was measured by Slaughter et al. (1978). Differences in thickness between horizontal and vertical folds are minimal (Chumlea & Roche, 1986).

Reliability

Using the value SD of difference/$\sqrt{2}$, the interobserver reliability was 1.47 mm in children aged 6 to 11 years in a National Center for Health Statistics Survey (Johnston et al., 1972) and was 0.36 mm for children and 0.64 mm for adults in the Fels Longitudinal Study (Chumlea & Roche, 1979). The intraobserver reliability has been reported also as the SE from a regression/$\sqrt{2}$ with values of about 1.0 mm (Wilmore & Behnke, 1969). Zavaleta and Malina (1982) reported a technical error of 0.95 mm for Mexican-American boys and of 2.08 mm for Health Examination Survey data. Lohman (1981) estimated the intrameasurer error as 1.22 mm.

Sources of Reference Data

Children
Johnston et al., 1972, 1974

Adults
Oberman et al., 1965
Young, 1964

Pectoral (Chest) Skinfold

Recommended Technique

It is recommended that the same pectoral (chest) skinfold site be used for both males and females (see Figure 8). Pectoral skinfold thickness is measured using a skinfold with its long axis directed

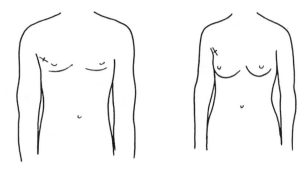

Figure 8 Illustration of location of pectoral skinfold in males and females.

to the nipple. The skinfold is picked up on the anterior axillary fold as high as possible; the thickness is measured 1 cm inferior to this (see Figure 9). The measurement is made to the nearest 0.1 cm while the subject stands with the arms hanging relaxed at the sides (see Figure 10).

For a patient confined to bed, the measurement is made while the patient is supine, with arms

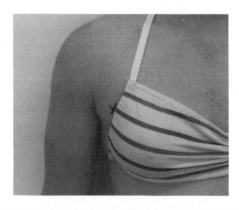

Figure 9 Location of pectoral skinfold on the anterior axillary fold.

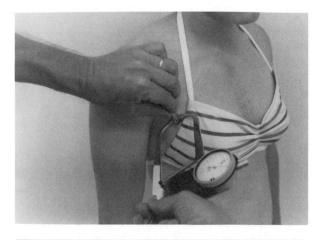

Figure 10 Measurement of the pectoral skinfold.

relaxed at the sides. For a patient confined to a wheelchair, the measurement can be made with the subject in a wheelchair with the arms relaxed at the sides.

Purpose

Pectoral skinfold thicknesses have high correlations with body density determined by hydrostatic weighing (Pollock et al., 1975, 1976). This measure has been selected by regression analysis for inclusion in equations to predict body density from anthropometric values (Pascale et al., 1956).

Literature

Pectoral skinfold thicknesses are not measured commonly. Its exclusion from many studies may result from the vague descriptions in the literature and the complexity of the measurement. Complications include the need for the removal of a T-shirt or undergarment and the need to measure away from the mammary gland in women. In most studies, a distinction is not made between the sexes in the methods for the measurement of pectoral skinfold thicknesses.

Three sites for the measurement of pectoral skinfold thicknesses are described: (a) the midpoint between the anterior axillary fold and the nipple (Pascale et al., 1956; Pollock et al., 1980); (b) juxtanipple (Pascale et al., 1956; Forsyth & Sinning, 1973); and (c) medial to the anterior axillary fold (Katch & Michael, 1968). Skěrlj et al. (1953) appear to describe a pectoral skinfold site located between those described in methods (b) and (c) above. Hertzberg et al. (1963) describe the pectoral skinfold site as juxtanipple, but their illustration shows the site as described under (a) above. The literature does not indicate the direction from the nipple of the juxtanipple skinfold site.

Skěrlj et al. (1953) describe the site as being at the axillary border of the pectoralis major muscle and state that the location is somewhat more proximal for women than for men. Pollock et al. (1984) describe the pectoral skinfold site as (a) above for males and used one third of the distance between the anterior axillary fold and the nipple for women. Depending on the size of of the mammary gland, this description for women would lead to variable site location. The main intent of describing a separate site for females was to keep the measurement away from the glandular tissue of the mammary gland.

The literature is vague, but the general impression is that most investigators measured the thickness of an oblique fold along the line of the anterior axillary fold. Hertzberg et al. (1963) measured the thickness of a vertical fold.

The same site for both males and females is desirable. Although the midpoint between the anterior axillary fold and the nipple is used most commonly for males, it is not appropriate for females. Because of the variability in the size of the mammary gland, it is difficult to use the nipple as a reference point to locate the site. Also, in most cases it would be difficult to exclude mammary tissue from measurements at the site described under (a). The recommended site allows the measurement to be made while a woman wears a two-piece bathing suit or bra.

Reliability

Intrameasurer reliability coefficients are very high, ranging from .91 to .97 (Pollock et al., 1975, 1976). The standard error of measurement *(SEM)* generally averages 1 to 2 mm. Data from 68 adults showed a correlation of .96 between trials measured on separate days with a *SEM* of 1.45 mm (Pollock, unpublished data, 1985).

Intermeasurer correlations are generally above .9, but the *SEM* may vary as much as 3 to 5 mm with inexperienced measurers, or when the site is not standardized (Lohman et al., 1984). Jackson et al. (1978) reported a correlation among measurers of .98 with a *SEM* of 2.1 mm. An intermeasurer correlation of .93 with a *SEM* of 1.7 mm has been recorded (Pollock, unpublished data, 1985).

Sources of Reference Data

Children
none reported

Adults
none reported

Abdominal Skinfold

Recommended Technique

For the measurement of abdominal skinfold thickness, the subject relaxes the abdominal wall musculature as much as possible during the procedure and breathes normally. The subject may be asked to hold his or her breath near the end of expiration if there is bothersome movement of the ab-

dominal wall with normal respiration. The subject stands erect with body weight evenly distributed on both feet. Children stand on a platform to allow the measurer appropriate access to the skinfold site.

Select a site 3 cm lateral to the midpoint of the umbilicus and 1 cm inferior to it (see Figure 11). The decision whether to measure to the left or right of the umbilicus should be consistent within a study. Raise a horizontal skinfold with the left hand and measure its thickness to the nearest 0.1 cm (see Figure 12).

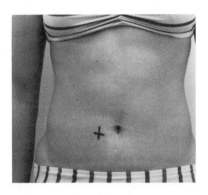

Figure 11 Location of abdominal skinfold site.

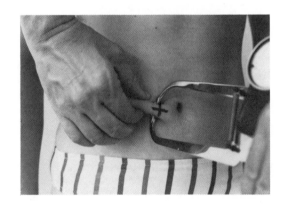

Figure 12 Measurement of abdominal skinfold.

Purpose

The abdominal skinfold is measured commonly and has been included in many studies of body fatness and in many regression equations (Lohman, 1981). Abdominal skinfold thickness changes markedly with weight reduction (Després et al., 1985). It is relatively easy to access, is relatively large, differs considerably among subjects, and is reasonably reproducible with the recommended technique.

Literature

Several locations have been used for measurement of the abdominal skinfold. These include adjacent to the umbilicus; level of the umbilicus but 5 cm to the left of it; slightly inferior to the umbilicus and 1 cm to the right of it, and a quarter of the distance between the umbilicus and the anterior superior iliac spine (Edwards, 1950; Lohman, 1981; Pařiźková & Zdenek, 1972; Skěrlj et al., 1953; Weiner & Lourie, 1981). Most have measured horizontal fold (Behnke & Wilmore, 1974), but others have measured a vertical fold (Sinning et al., 1985; Steinkamp et al., 1965). Some subjects have a "crease" in the region of the umbilicus that precludes selection of a single site for all, and in the obese it is difficult to raise a discrete skinfold.

Reliability

Wilmore and Behnke (1969) reported a test-retest correlation of .979 for measurements made 1 day apart in young men. An intrameasurer technical error of 0.89 mm was reported by Zavaleta and Malina (1982).

Sources of Reference Data

Children

None reported

Adults

None reported

Suprailiac Skinfold

Recommended Technique

The suprailiac skinfold is measured in the midaxillary line immediately superior to the iliac crest (see Figure 13). The subject stands with feet together and in an erect position. The arms hang by the sides or, if necessary, they can be abducted slightly to improve access to the site (see Figure 14). In those unable to stand, the measurement can be made with the subject supine. An oblique skinfold is grasped just posterior to the midaxillary line following the natural cleavage lines of the skin. It is aligned inferomedially at 45° to the horizontal (see Figure 14). The caliper jaws are applied about 1 cm from the fingers holding the skinfold, and the thickness is recorded to the nearest 0.1 cm (see Figure 15).

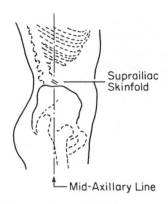

Figure 13   Diagram to illustrate the location of the suprailiac skinfold in the midaxillary line superior to the iliac crest.

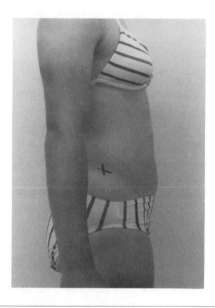

Figure 14   Subject position for measurement of the suprailiac skinfold.

Purpose

Suprailiac skinfold thicknesses are commonly used as indices of body fatness together with other skinfold thicknesses (Durnin & Womersley, 1974). Suprailiac skinfold thicknesses are useful in the study of subcutaneous adipose tissue distribution, which is important in regard to risk of disease (Lapidus et al., 1984; Larsson et al., 1984).

Literature

In most studies, the subjects stood for the measurement of suprailiac skinfold thicknesses. Considerable variation regarding the location and direction of the suprailiac skinfold occurs in the

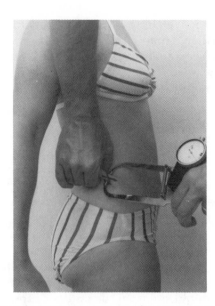

Figure 15 Measurement of the suprailiac skinfold.

literature. Thicknesses at the various locations appear highly correlated with each other and with body density (Sinning & Wilson, 1984), so that no one position appears to offer unique information. Relatively large systematic differences in thicknesses among locations emphasize the need to standardize the technique for the measurement of the suprailiac skinfold.

The selection of a site on the midaxillary line superior to the iliac creast has the advantage of being easily located in reference to anatomical landmarks. The direction of the fold parallel to the cleavage lines of the skin matches the general ap-

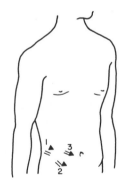

1. Standardized Suprailiac Site
2. After Pollock et al
3. After Ross and Marfell-Jones

Figure 16 Location of recommended suprailiac site in reference to other frequently measured suprailiac sites.

proach to skinfold measurement of this manual. The use of a vertical fold (Behnke & Wilmore, 1974), horizontal fold (Johnston et al., 1974), or oblique folds at more anterior locations (Pollock et al., 1975; Ross and Marfell-Jones, 1983) is common (see Figure 16).

The recommended site of measurement is very similar to the site sometimes described for the waist skinfold (Behnke & Wilmore, 1974; Brown & Jones, 1977; Skěrlj et al., 1953). Because of this similarity, the waist skinfold procedure is not described separately.

Reliability

Wilmore and Behnke (1969) reported a test–retest correlation of .970 for values recorded 1 day apart in young men. Technical errors of 1.53 mm in children and youth (Johnston et al., 1974) and of 1.7 mm in adults (Haas & Flegal, 1981) have been reported. In each study, the errors for suprailiac skinfold thicknesses were larger than those for other skinfold sites. Intrameasurer technical errors of 0.3 to 1.0 mm have been reported by others (Buschang, 1980; Meleski, 1980; Zavaleta & Malina, 1982).

Sources of Reference Data

Children

Baker et al., 1958
Ferris et al., 1979
Johnston et al., 1974 (horizontal fold)
Montoye, 1978
Schutte, 1979
Zavaleta, 1976

Adults

Katch & Michael, 1968

Thigh Skinfold

Recommended Technique

The thigh skinfold site is located in the midline of the anterior aspect of the thigh, midway between the inguinal crease and the proximal border of the patella (see Figure 17). The subject flexes the hip to assist location of the inguinal crease. The proximal reference point is on the inguinal crease at the midpoint of the long axis of the thigh. The distal reference point (proximal border of the patella) is located while the knee of the subject is extended.

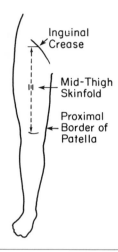

Figure 17   Location of the midthigh skinfold site.

The thickness of a vertical fold is measured while the subject stands. The body weight is shifted to the other foot while the leg on the side of the measurement is relaxed with the knee slightly flexed and the foot flat on the floor (see Figure 18). If the maintenance of balance is a problem, the subject holds the top of the measurer's shoulder, a counter top, or high-backed chair. For patients confined to a bed or wheelchair, the thigh skinfold is measured while the patient is supine. The caliper jaws are applied about 1 cm distal to the fingers holding the fold; the thickness of the fold is recorded to the nearest 0.1 cm.

Purpose

Thigh skinfold thicknesses have moderate to high correlations with body density determined by

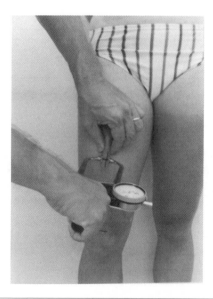

Figure 18   Measurement of midthigh skinfold.

hydrostatic weighing (Wilmore & Behnke, 1969, 1970). Thigh skinfold thickness has been selected by regression analysis as one of the skinfold measures included in equations to predict body density from anthropometric values.

Literature

A few early studies refer to both anterior and posterior thigh skinfold sites, but most refer only to the anterior site: thus, further discussion will relate to this site only.

Although description of the thigh skinfold site appears to be standardized among many studies, considerable variation can be found (Lohman et al., 1984). The most common description of the thigh skinfold site is on the anterior aspect of the thigh, midway between the hip and knee (Wilmore & Behnke, 1969; Zuti & Golding, 1973). Sloan et al. (1962) used the midpoint from the inguinal crease to the proximal margin of the patella. Others give a more general description, such as halfway down the rectus femoris muscle (Young et al., 1962).

The investigators mentioned previously described their measurements as being made with the subject in the standing position, leg relaxed. Some measure with the leg flexed 90° at the knee by placing the foot on a box. This technique is recommended by Ross and Marfell-Jones (1984). All investigators measure thigh skinfold thicknesses with a vertical fold aligned in the long axis of the thigh.

Reliability

Intrameasurer reliability coefficients are very high, ranging from .91 to .98 (Pollock et al., 1976; Wilmore & Behnke, 1969; Zuti & Golding, 1973), although the standard error of measurement (*SEM*) generally averages between 1 to 2 mm. Recent data on 68 adults showed a correlation of .985 between trials taken on separate days with a *SEM* of 1.4 mm (Pollock et al., unpublished data, 1985). Others have reported intrameasurer technical errors of 0.5 to 0.7 mm (Meleski, 1980; Zavaleta, 1976).

Intermeasurer correlations are generally above .9, but the *SEM* may be as much as 3 to 4 mm with inexperienced measurers or when the sites are not standardized (Lohman et al., 1984). Jackson et al. (1978) reported a correlation among measurers of .97 and a *SEM* of 2.4 mm for measurers of varying experience who had trained together. In an unpublished study, Pollock (1986) showed an intermeasurer correlation of .975, with a *SEM* of 2.1 mm.

Sources of Reference Data

Children
Malina & Roche, 1983
Michael & Katch, 1968
Novak et al., 1970

Adults
Shutte, 1979
Zavaleta, 1976

Suprapatellar Skinfold

Recommended Technique

The suprapatellar skinfold site is located in the midsagittal plane on the anterior aspect of the thigh, 2 cm proximal to the proximal edge of the patella (see Figure 19). A vertical fold is raised while the subject is standing. The leg on the side of the measurement is relaxed, with the body weight shifted to the other foot. The knee on the side of measurement is slightly flexed, but the sole of the corresponding foot remains in contact with the floor. If the maintenance of balance is a problem, the subject should hold onto the measurer's shoulder, a countertop, or a high-backed chair. The thickness of the fold is measured to the nearest 0.1 cm about 1 cm distal to the fingers holding the fold (see Figure 20). For patients confined to a bed or wheelchair, the suprapatellar skinfold should be measured while the patient is supine.

Purpose

Suprapatellar skinfold thicknesses have low to moderate correlations with body density, deter-

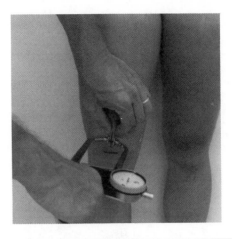

Figure 20   Measurement of suprapatellar skinfold.

mined by hydrostatic weighing or with a composite of skinfolds ($r = .2$ to $.5$; Nagamine & Suzuki, 1964; Pollock et al., 1975; Wilmore & Behnke, 1969, 1970; Young et al., 1961). Postmortem data have shown that suprapatellar skinfold thicknesses have a high correlation with total subcutaneous adipose tissue mass ($r = .86$; Martin, 1984). Because the subjects studied by Martin had more adipose tissue than usual, the suprapatellar skinfold thickness may be most valid with a moderately obese population.

Literature

The suprapatellar skinfold has not been used widely. Most investigators describe a vague site located over the knee or patella (Chen, 1953; Pollock et al., 1975; Wilmore & Behnke, 1969, 1970; Young et al., 1961, 1962). Skěrlj et al. (1953), Nagamine and Suzuki (1964), and Martin (1984) have described a site proximal to the superior edge of the patella. Most do not describe the direction of the skinfold, but Wilmore and Behnke (1969, 1970) and Martin (1984) measured vertical folds.

Reliability

Intrameasurer correlations for knee skinfold thicknesses exceed .9 (Pollock et al., 1975; Wilmore & Behnke, 1969).

Sources for Reference Data

Children
None reported

Adults
None reported

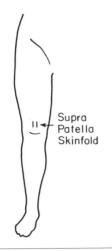

Figure 19   Location of suprapatellar skinfold site.

Medial Calf Skinfold

Recommended Technique

For the measurement of the medial calf skinfold, the subject sits with the knee on the side to be measured flexed to about 90°, with the sole of the corresponding foot on the floor. An alternative is for the subject to stand with the foot on a platform or box so that the knee and hip are flexed to about 90° (see Figure 21). The level of the maximum calf

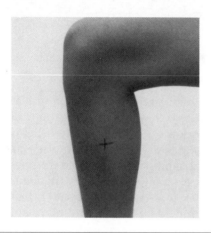

Figure 21 Foot placed on platform or box for location of medial calf skinfold site.

circumference is marked on the medial aspect of the calf (see technique for calf circumference). From a position in front of the subject, the measurer raises a skinfold parallel to the long axis of the calf on its medial aspect, when viewed from the front, at a level slightly proximal to the marked site (see Figure 22). The thickness of the fold is measured at the marked level to the nearest 0.1 cm (see Figure 23). Alternatively, the lateral calf skinfold can be measured using a corresponding procedure.

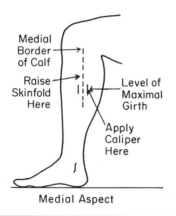

Medial
Border
of Calf

Raise
Skinfold
Here

Level of
Maximal
Girth

Apply
Caliper
Here

Medial Aspect

Figure 22 Medial calf skinfold site.

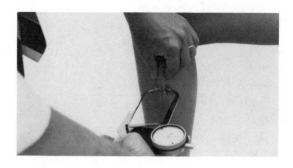

Figure 23 Measurement of medial calf skinfold.

Purpose

The medial and lateral calf skinfold thicknesses sample the adipose tissue in the lower leg region. These thicknesses are important in the prediction of total body fatness and in the evaluation of fat patterning.

Literature

It is important that the measurer's eyes be level with the subject's knees, or lower, so that the hands and the caliper can be placed correctly. The caliper must be horizontal, with its jaw faces parallel to the vertical axis of the fold. When the subject is seated, it may be necessary to move the other leg slightly posteriorly or laterally to allow more working room. It is necessary to elevate the limb slightly to make this measurement in recumbent subjects. Johnston et al. (1974) noted that the medial calf skinfold is technically difficult to measure and that, in about 1% of individuals, the skin and underlying tissues were "stretched" so tightly that a satisfactory fold could not be elevated. Occassionally, this measurement causes some pain or discomfort.

Medial calf skinfold thicknesses have been measured commonly (Clauser et al., 1972; De Garay et al., 1974; Heath & Carter, 1967; Johnston et al., 1974). Anterior, posterior, and lateral sites have been measured less commonly (Correnti & Zauli, 1964; De Garay et al., 1974; Škerlj et al., 1953). The lateral calf skinfold allows easier access than the medial calf skinfold, and its measurement is less likely to be painful. It is not the preferred calf site because of the paucity of reference data.

Reliability

Johnston et al. (1974) reported that the relative errors for medial calf skinfold thickness were similar to those for the suprailiac and midaxillary skinfold thicknesses. The absolute median error for all these skinfold thicknesses was 1.0 to 1.5 mm using a Lange caliper read to the nearest 0.5 mm. A test-retest correlation of .98 has been reported (Perez, 1981). In subjects with a wide range of ages, the intrameasurer correlations ranged from .94 to .99 (Carter, 1986).

Sources of Reference Data

Children

Johnston et al., 1974
Malina & Roche, 1983
Ross & Ward, 1984
Zavaleta, 1976

Adults

Clauser et al., 1972
Ross & Ward, 1984

Triceps Skinfold

Recommended Technique

The triceps skinfold is measured in the midline of the posterior aspect of the arm, over the triceps muscle, at a point midway between the lateral projection of the acromion process of the scapula and the inferior margin of the olecranon process of the ulna. The level of measurement is determined by measuring the distance between the lateral projection of the acromial process and the inferior border of the olecranon process of the ulna, using a tape measure, with the elbow flexed to 90° (see Figure 24). The tape is placed with its zero mark on the acromion and stretched along the upper arm, extending below the elbow. The midpoint

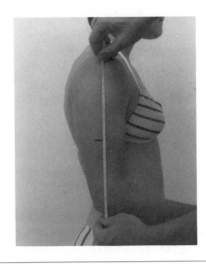

Figure 25 Marked midpoint for triceps skinfold site.

is marked on the lateral side of the arm (see Figure 25).

The subject is measured standing, except for infants and the handicapped. The skinfold is measured with the arm hanging loosely and comfortably at the subject's side (Figure 26). The caliper is held in the right hand. The measurer stands behind the subject and places the palm of his or her left hand on the subject's arm proximal to the marked level, with the thumb and index finger directed inferiorly. The triceps skinfold is picked up with the left thumb and index finger, approximately 1 cm proximal to the marked level, and the tips of the calipers are applied to the skinfold at the marked level (see Figure 26). The site of measurement must be in the midline posteriorly

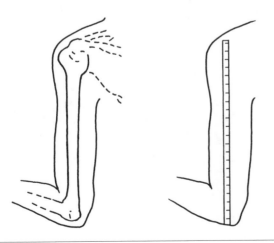

Figure 24 Location of mid-arm level for triceps skinfold.

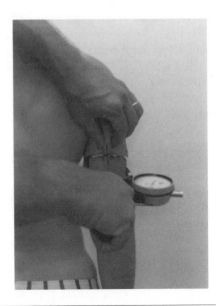

Figure 26 Measurement of triceps skinfold.

when the palm is directed anteriorly. Particular problems will be faced when measuring the obese and muscular subjects with little fat at this site. If necessary in the case of obese subjects, an assistant may pick up the fold with two hands, but this gives larger readings than if one hand is used (Damon, 1965).

Purpose

The triceps skinfold is measured more commonly than any other, partly because it is so accessible. It is closely correlated with percentage of body fat and with total body fat but is less well correlated with blood pressure than are trunk skinfolds. It is often included in studies of fat patterning.

Literature

The level of the site is marked with the arm flexed at a right angle at the elbow, and the skinfold is measured with the arm hanging loosely at the side. Positioning is not crucial, except that the subject should be relaxed and the palm directed anteriorly so that the posterior midline can be determined. Most measure subjects in a standing position, though nonambulatory patients may be measured when supine. Infants may be measured lying down, or being held on someone's lap. When supine or sitting positions are used, the recommended technique can still be applied with little modification.

Reliability

In general, measurement error increases with the age of the subject and with increasing levels of fatness. Intermeasurer technical errors vary from 0.8 to 1.89 mm (Johnston et al., 1974; Johnston & Mack, 1985). Intrameasurer technical errors vary from 0.4 to 0.8 mm (Johnston et al., 1974, 1975; Malina & Buschang, 1984; Martorell et al., 1975).

Sources of Reference Data

Children
Frisancho, 1981
Johnston et al., 1981

Adults
Frisancho, 1981
Johnston et al., 1981

Biceps Skinfold

Recommended Technique

Biceps skinfold thickness is measured as the thickness of a vertical fold raised on the anterior aspect of the arm, over the belly of the biceps muscle (see Figure 27). The skinfold is raised 1 cm superior to the line marked for the measurement of triceps

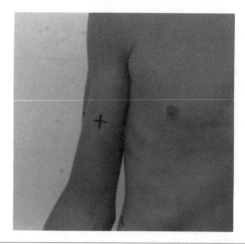

Figure 27   Location of biceps skinfold site.

skinfold thickness and arm circumference, on a vertical line joining the anterior border of the acromion and the center of the antecubital fossa (see Figure 28). The subject stands, facing the measurer, with the upper extremity relaxed at the side, and the palm directed anteriorly. The caliper jaws are applied at the marked level (see Figure 28). The thickness of the skinfold is recorded to the nearest 0.1 cm.

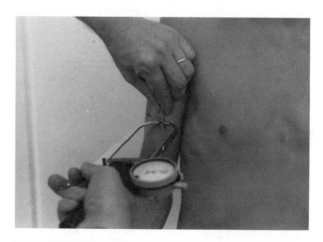

Figure 28   Measurement of biceps skinfold.

Purpose

The biceps skinfold is a measurer of subcutaneous adipose tissue and skin thickness on the anterior aspect of the arm. In combination with other skinfold measurements, it is a useful predictor of total body fat (Durnin & Womersley, 1974). Together with triceps skinfold thickness it may assist the calculation of the "muscle plus bone" cross-sectional area at this level. It can be useful in the obese, in whom many other skinfolds cannot be measured.

Literature

Biceps skinfold thickness is not measured commonly. Consequently, the site has been poorly described, and the reproducibility of measurement is not well established. The International Biological Programme included the biceps skinfold thickness as one of 10 possible skinfold thickness measurements for use in studies of growth and physique, nutritional status, and work capacity (Weiner & Lourie, 1981). More recently, Cameron (1978), based presumably on the work of Durnin and associates (Durnin & Rahaman, 1967; Durnin & Womersley, 1974), recommended biceps skinfold thickness in combination with the triceps, subscapular, and suprailiac skinfold thicknesses, as the fewest skinfold thicknesses representative of body fat; this recommendation is unlikely to be valid in both sexes and in different age groups. The biceps skinfold thickness is used mainly by workers who employ the Durnin equations to estimate percent body fat or study the obese.

Previous descriptions of the biceps skinfold have placed the site generally at the position recommended here. Subject positioning has varied between studies from sitting with the upper extremity resting supinated on the subject's thigh (Durnin & Rahaman, 1967), to standing with the upper extremity held relaxed at the side, palm facing forwards (Cameron, 1978), as is recommended. This brings the site into the anterior midline of the arm, and muscle contraction and skin tension are low.

Reliability

The standard deviation of differences for repeated measurements of biceps skinfold thicknesses by one investigator was 1.9 mm, and the standard deviation of the differences between three measurers was 1.9 mm (Edwards et al., 1955). Technical errors for intrameasurer differences are about 0.2 to 0.6 mm (Meleski, 1980; Zavaleta, 1976).

Sources of Reference Data

Children
Harsha et al., 1978
McGowan et al., 1975

Adults
Durnin & Rahaman, 1967
Durnin & Womersley, 1974
Edwards et al., 1955

Forearm Skinfold

Recommended Technique

The forearm skinfold thickness is measured with the subject standing and with shoulders and arms relaxed (see Figure 29). The arm is pendant and the palm faces the lateral aspect of the thigh. The forearm skinfold is measured at the same level as the maximum circumference of the forearm. The technique for locating the maximum circumference is described separately. The level of the maximum circumference should be marked on the skin (see Figure 30). A vertical fold is raised in the midline of the posterior aspect of the forearm between the thumb and index finger of the left hand, about 1 cm distal to the marked level. Its thickness is mea-

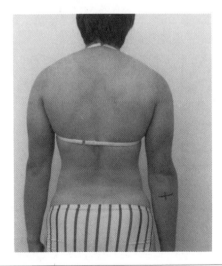

Figure 29 Subject positioning and location of forearm skinfold site on the posterior aspect of the forearm.

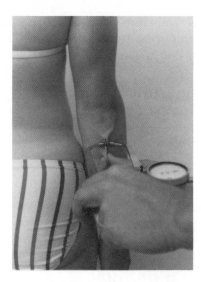

Figure 30   Measurement of forearm skinfold.

sured at the level of the marked circumference to the nearest 0.1 cm (see Figure 30).

Purpose

The forearm skinfold is measured to study adipose tissue distribution or to obtain data for a site where individual differences tend to be independent of general body fatness. This skinfold thickness is not as useful as that of the triceps skinfold for predicting total body fat or body density but may be more useful for studying individual variability in fat patterning. Albrink and Meigs (1964) claimed that forearm skinfold thickness was a good index of "inherited" fatness because it did not correlate with weight gain in adult life, nor was it closely correlated with subscapular and subcostal skinfold thicknesses. In contrast, the thicknesses of trunk skinfolds were well correlated with weight gain and with plasma triglyceride levels. More recently,

Szathmary and Holt (1983) have shown that forearm skinfold thickness is important in studies of adipose tissue patterning in relation to glucose intolerance.

Literature

The measurement is made with the arm pendant, because in this position the fold is vertical, the calipers are easier to read, and errors are less likely. Forearm skinfold thickness has been measured at the midpoint of the radius (Weiner & Lourie, 1981). The recommended site, at the level of the maximum circumference, is easier to locate. This should simplify the process and lead to fewer measuring errors. It is important that the forearm circumference and the forearm skinfold thickness be measured at the same level so that adipose tissue and muscle areas can be calculated.

The forearm skinfold has been measured on the medial (ulnar), lateral (radial), and posterior aspects of the forearm. Weiner and Lourie (1981) state the forearm skinfold "is picked up on the lateral aspect of the forearm." The posterior location is recommended, because thicknesses at this site have health-related significance (Feldman et al., 1969).

Reliability

Reliability data for forearm skinfold thicknesses are unavailable.

Sources of Reference Data

Children
Malina & Roche, 1983
Adults
None reported

References for Part I

Abraham, S., Johnson, C.L., & Najjar, M.F. (1979). *Weight by height and age for adults 18–74 years, U.S. 1971–1974, vital and health statistics* (Series 11, No. 211, Department of Health, Education, and Welfare). Washington, DC: U.S. Government Printing Office.

Albrink, M.J., & Meigs, J.W. (1964). Interrelationship between skinfold thickness, serum lipids and blood sugar in normal men. *American Journal of Clinical Nutrition, 15,* 255–261.

Allen, T-H, Peng, M-T., Cheng, K-P., Huang, T-F., Chang, C., & Fang, H-S. (1956). Prediction of total adiposity from skinfolds and the curvilinear relationship between external and internal adiposity. *Metabolism, 5,* 546–552.

Bailey, D. (1967). *Saskatchewan child growth and development study* (Report No. 5). Saskatoon, Canada: University of Saskatchewan.

Baker, P.T., Hunt, E.E., Jr., & Sen, T. (1958). The growth and interrelations of skinfolds and brachial tissues in man. *American Journal of Physical Anthropology, 16,* 39–58.

Becque, M.D., Katch, V.L., & Moffatt, R.J. (1986). Time course of skin-plus-fat compression in males and females. *Human Biology, 58,* 33–42.

Behnke, A.R. (1963). Anthropometric estimate of body size, shape, and fat content. *Postgraduate Medicine, 34,* 190–198.

Behnke, A.R., & Wilmore, J.H. (1974). *Evaluation and regulation of body build and composition.* Englewood Cliffs, NJ: Prentice-Hall.

Bishop, C.W., Bowen, P.E., & Ritchey, S.S. (1981). Norms for nutritional assessment of American adults by upper arm anthropometry. *American Journal of Clinical Nutrition, 34,* 2830–2839.

Blackburn, G.L., Bristrian, B.R., Maini, B.S., Schlamm, H.T., & Smith, M.F. (1977). Nutritional and metabolic assessment of the hospitalized patient. *Journal of Parenteral and Enteral Nutrition, 1,* 11–22.

Boileau, R.A., Wilmore, J.H., Lohman, T.G., Slaughter, M.H., & River, W.F. (1981). Estimation of body density from skinfold thicknesses, body circumferences and skeletal widths in boys aged 8 to 11 years: Comparison of two samples. *Human Biology, 53,* 575–592.

Bolton, C.B., Kenward, M., Simpson, R.E., & Turner, G.M. (1973). *An anthropometric survey of 2000 Royal Air Force Aircrew* (TR-73083). Farnborough, England: Royal Aircraft Establishment.

Borkan, G., Glynn, S., Bachman, S., Bossé, R., & Weiss, S. (1981). Relationship between cigarette smoking, chest size and body size in health-screened adult males. *Annals of Human Biology, 8,* 153–160.

Borkan, G.A., Hults, D.E., Gerzof, S.G., Burrows, B.A., & Robbins, A.H. (1983). Relationships between computed tomography tissue areas, thicknesses and total body composition. *Annals of Human Biology, 10,* 537–546.

Brans, Y.W., Summers, J.E., Dweck, H.S., & Cassidy, G. (1974). A noninvasive approach to body composition in the neonate: Dynamic skinfold measurement. *Pediatric Research, 8,* 215–222.

Bray, G.A., Greenway, F.L., Molich, M.E., Dahms, W.T., Atkinson, R.L., & Hamilton, K. (1978). Use of anthropometric measures to assess weight loss. *American Journal of Clinical Nutrition, 31,* 769–773.

Brown, K.R. (1984). *Growth, physique and age at menarche of Mexican American females ages 12 through 17 years residing in San Diego County, California.* Unpublished doctoral dissertation, University of Texas, Austin.

Brown, O.T., & Wigzell, F.W. (1964). The significance of span as a clinical measurement. In W.F. Anderson & B. Issaacs (Eds.), *Current achievements in geriatrics* (pp. 246–251). London: Cassell.

Brown, W.J., & Jones, P.R.M. (1977). The distribution of body fat in relation to habitual activity. *Annals of Human Biology, 4,* 537–550.

Brožek, J. (1961). Body measurements, including skinfold thickness, as indicators of body composition. In J. Brožek & A. Henschel (Eds.),

Techniques for measuring body composition (proceedings of a conference, Quartermaster Research and Engineering Center; pp. 3-35). Washington, DC: National Academy of Science.

Buschang, P.H. (1980). *Growth status and rate in school children 6 to 13 years of age in a rural Zapotec-speaking community in the Valley of Oaxaca, Mexico.* Unpublished doctoral dissertation: University of Texas, Austin.

Cameron, N. (1978). The methods of auxological anthropometry. In F. Falkner & J.M. Tanner (Eds.), *Human growth: Vol. 2. Post natal growth* (pp. 35-90). New York: Plenum Press.

Cameron, N. (1984). *The measurement of human growth.* London: Coom Helm.

Carter, J.E.L. (1980). *The Heath-Carter Somatotype Method.* San Diego, CA: San Diego State University Syllabus Service.

Carter, J.E.L. (1986). Unpublished data. San Diego State University, Department of Physical Education. San Diego, CA.

Chen, K. (1953). Report on total body fat in American women estimated on the basis of specific gravity as an evaluation of individual fatness and leanness. *Journal of the Formosan Medical Association,* **52,** 271-276.

Chumlea, W.C. (1983). Unpublished data. Wright State University School of Medicine, Department of Pediatrics, Yellow Springs, OH.

Chumlea, W.C. (1985). Accuracy and reliability of a new sliding caliper. *American Journal of Physical Anthropology,* **68,** 425-427.

Chumlea, W.C., & Roche, A.F. (1979). Unpublished data. Wright State University School of Medicine, Department of Pediatrics, Yellow Springs, OH.

Chumlea, W.C., & Roche, A.F. (1986). Unpublished data. Wright State University School of Medicine, Department of Pediatrics, Yellow Springs, OH.

Chumlea, W.C., Roche, A.F., & Mukherjee, D. (1984a). *Nutrional assessment of the elderly through anthropometry.* Columbus, OH: Ross Laboratories.

Chumlea, W.C., Roche, A.F., & Rogers, E. (1984b). Replicability for anthropometry in the elderly. *Human Biology,* **56,** 329-337.

Chumlea, W.C., Roche, A.F., & Webb, P. (1984c). Body size, subcutaneous fatness and total body fat in older adults. *International Journal of Obesity,* **8,** 311-317.

Chumlea, W.C., Steinbaugh, M.L., Roche, A.F., Mukherjee, D., & Gopalaswamy, N. (1985). Nutritional anthropometric assessment in elderly persons 65 to 90 years of age. *Journal of Nutrition for the Elderly,* **4,** 39-51.

Churchill, E., Churchill, T., McConville, J.T., & White, R.M. (1977). *Anthropometry of women of the U.S. Army 1977* (Report No. 2—The basic univariate statistics. [AD-A044-806] Natick/TR-77/024). Natick, MA: United States Army.

Clarys, J.P., Martin, A.D., & Drinkwater, D. (1984). Gross tissue weights in the human body by cadaver dissection. *Human Biology,* **56,** 459-473.

Clauser, C.E., Tucker, P.E., McConville, J.T., Churchill, E., Laubach, L.L., & Reardon, J.A. (1972). *Anthropometry of Air Force women* (Report No. AMRL-TR-70-5). Dayton, OH: Aerospace Medical Research Laboratory, Aerospace Medical Division, Air Force Systems Command, Wright-Patterson Air Force Base.

Comas, J. (1960). *Manual of physical anthropology.* Springfield, IL: Charles C Thomas.

Cooke, R.W.I., Lucas, A., Yudkin, P.L.N., & Pryse-Davies, J. (1977). Head circumference as an index of brain weight in the fetus and newborn. *Early Human Development,* **1,** 145-149.

Correnti, V., & Zauli, B. (1964). *Olimpionici, 1960.* Rome: Marves.

Damon, A. (1964). Notes on anthropometric technique I. Stature against a wall and standing free. *American Journal of Physical Anthropology,* **22,** 73-77.

Damon, A. (1965). Notes on anthropometric technique: II. Skinfolds— right and left sides; held by one or two hands. *American Journal of Physical Anthropology,* **23,** 305-311.

Damon, A., Stoudt, H.W., & McFarland, R.A. (1966). *The human body in equipment design.* Cambridge, MA: Harvard University Press.

Davenport, C.B. (1921). *The medical department of the United States Army in the World War: Volume XV. Statistics: Part One. Army anthropology.* Washington, DC: U.S. Government Printing Office.

De Garay, A.L., Levine, L., & Carter, J.E.L. (1974). *Genetic and anthropological studies of Olympic athletes.* New York: Academic Press.

Demirjian, A. (1980). *Anthropometry report: Height, weight and body dimensions.* Ottawa, Canada: Ministry of National Health and Welfare.

Demirjian, A., & Jeniček, M. (1972). Latéralité corporelle des enfants Canadiens Français à Montréal. *Kinanthropologie,* **4,** 158-185.

Demirjian, A., Jeniček, M., & Dubuc, M.B. (1972). Les normes staturopondérales de l'enfant urbain Canadien français d'age scolaire. *Canadian Journal of Public Health,* **63,** 14-30.

Dequeker, J.V., Baeyens, J.P., & Claessens, J. (1969). The significance of stature as clinical measurement of aging. *Journal of the American Geriatric Society*, **17**, 169–179.

Després, J.P., Bouchard, C., Tremblay, A., Savard, R., & Marcotte, M. (1985). Effects of aerobic training on fat distribution in male subjects. *Medicine and Science in Sports and Exercise*, **17**, 113–118.

Durnin, J.V.G.A., & Rahaman, M.M. (1967). The assessment of the amount of fat in the human body from measurements of skinfold thickness. *British Journal of Nutrition*, **21**, 681–689.

Durnin, J.V.G.A., & Womersley, J. (1974). Body fat assessed from total body density and its estimation from skinfold thickness: Measurements on 481 men and women aged 16 to 72 years. *British Journal of Nutrition*, **32**, 77–97.

Edwards, D.A.W. (1950). Observations on the distribution of subcutaneous fat. *Clinical Science*, **9**, 259–270.

Edwards, D.A.W., Hammond, W.H., Healy, M.J.R, Tanner, J.M., & Whitehouse, R.H. (1955). Design and accuracy of calipers for measuring subcutaneous tissue thickness. *British Journal of Nutrition*, **9**, 133–143.

Engelbach, W. (1932). *Endocrine medicine: Vol. 1: General considerations.* Springfield, IL: Charles C Thomas.

Engstrom, F.M., Roche, A.F., & Mukherjee, D. (1981). Differences between arm span and stature in white children. *Journal of Adolescent Health Care*, **2**, 19–22.

Eveleth, P.B., & Tanner, J.M. (1976). *Worldwide variation in human growth.* Cambridge, England: Cambridge University Press.

Faulhaber, J. (1970). Anthropometry of living Indians. In R. Wauchope (Ed.), *Physical anthropology*: Vol. 9. *Handbook of middle American Indians* (pp. 82–104). Austin, TX: University of Texas Press.

Feldman, R., Sender, A.J., & Siegelaub, A.B. (1969). Difference in diabetic and non-diabetic fat distribution patterns by skinfold measurements. *Diabetes*, **18**, 478–486.

Ferris, A.G., Beal, V.A., Laus, M.J., & Hosmer, D.W. (1979). The effect of feeding on fat deposition in early infancy. *Pediatrics*, **64**, 397–401.

Forsyth, H.L., & Sinning, W.E. (1973). The anthropometric estimation of body density and lean body weight of male athletes. *Medicine and Science in Sports and Exercise*, **5**, 174–180.

Friedlander, J.S., Costa, P.T., Bossé, R., Ellis, E., Rhoads, J.G., & Stoudt, H.W. (1977). Longitudinal physique changes among healthy white veterans of Boston. *Human Biology*, **49**, 541–558.

Frisancho, A. (1974). Triceps skinfold and upper arm muscle size norms for assessment of nutritional status. *American Journal of Clinical Nutrition*, **27**, 1052–1057.

Frisancho, A.R. (1976). Growth and morphology at high altitude. In P.T. Baker & M.A. Little (Eds.), *Man in the Andes* (pp. 180–207). Stroudsburg, PA: Dowden, Hutchinson, Ross, Inc.

Frisancho, A.R. (1981). New norms of upper limb fat and muscle areas for assessment of nutritional status. *American Journal of Clinical Nutrition*, **34**, 2540–2545.

Frisancho, A.R. (1984). New standards of weight and body composition by frame size and height for assessment of nutritional status of adults and the elderly. *American Journal of Clinical Nutrition*, **40**, 808–819.

Frisancho, A.R. (1986). *Desirable anthropometric standards by frame size for the assessment of growth and nutritional status of children and adults for use with the Frameter.* Ann Arbor, MI: Health Products.

Frisancho, A.R., & Baker, P.T. (1970). Altitude and growth: A study of the patterns of physical growth of a high altitude Peruvian Quecha population. *American Journal of Physical Anthropology*, **32**, 279–292.

Frisancho, A.R., & Flegel, P.N. (1983). Elbow breadth as a measure of frame size for U.S. males and females. *American Journal of Clinical Nutrition*, **37**, 311–314.

Garrett, J.W. (1971). The adult human: Some anthropometric and biomechanical considerations. *Human Factors*, **13**, 117–131.

Garrett, J.W., & Kennedy, K.W. (1971). *A collation of anthropometry* (AMRL-TR-68-1, 2 Vols). Dayton, OH: Aerospace Medical Research Laboratory, Aerospace Medical Division, Air Force Systems Command, Wright-Patterson Air Force Base.

Gavan, J.A. (1950). The consistency of anthropometric measurements. *American Journal of Physical Anthropology*, **8**, 417–426.

Gleń, E., Glab, H., Jasicki, B., Kaczanowski, K., Karás, B., Schmager, J., Sikora, P., & Tadeusiewicz, R. (1982). Rozwój dzieci i mlodzieży w rejonie Huty Katowice na tle populacji doroslych (normy rozwojowe). *Prace Zoologiczne, Zeszyt*, **28**, 1–198.

Guo, S., Roche, A.F., Chumlea, W.C., Miles, D.S., & Pohlman, R.L. (1987). Body composition predictions from bioelectric impedance. *Human Biology*, **59**, 221–233.

Gurney, J.M., & Jelliffe, D.B. (1973). Arm anthropometry in nutritional assessment: Nomogram for rapid calculation of muscle circumference and cross-sectional muscle and fat areas. *American Journal of Clinical Nutrition*, **26**, 912–915.

Haas, J.D., & Flegal, K.M. (1981). Anthropometric measurements. In G.R. Newell & N.M. Ellison (Eds.), *Progress in cancer research: Vol. 17. Nutrition and cancer: Etiology and treatement* (pp. 123–140). New York: Raven Press.

Hall, J.C., O'Quigley, J., Giles, G.R., Appleton, N., & Stocks, H. (1980). Upper limb anthropometry: The value of measurement variance studies. *American Journal of Clinical Nutrition*, **33**, 1846–1851.

Hamill, P.V.V., Drizd, T.A., Johnson, C.L., Reed, R.B., & Roche, A.F. (1977). *NCHS growth curves for children birth–18 years, U.S.* (Vital and Health Statistics, Series 11, No. 165, Department of Health, Education and Welfare). Washington, DC: U.S. Government Printing Office.

Hamill, P.V.V., Drizd, T.A., Johnson, C.L., Reed, R.B., Roche, A.F., & Moore, W.M. (1979). Physical growth: National Center for Health Statistics percentiles. *American Journal of Clinical Nutrition*, **32**, 607–609.

Hamill, P.V.V., Johnston, F.E., & Grams, W. (1970). *Height and weight of children* (Vital and Health Statistics, Series 11, No. 104, Department of Health, Education and Welfare). Washington, DC: U.S. Government Printing Office.

Hamill, P.V.V., Johnston, F.E., & Lemeshow, S. (1973a). *Height and weight of youths 12–17 years* (Vital and Health Statistics, Series 11, No. 124, Department of Health, Education, and Welfare). Washington, DC: U.S. Government Printing Office.

Hamill, P.V.V., Johnston, F.E., & Lemeshow, S. (1973b). *Body weight, stature, and sitting height: White and Negro youths 12–17 years, United States* (Vital and Health Statistics, Series 11, No. 126, Department of Health, Education and Welfare). Washington, DC: U.S. Government Printing Office.

Harrison, G.A., Weiner, J.S., Tanner, J.M., & Barnicot, N.A. (1964). *Human biology: An introduction to human evolution, variation and growth*. New York: Oxford University Press.

Harsha, D.W., Frericks, R.R., & Berenson, G.S. (1978). Densitometry and anthropometry of black and white children. *Human Biology*, **50**, 261–280.

Hartz, A.J., Rupley, D.C., & Rimm, A.A. (1984). The association of girth measurements with disease in 32,856 women. *American Journal of Epidemiology*, **119**, 71–80.

Heath, B.H., & Carter, J.E.L. (1967). A modified somatotype method. *American Journal of Physical Anthropology*, **27**, 57–74.

Hendy, K.C. (1979). *Australian Tri-Service Anthropometric Survey. 1977: Part 1. Survey planning, conduct, data handling and methods of analysis* (ARL-SYS-REPORT-15). Melbourne, Australia: Aeronautical Research Laboratories.

Hertzberg, H.T.E. (1968). The Conference on Standardization of Anthropometric Technique and Terminology. *American Journal of Physical Anthropology*, **28**, 1–16.

Hertzberg, H.T.E., Churchill, E., Dupertuis, C.W., White, R.M., & Damon, A. (1963). *Anthropometric survey of Turkey, Greece and Italy*. New York: Macmillan Company.

Heymsfield, S.B., Clifford, B., McManus, C., Sietz, S.B., Nixon, D.W., & Andrews, J.S. (1984). Anthropometric assessment of adult protein-energy malnutrition. In R.A. Wright & S. Heymsfield (Eds.) *Nutritional assessment* (pp. 27–82). Boston: Blackwell Scientific Publications.

Himes, J.H., & Bouchard, C. (1985). Do the new Metropolitan Life Insurance weight-height tables correctly assess body frame and body fat relationships? *American Journal of Public Health*, **75**, 1076–1079.

Hrdlička, A. (1920). *Anthropometry*. Philadelphia: Wistar Institute of Anatomy and Biology.

Hrdlička, A. (1939). *Practical anthropometry*. Philadelphia: Wistar Institute of Anatomy and Biology.

Huenemann, R.L., Hampton, M.C., Behnke, A.R., Shapiro, L.R., & Mitchell, B.N. (1974). *Teenage nutrition and physique*. Springfield, IL: Charles C Thomas.

Illingworth, R.S., & Eid, E.E. (1971). The head circumference in infants and other measurements to which it may be related. *Acta Paediatrica Scandinavica*, **60**, 333–337.

Jackson, A.S., & Pollock, M.L. (1976). Factor analysis and multivariate scaling of anthropometric variables for the assessment of body composition. *Medicine and Science in Sports and Exercise*, **8**, 196–203.

Jackson, A.S., & Pollock, M.L. (1978). Generalized equations for predicting body density of men. *British Journal of Nutrition*, **40**, 497-504.

Jackson, A.S., Pollock, M.L., & Gettman, L.R. (1978). Intertester reliability of selected skinfold and circumference measurements and percent fat estimates. *Research Quarterly for Sport and Exercise*, **49**, 546-551.

Johnson, C.L., Fulwood, R., Abraham, S., & Bryner, J.D. (1981). *Basic data on anthropometric and angular measurements of the hip and knee joints for selected age groups 1–74 years of age, United States, 1971–1975* (Vital and Health Statistics, Series 11, No. 219. U.S. Department of Health and Human Services). Washington, DC: U.S. Government Printing Office.

Johnston, F.E., Dechow, P.C., & McVean, R.B. (1975). Age changes in skinfold thickness among upper class school children of different ethnic backgrounds residing in Guatemala. *Human Biology*, **47**, 251-262.

Johnston, F.E., Hamill, P.V.V., & Lemeshow, S. (1972). *Skinfold thickness of children 6-11 years, United States, 1963–1965* (Vital and Health Statistics, Series 11, No. 120, Department of Health, Education and Welfare). Washington, DC: U.S. Government Printing Office.

Johnston, F.E., Hamill, P.V.V., & Lemeshow, S. (1974). *Skinfold thickness of youth 12-17 years, United States, 1966–1970* (Vital and Health Statistics, Series 11, No. 132, Department of Health, Education and Welfare). Washington, DC: U.S. Government Printing Office.

Johnston, F.E., & Mack, R.W. (1985). Interobserver reliability of skinfold measurements in infants and young children. *American Journal of Physical Anthropology*, **67**, 285-290.

Kalkhoff, R.R., Hartz, A.H., Rupley, D., Kissebah, A.H., & Kelber, S. (1983). Relationship of body fat distribution to blood pressure, carbohydrate tolerance, and plasma lipids in healthy obese women. *Journal of Laboratory and Clinical Medicine*, **102**, 621-627.

Kannel, W.B., & Gordon, T. (1980). Physiological and medical concomitants of obesity: The Framingham Study, *Obesity in America*, In G.A. Bray (Ed.). (pp. 125-163; Department of Health, Education and Welfare, National Institutes of Health, Publication No. 80-359). Washington DC: U.S. Government Printing Office.

Karlberg, P., Taranger, J., Engström, I., Karlberg, J., Landström, T., Lichtenstein, H., Lindström, B., & Svennberg-Redegren, I. (1976). I. Physical growth from birth to 16 years and longitudinal outcome of the study during the same age period. In J. Taranger (Ed.), *The somatic development of children in a Swedish urban community* (pp. 7-76). Göteborg, Sweden: Gotab Kungalv.

Katch, F.I., & McArdle, W.D. (1973). Prediction of body density from simple anthropometric measurements in college-age men and women. *Human Biology*, **45**, 445-454.

Katch, F.I., & Michael, E.D. (1968). Prediction of body density from skinfold and girth measurements of college females. *Journal of Applied Physiology*, **25**, 92-94.

Keys, A., & Brožek, J. (1953). Body fat in adult man. *Physiological Reviews*, **33**, 245-325.

Kondo, S., & Eto, M. (1975). Physical growth studies on Japanese-American children in comparison with native Japanese. In S.M. Horvath, S. Kondo, H. Matsui, & H. Yoshimura (Eds.), *Human adaptability: Vol. 1. Comparative studies on human adaptibility of Japanese, Causasians and Japanese-Americans* (pp. 13-45). Tokyo: University of Tokyo Press.

Krogman, W.M. (1950). A handbook of the measurement and interpretation of height and weight in the growing child. *Monographs of the Society for Research in Child Development*, **13**, Serial No. 48.

Krogman, W.M. (1970). Growth of the head, face, trunk and limbs in Philadelphia white and Negro children of elementary and high school age. *Monographs of the Society for Research in Child Development, 35*, Serial No. 136.

Krotkiewski, M., Björntorp, P., Sjöström, L., & Smith, U. (1983). Impact of obesity on metabolism in men and women. Importance of regional adipose tissue distribution. *Journal of Clinical Investigation*, **72**, 1150–1162.

Lapidus, L., Bengtsson, C., Larsson, B., Pennert, K., Rybo, E., & Sjöström, L. (1984). Distribution of adipose tissue and risk of cardiovascular disease and death: A 12 year follow up of participants in the population study of women in Gothenburg, Sweden. *British Medical Journal*, **289**, 1261–1263.

Larsson, B., Svärdsudd, K., Welin, L., Wilhelmsen, L., Björntorp, P., & Tibblin, G. (1984). Abdominal adipose tissue distribution, obesity and risk of cardiovascular disease and death: A 13 year follow up of participants in the study of men born in 1913. *British Medical Journal*, **288**, 1401–1404.

Laubach, L.L., McConville, J.T., Churchill, E., & White, R.M. (1977). *Anthropometry of women of the U.S. Army—1977* (Report No. 1: methodology and survey plan. Technical Report TR-77/021). Natick, MA: U.S. Army Natick Research & Development Command.

Lohman, T.G. (1981). Skinfolds and body density

and their relation to body fatness: A review. *Human Biology, 53*, 181–225.

Lohman, T.G., Boileau, R.A., & Massey, B.H. (1975). Prediction of lean body mass in young boys from skinfold thickness and body weight. *Human Biology, 47*, 245–262.

Lohman, T.G., Pollock, M.L., Slaughter, M.H., Brandon, L.J., & Boileau, R.A. (1984). Methodological factors and the prediction of body fat in female athletes. *Medicine and Science in Sports and Exercise, 16*, 92–96.

MacDonald, G.A.H., Sharrard, K.A., & Taylor, M.C. (1978). *Preliminary anthropometric survey of Canadian Forces women* (Technical Report No. 78x20). Toronto, Canada: Defense and Civil Institute of Environmental Medicine.

MacDougall, J.D., Wenger, H.A., & Green, H.J. (1981). *Physiological testing of the elite athlete.* Ottawa, Canada: Canadian Association of Sport Sciences.

Malina, R.M. (1968). *Growth, maturation, and performance of Philadelphia Negro and white elementary school children.* Unpublished doctoral dissertation, University of Pennsylvania, Philadelphia.

Malina, R.M. (1986). Unpublished data. University of Texas, Department of Anthropology, Austin.

Malina, R.M., & Buschang, P.H., (1984). Anthropometric asymmetry in normal and mentally retarded males. *Annals of Human Biology, 11*, 515–531.

Malina, R.M., Hamill, P.V.V., & Lemeshow, S. (1973). *Selected body measurements of children 6–11 years, United States* (Vital and Health Statistics, Series 11, No. 123. Department of Health, Education and Welfare). Washington, DC: U.S. Government Printing Office.

Malina, R.M., Hamill, P.V.V., & Lemeshow, S. (1974). *Body dimensions and proportions, White and Negro children 6–11 years, United States* (Vital and Health Statistics, Series 11, No. 143. Department of Health, Education and Welfare). Washington, DC: U.S. Government Printing Office.

Malina, R.M., & Roche, A.F. (1983). *Manual of physical status and performance in childhood: Vol. 2. Physical performance.* New York: Plenum Publishing Corporation.

Martin, A.D. (1984). *An anatomical basis for assessing human body composition: Evidence from 25 dissections.* Unpublished doctoral dissertation, Simon Fraser University, Burnaby, British Columbia, Canada.

Martin, A.D. (1986). Unpublished data. Simon Fraser University, Burnaby, British Columbia, Canada.

Martin, R., & Saller, K. (1959). *Lehrbuch der Anthropologie.* Stuttgart, West Germany: Fischer.

Martin, W.E. (1954). *The functional body measurements of school age children: A handbook for manufacturers, design engineers, architects, and school officials for use in planning school furniture, equipment, and buildings.* Chicago: National School Service Institute.

Martin, W.E. (1955). *Children's body measurements for planning and equipping schools* (Special Public. No. 4. Office of Education, Department of Health, Education and Welfare). Washington, DC: U.S. Government Printing Office.

Martorell, R., Habicht, J-P., Yarbrough, C., Guzmán, G., & Klein, R.E. (1975). The identification and evaluation of measurement variability in the anthropometry of preschool children. *American Journal of Physical Anthropology, 43*, 347–352.

Matheny, W.D., & Meredith, H.V. (1947). Mean body size of Minnesota schoolboys of Finnish and Italian ancestry. *American Journal of Physical Anthropology, 5*, 343–355.

Matiegka, J. (1921). The testing of physical efficiency. *American Journal of Physical Anthropology, 4*, 223–230.

McCammon, R. (1970). *Human growth and development.* Springfield, IL: Charles C Thomas.

McCloy, C.H. (1936). *Appraising physical status. The selection of measurements* (Vol. 12). University of Iowa Studies in Child Welfare, Iowa City, IA.

McConville, J.T., Churchill, E., Churchill, T., & White, R.M. (1977). *Anthropometry of women of the U.S. Army—1977* (Report No. 5, Comparative Data for U.S. Army Men. TR-7-029). Natick, MA: United States Army.

McGowan, A., Jordan, M., & MacGregor, J. (1975). Skinfold thickness in neonates. *Biology of the Neonate, 23*, 66–84.

McPherson, J.R., Lancaster, D.R., & Carroll, J.C. (1978). Stature change with aging in black Americans. *Journal of Gerontology, 33*, 20–25.

Meleski, B.W. (1980). *Growth, maturity, body composition and familial characteristics of competitive swimmers 8 to 18 years of age.* Unpublished doctoral dissertation, University of Texas, Austin.

Meredith, H. (1970). Body size of contemporary groups of one-year-old infants studied in different parts of the world. *Child Development, 41*, 551–600.

Meredith, H.V., & Spurgeon, J.H. (1980). Somatic comparisons at age 9 years for South Carolina white girls and girls of other ethnic groups. *Human Biology, 52*, 401–411.

Michael, E.D., Jr., & Katch, F.I. (1968). Prediction

of body density from skinfold and girth. Measurements of 17 year-old boys. *Journal of Applied Physiology, 25,* 747-750.

Montagu, M.F.A. (1960). *A handbook of anthropometry.* Springfield, IL: Charles C Thomas.

Montoye, H.J. (1978). *An introduction to measurement in physical education.* Boston: Allyn and Bacon.

Moore, W.M., & Roche, A.F. (1983). *Pediatric anthropometry* (2nd ed.). Columbus, OH: Ross Laboratories.

Morris, A., Wilmore, J., Atwater, A., & Williams, J. (1980). Anthropometric measurements of 3-4 and 5-6 year old boys and girls. *Growth, 40,* 253-267.

Mueller, W.H., & Wohlleb, J.C. (1981). Anatomical distribution of subcutaneous fat and its description by multivariate methods: How valid are principle components? *American Journal of Physical Anthropology, 54,* 25-35.

Nagamine, S., & Suzuki, S. (1964). Anthropometry and human composition of Japanese young men and women. *Human Biology, 36,* 8-15.

National Aeronautics and Space Administration. (1978). *Anthropometric source book vol. I: Anthropometry for designers: Vol. II: A handbook of anthropometric data* (No. 1024). Houston, TX: Lyndon B. Johnson Space Center.

Nellhaus, G. (1968). Head circumference from birth to eighteen years: Practical composite international and interracial graphs. *Pediatrics, 41,* 106-114.

Newman, R.W. (1952). *The assessment of military personnel by 1912 height-weight standards* (Report No. 194). Natick, MA: Environmental Protection Branch, Office of the Quartermaster General, U.S. Army.

Novak, L.P., Hamamoto, K., Orvis, A.L., & Burke, E.C. (1970). Total body potassium in infants. Determination by whole-body counting of radioactive potassium (^{40}K). *American Journal of Diseases of Children., 119,* 419-423.

Oberman, A., Lane, N.E., Mitchell, R.E., & Graybiel, A. (1965). *The thousand aviator study: Distributions and intercorrelations of selected variables* (Monograph 12). Pensacola, FL: U.S. Naval Aerospace Medical Institute.

O'Brien, R., & Shelton, W.C. (1941). *Women's measurements for garment and pattern construction* (Public. No. 454, Department of Agriculture). Washington, DC: U.S. Government Printing Office.

Ohlson, L.O., Larsson, B., Svärdsudd, K., Welin, L., Eriksson, H., Wilhelmsen, L., Björntorp, P., & Tibblin, G. (1985). The influence of body fat distribution on the incidence of diabetes mellitus. *Diabetes, 34,* 1055-1058.

Olivier, G. (1969). *Practical anthropology.* Springfield, IL: Charles C Thomas.

Osborne, R., & De George, F. (1959). *Genetic bases of morphological variation.* Cambridge, MA: Harvard University Press.

Pařízková, J. (1961). Total body fat and skinfold thickness in children. *Metabolism, 10,* 794-807.

Pařízková, J. (1977). *Body fat and physical fitness.* The Hague, The Netherlands: Martinus Nijhoff.

Pařízková, J., & Zdenek, R. (1972). The assessment of depot fat in children from skinfold thickness measurements by Holtain (Tanner/Whitehouse caliper). *Human Biology, 44,* 613-620.

Parnell, W.R. (1954). Somatotyping by physical anthropometry. *American Journal of Physical Anthropology, 12,* 209-239.

Pascale, L.R., Grossman, M.I., Sloane, H.S., & Frankel, T. (1956). Correlations between thickness of skinfolds and body density in 88 soldiers. *Human Biology, 28,* 165-176.

Patton, J.L. (1979). *A study of distributional normality of skinfold measurements.* Unpublished master's thesis, University of Washington, Seattle.

Perez, B.M. (1981). *Los atletas venezolanos. Su tipo físico.* Caracas, Venezuela: Universidad Central de Venezuela.

Pett, L.B., & Ogilvie, G.F. (1957). The report on Canadian average weights, heights and skinfolds. *Canadian Bulletin of Nutrition, 5,* 1-81.

Pieper, U., & Jürgens, H.W. (1977). *Anthropometriche Untersuchungen zv Bav und Funktion des Kindlichen Körpers.* Bundesanstaldt für Arbeitsschutz und Unfallforsehung, Dortmund. Furschungbericht No. 178.

Pollock, M.L. (1986). Unpublished data. University of Florida, Department of Exercise Science, Gainesville.

Pollock, M.L., Hickman, T., Kendrick, Z., Jackson, A., Linnerud, A.C., & Dawson, G. (1976). Prediction of body density in young and middle-aged men. *Journal of Applied Physiology, 40,* 300-304.

Pollock, M.L., & Jackson, A. (1984). Research progress in validation of clinical methods of assessing body composition. *Medicine and Science in Sports and Exercise, 16,* 606-613.

Pollock, M.L., Laughridge, E.E., Coleman, B., Linnerud, A.C., & Jackson, A. (1975). Prediction of body density in young and middle-aged women. *Journal of Applied Physiology*, **38**, 745-749.

Pollock, M.L., Schmidt, D.H., & Jackson, A.S. (1980). Measurement of cardio-respiratory fitness and body composition in the clinical setting. *Comprehensive Therapy*, **6**, 12-27.

Pollock, M.L., Wilmore, J.H., & Fox, S.M. (1984). *Exercise in health and disease. Evaluation and prescription for prevention and rehabilitation.* Philadelphia: W.B. Saunders.

Randall, F.E., & Baer, M.J. (1951). *Survey of body sizing of army personnel, male and female: 1. Methodology.* (Report No. 122). Lawrence, MA: US Quartermaster Climatic Research Laboratory.

Robinow, M., & Chumlea, W.C. (1982). Standards for limb bone length ratios in children. *Radiology*, **143**, 433-436.

Roche, A.F., & Chumlea, W.C. (1985). Unpublished data. Wright State University School of Medicine, Department of Pediatrics, Yellow Springs, OH.

Roche, A.F., & Davila, G.H. (1974). Differences between recumbent length and stature within individuals. *Growth*, **38**, 313-320.

Roche, A.F., & Himes, J.H. (1980). Incremental growth charts. *American Journal of Clinical Nutrition*, **33**, 2041-2052.

Roche, A.F., & Malina, R.M. (1983). *Manual of physical status and performance in childhood: Vol. 1. Physical status.* New York: Plenum.

Roche, A.F., Mukherjee, D., Guo, S., & Moore, W.M. (1987). Head circumference reference data: Birth to 18 years. *Pediatrics*, **79**, 706-712.

Roebuck, J.A., Kroemer, K.H.E., & Thomson, W.G. (1975). *Engineering anthropometry methods.* New York: Wiley.

Ross, W.D., Brown, S.R., Hebbelinck, M., & Falkner, R.A. (1978). Kinanthropometry terminology and landmarks. In R.J. Shepard & H. Lavallee (Eds.), *Physical fitness assessment* (pp. 44–50). Springfield, IL: Charles C Thomas.

Ross, W.D., & Marfell-Jones, M.J. (1982). Kinanthropometry. In J.D. MacDougall, H.A. Wenger, & H.J. Green (Eds.), *Physiological testing of the elite athlete* (pp. 75–115). Ottawa, Canada: Canadian Association of Sport Sciences.

Ross, W.D., & Ward, R. (1984). *The O-Scale System.* Surrey, British Columbia, Canada: Rosscraft.

Rossman, I. (1979). The anatomy of aging. In I. Rossman (Ed.), *Clinical geriatrics* (2nd ed., pp. 3–22). Philadelphia: J.B. Lippincott.

Schutte, J.E. (1979). *Growth and body composition of lower and middle income adolescent black males.*

Unpublished doctoral dissertation, Southern Methodist University, Dallas, TX.

Simmons, K. (1944). The Brush Foundation Study of Child Growth and Development: II. Physical growth and development. *Monographs of the Society for Research in Child Development*, **9**, No. 1, Serial No. 37.

Singh, I., & Bhasin, M. (1968). *Anthropometry.* Delhi, India: Bharti Bhawan.

Sinning, W.E., Dolny, D.G., Little, K.D., Cunningham, L.N., Racaniello, A., Sicnolfi, S.F., & Sholes, J.L. (1985). Validity of ''generalized'' equations for body composition analysis in male athletes. *Medicine and Science in Sports and Exercise*, **17**, 124–130.

Sinning, W.E., & Wilson, J.R. (1984). Validity of ''generalized'' equations for body composition analysis in women athletes. *Research Quarterly for Exercise and Sport*, **55**, 153–160.

Skěrlj, B., Brožek, J., & Hunt, E.E., Jr. (1953). Subcutaneous fat and age changes in body build and body form in women. *American Journal of Physical Anthropology*, **11**, 577–600.

Slaughter, M.H., Lohman, T.G., & Boileau, R.A. (1978). Relationship of anthropometric dimensions to lean body mass in children. *Annals of Human Biology*, **5**, 469–482.

Sloan, A.W. (1967). Estimation of body fat in young men. *Journal of Applied Physiology*, **23**, 311–315.

Sloan, A.W., Burt, J.J., & Blyth, C.S. (1962). Estimation of body fat in young women. *Journal of Applied Physiology*, **17**, 967–970.

Sloan, A.W., & Shapiro, M. (1972). A comparison of skinfold measurements with three standard calipers. *Human Biology*, **44**, 29–36.

Smith, D.W. (1976). *Recognizable patterns of human malformation, genetic, embryologic and clinical aspects* (2nd ed.). Philadelphia: W.B. Saunders.

Snow, C.C., Reynolds, H.M., & Allgood, M.A. (1975). *Anthropometry of airline stewardesses* (Report No. FAA-AM-75-2). Oklahoma City, OK: Office of Aviation Medicine, Federal Aviation Administration, Department of Transportation.

Snyder, R.G., Schneider, L.W., Owings, C.L., Reynolds, H.M., Golomb, D.H., & Schork, M.A. (1977). *Anthropometry of infants, children and youths to age 18 for product safety design* (Publication 77-177). Ann Arbor, University of Michigan, Highway Safety Research Institute.

Snyder, R.G., Spencer, M.L., Owings, C.L., & Schneider, L.W. (1975). *Anthropometry of U.S. infants and children* (Publication SP-394, Paper

No. 750423). Warrendale, PA: Society of Automotive Engineers.

Steel, M.F. & Mattox, J.W. (1987). Unpublished raw data. Department of Food, Nutrition, and Institute Management, East Carolina University, Greenville, NC.

Steinkamp, R.C., Cohen, N.L., Siri, W.E., Sargent, T.W., & Walsh, H.E. (1965). Measures of body fat and related factors in normal adults: I. Introduction and methodology. *Journal of Chronic Diseases, 18,* 1279–1289.

Stewart, L.E. (1985). *Anthropometric survey of Canadian Forces aircrew* (Tech. Rep. No. 85-12-01). Toronto, Canada: Human Elements Incorporated.

Stolz, H.R., & Stolz, L.M. (1951). *Somatic development of adolescent boys.* New York: Macmillan.

Stoudt, H., Damon, A., & McFarland, R. (1970). *Skinfolds, body girths, biacromial diameter and selected anthropometric indices of adults, United States, 1960–1962* (Vital and Health Statistics, Series 11, No 35. U.S. Department of Health, Education and Welfare). Washington, DC: U.S. Government Printing Office.

Stoudt, H., Damon, A., McFarland, R., & Roberts, J. (1965). *Weight, height and selected body dimensions of adults, United States, 1960–1962* (Vital and Health Statistics, Series 11, No. 8. U.S. Department of Health, Education and Welfare). Washington, DC: U.S. Government Printing Office.

Sumner, E.E., & Whitacre, J. (1931). Some factors affecting accuracy in the collection of data on the growth of weight in school children. *Journal of Nutrition, 4,* 15–33.

Szathmary, E.J.E., & Holt, N. (1983). Hyperglycemia in Dogrib Indians of the Northwest Territories, Canada: Association with age and a centripetal distribution of body fat. *Human Biology, 55,* 493-515.

Tuddenham, R.D., & Snyder, M.M. (1954). *Physical growth of California boys and girls from birth to eighteen years.* Berkeley, CA: University of California Press.

Valk, I.M. (1971). Accurate measurement of the length of the ulna and its application in growth measurement. *Growth, 35,* 297–310.

Valk, I.M. (1972). Ulnar length and growth in twins with a simplified technique for ulnar measurement using a condylograph. *Growth, 36,* 291–309.

Valk, I.M., Langhout Chabloz, A.M.E., & Gilst, W. van. (1983b). Intradaily variation of the human lower leg length and short term growth—A longitudinal study in fourteen children. *Growth, 47,* 397–402.

Valk, I.M., Langhout Chabloz, A.M.E., Smals, A.G.H., Kloppenborg, P.W.C., Cassorla, F.G., & Schutte, E.A.S.T. (1983a). Accurate measurements of the lower leg length and the ulnar length and its application in short term growth measurement. *Growth, 47,* 53–66.

Van Wieringen, J.C., Wafelbakker, F., Verbrugge, H.P., & de Haas, J.H. (1971). *Growth diagrams 1965 Netherlands.* Groningen, The Netherlands: Wolters-Noordhoff Publishing.

Verghese, K.P., Scott, R.B., Teixeira, G., & Ferguson, A.D. (1969). Studies in growth and development: XII. Physical growth of North American Negro children. *Pediatrics, 44,* 243-247.

von Döbeln, W. (1964). Determination of body constituents. In G. Blix (Ed.), *Occurrences, causes and prevention of overnutrition* (pp. 103–106). Uppsala, Sweden: Almquist and Wiksell.

Weiner, J.S., & Lourie, J.A. (1981). *Practical human biology.* New York: Academic Press.

Welham, W.C., & Behnke, A.R. (1942). The specific gravity of healthy men. *Journal of the American Medical Association, 118,* 498–501.

Weltman, A., & Katch, V. (1975). Preferential use of casing (girth) measures for estimating body volume and density. *Journal of Applied Physiology, 38,* 560–563.

White, R., & Churchill, E. (1971). *The body size of soldiers.* (TR72-51-CE). Natick, MA: U.S. Army Natick Laboratories.

Whitehouse, R.H., Tanner, J.M., & Healy, M.J.R. (1974). Diurnal variation in stature and sitting-height in 12–14 year old boys. *Annals of Human Biology, 1,* 103–106.

Wilder, H.H. (1920). *A laboratory manual of anthropometry.* Philadelphia: Blakiston's Son and Company.

Wilmore, J.H., & Behnke, A.R. (1969). An anthropometric estimation of body density and lean body weight in young men. *Journal of Applied Physiology, 27,* 25–31.

Wilmore, J.H., & Behnke, A.R. (1970). An anthropometric estimation of body density and lean body weight in young women. *American Journal of Clinical Nutrition, 23,* 267–274.

Wilson, R.S. (1979). Twin growth: Initial deficit, recovery, and trends in concordance from birth to nine years. *Annals of Human Biology, 6,* 205–220.

Wolański, N., Niemiec, S., & Pyżuk, M. (1975). *Anthropometria Inzynieryjna.* Warsaw, Poland: Ksiazka i Wiedza.

Young, C.M. (1964). Predicting specific gravity and

body fatness in older women. *Journal of the American Dietetic Association, 45,* 333–338.

Young, C.M., Martin, M., Chihan, M., McCarthy, M., Manniello, M., Harmuth, E., & Fryer, J. (1961). Body composition of young women. *Journal of the American Dietetic Association* **38,** 332–340.

Young, C.M., Martin, M., Tensuan, R., & Blondin, J. (1962). Predicting specific gravity and body fatness in young women. *Journal of the American Dietetic Association,* **40,** 102–107.

Zavaleta, A.N. (1976). *Densitometric estimates of body composition in Mexican Americans.* Unpublished doctoral dissertation, University of Texas, Austin.

Zavaleta, A.N., & Malina, R.M. (1982). Growth and body composition of Mexican-American boys 9 through 14 years of age. *American Journal of Physical Anthropology,* **57,** 261-271.

Zuti, W.B., & Golding, L.A. (1973). Equations for estimating percent body fat and body density in active adults. *Medicine and Science in Sports and Exercise,* **5,** 262–266.

Part II

SPECIAL ISSUES

In this section three chapters address important issues related to measurement error, which side to measure, and special considerations for measurement of the non-ambulatory populations. In chapter 6, concepts of reliability, dependability, and accuracy are presented. The importance of estimating reliability of anthropometric dimensions is explained with emphasis on the estimation of the essential statistics. In chapter 7, results are summarized for assessing systematic differences between right and left side for many anthropometric dimensions as well as considerations for selecting one side or the other. In chapter 8, anthropometric assessment procedures of various nonambulatory populations are outlined and formulas are given to derive stature and body weight from other readily obtained anthropometric dimensions in the bedfast elderly population.

Chapter 6

Reliability and Accuracy of Measurement

William H. Mueller and
Reynaldo Martorell

Reliability studies have received scant attention in anthropometric studies, and according to Cameron (1986) one reason might be the "lack of standardized terminology to describe the reliability of measurement in a clearly understandable statistical format" (p. 30).

Habicht et al. (1979) have described the various sources of measurement error and propose that these have two different kinds of effects on the quality of data. Certain factors limit the degree to which repeated measurements yield the same value, whereas others affect the extent to which measurements depart from "true" values. Most authors refer to these two qualities of measurement as "reliability" or "reproducibility" on the one hand and as "accuracy" or "bias" on the other. The following summarizes the statistical format proposed by Habicht et al. (1979) and also contains recommendations regarding the minimum data on sources of error that all studies should report.

Reliability

Within-subject variability, called *unreliability* by Habicht et al. (1979), can be broken down into two components of variance: measurement error variance, or *imprecision*, and physiological variation, or *undependability* (unreliability = imprecision + undependability).

Components of Reliability

Imprecision is the within-subject variance obtained from replicate measures taken within a very short span of time. The square root of this term is often called the *technical error of measurement*. The main sources of error of imprecision are random imperfections in the measuring instruments or in the measuring and the recording techniques. Undependability, the component of error due to physiological variation, cannot be estimated directly. Rather, unreliability is first estimated from within-subject variance in subjects measured within a span of time long enough to capture physiological variation. Subtracting imprecision from unreliability yields estimates of undependability (undependability = unreliability − imprecision).

Weight is an example of a measure subject to considerable physiological variation (e.g., fluctuations in body weight caused by degree of gastric emptying and level of hydration) for which replicate measures several days or 1 week apart are desirable. For stature, as little as a few hours between replicates may be required. For most anthropometric variables undependability is not the major problem; the greater concern for most dimensions is imprecision (Cameron, 1986; Haas & Flegal, 1980; Habicht et al., 1977; Martorell et al., 1975; Mueller et al., in press). Unreliability and its two components, imprecision and undependability, are given in the units of measurement (e.g., cm, mm, kg).

Investigators also need to assess whether the degree of unreliability is large or small and whether it varies by anthropometric dimension. This assessment cannot be achieved by simple comparisions of error variances. Rather, one must express error variances as a function of the population or between-subject variance in order to assess the relative magnitude of the sources of error (Martorell et al., 1975). Because the values so obtained are unitless, direct comparison of the reproducibility of anthropometric dimensions becomes possible (e.g., stature may be compared to weight). In the terminology of Habicht et al. (1979) one can thus refer to unreliability, reported in the original units of measurement, as well as to "reliability," reported as a unitless quantity. Parallel concepts are "precision" and "dependability."

Algebraic Expression

The preceding concepts can be stated in algebraic terms. Let the variance component of unreliability be r^2 and its corresponding technical error of measurement be r. Let the variance of imprecision be p^2 and its technical error of measurement be p, and finally, let the undependability variance component be d^2 and its technical-error measurement be d.

Assuming that the components of within-subject variation are additive and independent, then:

$$r^2 = p^2 + d^2 \tag{1}$$

Reliability is a coefficient that has values ranging from 0 to 1 and is estimated as follows:

$$R = 1 - (r^2/s^2) \tag{2}$$

where s^2 is the intersubject variance. The closer the value is to 1, the greater is the degree of reliability.

Imprecision is what is usually assessed in typical measurement-error protocols where subjects are remeasured within minutes or hours. Precision is defined as

$$P = 1 - (p^2/s^2) \tag{3}$$

Within-subject variance *over time* estimates unreliability (r^2) because repeated measures separated by enough time reflect both measurement errors (imprecision) as well as physiological fluctuations (undependability). Undependability is obtained by subtraction:

$$d^2 = r^2 - p^2 \tag{4}$$

and dependability is

$$D = 1 - (d^2/s^2) \tag{5}$$

Because undependability is obtained by subtraction, in practice it can have a negative value, although in theory this could never be so. This may be true especially when r^2 and p^2 are close in value.

Analytic Equations

Analytic equations are those needed for the actual estimation of variance components from data on repeated measures. There is one fundamental equation. It is widely know as the *technical error of measurement* (Malina et al., 1973) or the *measurement error standard deviation* (Mueller et al., 1985). Suppose N subjects have been measured twice and that the time interval is long enough so that the variance is an estimate of unreliability. The technical error of measurement is as follows:

$$r = \sqrt{\frac{\sum\limits_{i=1}^{N} z_i^2}{2N}} \tag{6}$$

where r is the unreliability standard deviation (or technical error of measurement), z_i^2 is the difference squared between the two measurements on the ith subject, and the sum is over N subjects. When more than two measurements per subject are taken, the formula is only slightly more complex, and the case for K measurements per subject would be as follows:

$$r = \sqrt{\frac{\sum\limits_{i=1}^{N}\left[\sum\limits_{j=1}^{K} x_j^2 - \frac{(\sum\limits_{j=1}^{K} x_j)^2}{K}\right]_i}{N(K-1)}} \tag{7}$$

where x_j^2 is the squared value of the jth replicate ($j = 1,2,...,K$), K is the number of determinations of the variable taken of each subject, and N is the number of subjects.

Interpretation

The technical error of measurement squared gives us the imprecision variance (p^2), if the repeated measures are taken very close together in time, or the unreliability variance (r^2), if the time between repeated measures is longer. Equation 6 or 7 provides us with an estimate of measurement error that is in the units of measurement of the variable in question. Its interpretation is clear: It says that two thirds of the time a measurement should come within ± the value of the technical error of measurement. The technical error of measurement of observers should be compared to values obtained by a well-trained anthropometrist (by F ratio of variances). If the observers come close to this reference value in a series of repeated measures taken in the field, and if there are no biases in measurement (see the following section on accuracy), then they are trained and set to go. Also, knowing measurement error values for each variable under study allows the investigators to set permissible limits in order to correct or retake measurements in which differences between replicates are greater than expected. The limits may be set at the discretion of the investigator as one or more magnitudes of the measurement error.

Reliability *(R)*, precision *(P)*, and dependability *(D)*, in contrast to the technical error of measurement, are not in the units of measurement of the variable in question but are scaled from 0 to 1.0. Their estimation requires the appropriate variance component and the intersubject variance (s^2). The latter (s^2) can be derived from the sample of subjects upon which replicate measures were obtained if the sample is large enough and if it is representative of the study population at large. Otherwise, s^2 can be drawn from the literature or from some other representative data sets available to the researcher.

Reliability (Equation 2), precision (Equation 3), or dependability (Equation 5) have clear interpretations. The coefficients tell us how much of the between-subject variance is error free. For example, a measurement of reliability $R = 0.80$ is 80% error free. The within-subject variance comprises 20% of the between-subject variance. This knowledge can be used in predicting the maximum degree of association that would be expected with an otherwise perfectly correlated variable (Habicht et al., 1979). Comparison of reliability estimates for various dimensions can help investigators decide which to retain and which to delete from the anthropometric battery. Finally, the reliability information can also be used in estimating sample-size requirements.

Accuracy

Accuracy is the extent to which an observer achieves the "true" value of a measurement. The true measurement can be approximated only if many observations are taken on the subject by a well-trained observer. This is impractical in any study. Rather, accuracy is assessed by comparing the values obtained by a well-trained supervisor and the observers being evaluated. A simple way to assess differences is by paired *t*-test. If there is a systematic difference, careful observation of measurement techniques is required to identify the problem.

In studies that involve several observers, an effort should be made to obtain replicate measurements for all observers on the same group of subjects. These data can then be used to test the significance of within-observer and between-observer sources of variation in an analysis of variance. Alternatively, Equation 6 can be used to estimate within- and between-observer variances. Measures with high between-observer relative to within-observer variance (comparison by F ratio) are those in which accuracy needs to be improved.

Validity is a sense of accuracy that is unrelated to the quality of measurement. *Validity* refers to the extent to which the variable being measured reflects the aspect one would ideally like to measure. For example, skinfold thicknesses might be included in an investigation because one desires to study the correlates of total body fat. The selection of the more valid indicators involves a different process in which, to use the above example, various skinfold thicknesses would be compared to direct estimates of fat to identify those that are more reflective of total body fat.

Recommendations

Two pieces of information will, in principle, tell all one needs to know about the reliability of a particular variable. These are (a) the technical error of measurement (Equations 6 and 7), which provides information on reliability in the units of measurement much like a standard deviation, and (b) reliability (Equation 2), which provides a correlation-like coefficient that allows comparison of measurement errors for different variables and an estimate of the degree to which the intersubject variance is compromised by error. Whether the researcher wishes to estimate reliability, precision, or dependability will depend on the needs of the particular research project.

Large samples are not required; for most purposes a sample of 50 subjects should be enough. Sample sizes will be larger if different subgroups of the population are under study (e.g., pregnant women and infants). Obviously, the sample selected should be representative of the study population, and all replicate measurements should be blind. Accuracy estimates can also be obtained from the same exercise if desired.

It is recommended that all researchers use the methods outlined above. Analysis of variance techniques may also be used to identify significant sources of variance (e.g., within subject, between observers). The availability of reliability information allows researchers to make informed decisions about whether or not to include particular variables in the study. The timely collection and analysis of reliability data throughout the life of a study is also recommended because it is a useful quality control measure. If the method of reporting measurement-error results described above were to be adopted, readers would be able to easily compare anthropometric studies in terms of adequacy of measurement.

References

Cameron, N. (1986). The methods of auxological anthropometry. In F. Falkner & V.M. Tanner (Eds.), *Human growth, a comprehensive treatise: Vol. 3. Methodology. ecological, genetic and nutritional effects on growth* (2nd ed., pp. 3-46). New York: Plenum Press.

Haas, J.D., & Flegal, K.M. (1981). Anthropometric measurements. In G.R. Newell & N.M. Ellison (Eds.), *Nutrition and cancer: Etiology and treatment* (pp. 123-140). New York: Rowan Press.

Habicht, J.-P., Yarbrough, C., & Martorell, R. (1979). Anthropometric field methods: Criteria for selection. In D.B. Jelliffe & E.E.P. Jelliffe (Eds.), *Nutrition and growth* (pp. 365-387). New York: Plenum Press.

Johnston, F.E., Hammill, P.V.V., & Lemeshow, S. 1972. *Skinfold thicknesses of children 6-11 years. United States* (Vital and Health Statistics Series 11, No. 120, U.S.D.H.H.S.). Washington, DC: U.S. Government Printing Office.

Malina, R.M., Hamill, P.V.V., & Lemeshow, S. (1973). *Selected measurements of children 6-11 years. United States* (Vital and Health Statistics Series 11, No. 123, U.S.D.H.H.S.). Washington, DC: U.S. Government Printing Office.

Martorell, R., Habicht, J.-P., Yarbrough, C., Guzmán, G., & Klein, R.E. (1975). The identification and evaluation of measurement variability in the anthropometry of preschool children. *American Journal of Physical Anthropology*, **43**, 347-352.

Mueller, W.H., Joos, S.K., & Schull, W.J. (1985). Alternative measurements of obesity: Accuracy of body silhouettes and reported weights and heights in a Mexican American sample. *International Journal of Obesity*, **9**, 193–200.

Mueller, W.H., Slater, C.H., & Habicht, J-P. (in press). Reliability, dependability and precision of anthropometric measurements—NHANES II. *American Journal of Epidemiology*.

Chapter 7

Which Side to Measure: Right or Left?

Reynaldo Martorell,
Fernando Mendoza,
William H. Mueller, and
Ivan G. Pawson

Some investigators systematically measure subjects on the right, whereas others do so on the left side of the body. This may be an inconsequential detail. On the other hand, some anthropometric dimensions may be influenced by handedness of the subject, and values obtained from the dominant side may be significantly larger than those of the nondominant side. In this case, studies based on right-side measurements would have systematically larger averages values than those on left-side measurements. It is, therefore, important that we determine the extent of measurement bias associated with side of measurement in order to interpret past studies.

The purposes of this technical note are twofold. First, the biases associated with side of measurement are estimated for a number of anthropometric dimensions. Second, the necessity for recommendations on side of measurement is discussed in light of the findings.

Previous Research

Damon (1965) found that right-side measurements for triceps skinfold thicknesses were 1.2 mm larger than left measurements and that these differences were statistically significant. For subscapular skinfold thicknesses, the differences were smaller (0.6

mm and not statistically significant. Schell et al. (1985), in a study of 135 teenagers, reported similar results. Their analysis demonstrated that the right upper arm circumference was also significantly larger than the left, the mean difference being 0.22 mm.

Laubach and McConville (1967) carried out a study of right-left differences for 21 anthropometric dimensions. The results of their study and some additional statistics are presented in Table 1. Right values were significantly larger ($p < .01$) than left values for arm circumference (at axilla), biceps circumference (relaxed or tensed), forearm circumference, wrist circumference, acromial height, ankle height, and hand breadth. Laubach and McConville (1967) indicated that the fact that measured circumferences of the arm were significantly larger for right-side measurements indicated the importance of handedness of the subjects. With regard to the magnitude of the differences, the author stated: "Whether or not these differences are of practical significance is another question and can only be judged within the framework of the specific problem" (p. 368). A helpful statistic in this regard is the ratio of the difference between right and left (D in table 1) to the standard deviation (S in Table 1). For most of the variables, D/S is trivially small, but for the arm-circumference variables, it is about a quarter of a standard deviation. Cohen

Table 1   Statistics for Anthropometric Measurements of the Right and Left Sides

Variable	Right Side X	Right Side S	Left Side X	Left Side S	t-ratio	D	D/S
Arm circumference at axilla[a]	30.36	2.68	29.64	2.62	10.29	.72	.27
Biceps circumference, relaxed[a]	28.71	2.66	28.16	2.62	9.05	.55	.21
Biceps circumference, tensed[b]	31.56	2.59	30.82	2.59	7.80	.74	.29
Forearm circumference[a]	26.54	1.54	25.99	1.48	10.58	.55	.36
Wrist circumference[a]	16.72	0.82	16.58	0.82	4.67	.14	.17
Upper thight circumference[a]	55.28	4.54	55.22	4.55	0.71	.06	.01
Lower thigh circumference[a]	38.41	2.55	38.45	2.74	0.47	− .04	− .02
Calf circumference[a]	36.58	2.32	36.50	2.54	1.11	.08	.03
Ankle circumference[a]	22.41	1.30	22.45	1.37	1.11	− .04	− .03
Acromial height[a]	143.57	5.98	144.19	5.87	5.66	− .62	− .10
Trochanteric height[a]	92.69	4.42	92.60	4.38	0.90	.09	.02
Height of lower thigh circumference[c]	52.46	2.97	52.63	3.01	1.51	− .17	− .06
Tibiale height[a]	48.21	2.50	48.23	2.46	0.44	− .02	.01
Ankle height[c]	13.79	1.15	13.50	1.00	3.52	.29	.25
Sphyrion height[a]	7.46	0.59	7.48	0.60	1.00	− .02	− .03
Acromion-to-radiale length[a]	33.44	1.80	33.51	1.79	1.46	− .07	− .04
Radiale-to-ulnar stylion length[a]	25.56	1.37	25.61	1.34	1.04	− .05	− .04
Hand length[a]	19.21	0.98	19.20	0.97	0.58	.01	.01
Hand breadth[b]	8.49	0.55	8.43	0.52	3.47	.06	.11
Humerus breadth[b]	7.13	0.38	7.13	0.39	0.00	.00	.00
Femur breadth[b]	9.91	0.97	9.86	0.92	2.23	.05	.05

Note. Data from Laubach and McConville (1967). [a]$n = 117$, [b]$n = 75$, [c]$n = 42$.

(1977) calls a difference between two means equivalent to 0.20 of standard deviation a small effect size, 0.50 a medium effect, and 0.80 a large effect.

Analyses of HANES I Data

Data from the first Health and Nutrition Examination Survey (HANES I) are available for left and right measurements on 4,553 subjects aged 1 to 74 years. Unfortunately, these data are only available for four dimensions: arm circumference, triceps skinfold thickness, elbow breadth, and subscapular skinfold thickness. Average right-minus-left differences (D) and standard deviations (S) are presented for these four variables in Figures 1 to 4. These standard deviations are based on the entire N HANES I population (~ 20,000) to provide more stable estimates. The values given are for right-side measurements.

D values are systematically positive for arm circumference and triceps skinfold but not for elbow breadth or subscapular skinfold. There is a weak tendency for values of young children to be somewhat smaller, but no major associations between

D and age are evident. For all four variables, D is very small, average values being 0.23 cm for arm circumference, 0.48 mm for triceps skinfold, 0.06 cm for elbow breadth, and -0.11 mm for subscapular skinfold. Figures 1 to 4 also present standard deviation values, and comparisons of the magnitudes of D and S indicate that the bias associated with side of measurement, although evident for arm circumference and triceps skinfold, is small. For all four anthropometric variables under consideration, D is generally less than a tenth of S, a trivial quantity (Cohen, 1977). D is also small in relationship to measurement error as exemplified by HANES II data (see Table 2).

Recommendations

The evidence presented points out convincingly that handedness does influence some anthropometric dimensions, particularly dimensions of the arm. For such variables, measurements on the right exceed those on the left by about 0.2 to 0.3 standard deviation units. This is not a large difference in regard to the purposes of most anthropo-

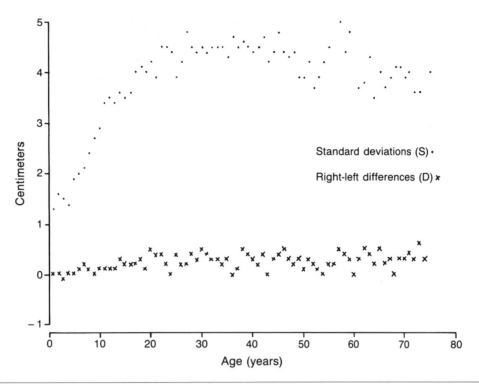

Figure 1   Right-left differences (D) and standard deviations (S) for upper arm circumference (n = 4553).

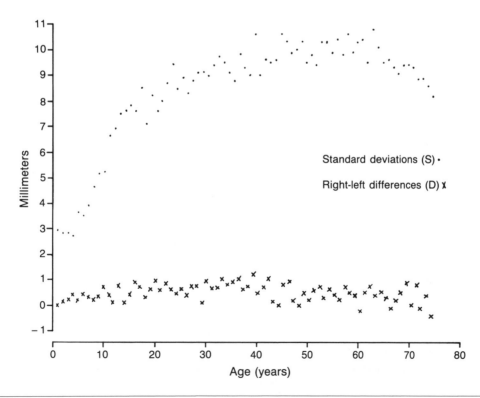

Figure 2   Right-left differences (D) and standard deviations (S) for triceps skinfold (n = 4553).

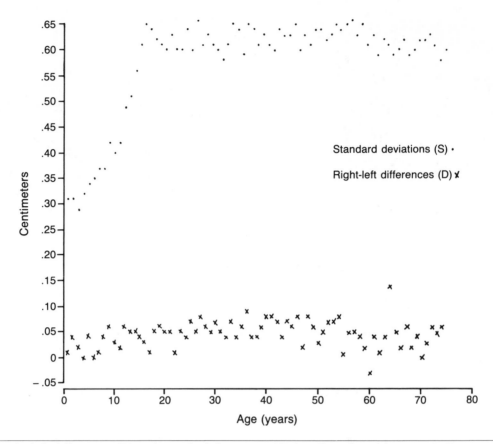

Figure 3 Right-left differences (D) and standard deviations (S) for elbow breadth (n = 4553).

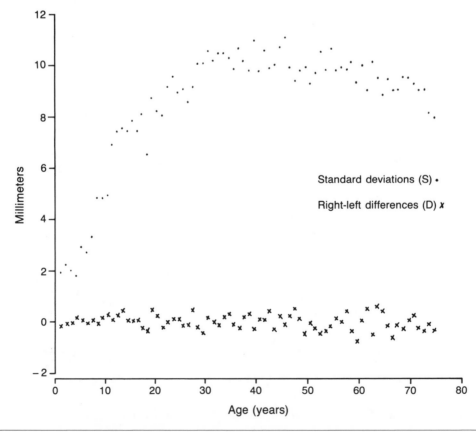

Figure 4 Right-left differences (D) and standard deviations (S) for subscapular skinfold (n = 4553).

Table 2 Measurement Error in HANES II and Side of Measurement Bias (D) in HANES I

Dimensions	Measurement error (ref)	D
Arm circumference (cm)	0.39–0.43	0.23
Triceps skinfold thickness (mm)	2.5–3.1	0.48
Elbow breadth (cm)	0.14–0.19	0.06
Subscapular skinfold thickness (mm)	2.7–3.1	−0.11

Note. HANES II data from Mueller et al., in press.

metric studies. If concern were to exist regarding the comparability of studies, adjustments of the data could easily be made.

A partial answer to the question of whether to measure on the right or the left is that the choice matters very little, if at all. In all cases, the bias associated with side of measurement is less than measurement error. Although it would be advisable, simply on the grounds of greater scientific uniformity, to recommend one side for measurement, consensus would be difficult to achieve. Some researchers in the United States measure on the right side of the body. The large national surveys of the U.S. population, HES and HANES, which form the basis for worldwide reference data, took measurements on the right side. On the other hand, the vast majority of anthropometric measurements in developing countries are carried out on the left. The International Biological Program recommends measurement on the left (Weiner & Lourie, 1981), as is the general practice in Europe. In conclusion, because it matters little on which side measurements are taken, it is best to leave the choice of side to the discretion of investigators.

References

Cohen, J. (1977). *Statistical power analysis for the behavioral sciences* (rev. ed.). New York: Academic Press.

Damon, A. (1965). Notes on anthropometric technique: II. Skinfolds—right and left sides; held by one or two hands. *American Journal of Physical Anthropology*, **23**, 305-306.

Laubach, L.L., & McConville, J.T. (1967). Notes on anthropometric technique: Anthropometric measurements—right and left sides. *American Journal of Physical Anthropology*, **26**, 367-370.

Mueller, W.H., Slater, C.H., & Habicht, J.P. (in press). Reliability, dependability and precision of anthropometric measurements—NHANES II. *American Journal of Epidemiology*.

Schell, L.M., Johnston, F.E., Smith, D.R., & Paolone, A.M. (1985). Directional asymmetry of body dimensions among white adolescents. *American Journal of Physical Anthropology*, **67**, 317-322.

Weiner, J.S., & Lourie, J.A. (1981). *Practical human biology*. New York: Academic Press.

Chapter 8

Methods of Nutritional Anthropometric Assessment for Special Groups

William Cameron Chumlea

If a child or adult is ambulatory and cooperative, standard anthropometric techniques can be used to collect body measurements. However, if a person is confined to a bed or wheelchair, is incompetent, elderly, and/or handicapped, the use of standard techniques to take body measurements may not be possible or their attempted use may provide spurious information. As a result, the clinical management and treatment of such individuals may be hampered by the absence or inability to collect certain body measurements. Nevertheless, the collection of nutritional anthropometry from these special groups of individuals is important because many of them may be at risk for obesity or emaciation.

Methods of "recumbent anthropometry" have been developed for elderly persons so as to remove the effects of their mobility status that prevent accurate collection of body measurements using standard techniques for ambulatory persons. The recommended recumbent measurements are arm and calf circumferences, triceps and subscapular skinfolds, and knee height. Using recumbent techniques, accurate anthropometry can be collected from elderly persons who are nonambulatory or from those who are ambulatory but too frail to stand for the time required for an examination (Chumlea et al., in press). These recumbent measurement techniques can be used to collect nutritional anthropometry from handicapped children and adults also (Chumlea & Roche, 1984), but there have been no tests to determine the relation

of these recumbent techniques to nutritional status in such individuals.

Methods

The subject is placed in a supine position for measurements of arm and calf circumference and knee height. Persons in wheelchairs should be measured in a recumbent position because measurements made in wheelchairs are difficult to collect and prone to error (Chumlea et al., in press).

Arm Circumference

Arm circumference is measured at the midpoint of the upper arm with a tape measure. To identify the midpoint, the elbow is bent to 90°, and the forearm is placed palm down across the middle of the body. The upper arm should be approximately parallel to the trunk. The midpoint of the arm is located with an insertion tape and marked.

To measure arm circumference, the arm is extended alongside the body, with the palm facing upward. The arm should be raised slightly off the surface of the bed or examination table by placing a sandbag under the elbow. The tape should be perpendicular to the long axis of the upper arm and held snug around the arm but not tight to avoid compressing the tissue.

Calf Circumference

Calf circumference is also taken with the person supine and the knee bent to a 90° angle. The tape measure is placed around the calf and moved up and down the calf in a plane perpendicular to the long axis of the lower leg to locate the maximum circumference. When this is located, the tape is held snug around the calf but not tight enough to compress the tissue.

Knee Height

While lying supine, the person being measured bends the knee and ankle each to a 90° angle. One blade of a sliding Mediform caliper is placed under the heel of the foot, and the other blade is placed on the anterior surface of the thigh over the condyles of the femur. The shaft of the caliper is held parallel to the long axis of the lower leg, and pressure is applied to compress the tissue.

Triceps Skinfold Thickness

Measurements of triceps skinfold thickness are made with the subject lying on the right or left side. The arm not measured extends from the front of the body at a 45° angle; the trunk is in a straight line, and the legs are bent and tucked up slightly. The arm to be measured rests along the trunk, palm down. An imaginary line connecting the acromial processes should be perpendicular to the surface of the bed and the spine.

The triceps skinfold is measured on the back of the arm over the triceps muscle at the level of the marked midpoint. The measurer grasps a double fold of skin and subcutaneous tissue between index finger and thumb. The fold must be on the back of the arm, in the midline, parallel to the long axis of the upper arm. The skinfold is held while the jaws of the caliper are placed perpendicular to the fold at the marked level. To avoid errors due to parallax, the measurer should bend down to read the caliper, which is held horizontal.

Subscapular Skinfold Thickness

Measurements of subscapular skinfold thickness are made with the subject lying on the right or left side. The arm not measured extends from the front of the body at a 45° angle; the trunk is in a straight line, and the legs are bent and tucked up slightly. The arm to be measured rests along the trunk, palm down. An imaginary line connecting the acromial processes should be perpendicular to the surface of the bed and the spine.

The subscapular skinfold is measured just below the scapula, or shoulder blade. The measurer grasps a double fold of skin and subcutaneous tissue between index finger and thumb, in a line from the inferior angle of the left scapular to the left elbow. The jaws of the caliper are applied perpendicular to the fold, medial to the fingers, at a point lateral to and just below the inferior angle of the scapula.

Computed Measurements

Some standard or recumbent measurement data can be used to derive additional quantitative nutritional indices: An estimate of stature can be computed from the knee height, and an estimate of weight can be computed from arm and calf circumferences and subscapular skinfold thickness. These computed measurements are derived by using a calculator and the appropriate formulae, or by using the appropriate nomograms (Chumlea et al., 1984).

Stature From Knee Height

Knee height is highly correlated with stature and is used to estimate the stature of an elderly person who cannot stand or who has such spinal curvature that a measurement of stature would be spurious (Chumlea et al., 1985). Computing stature requires an elderly person's knee height, age, and sex. Knee height must be measured in centimeters, and age is rounded to the nearest whole year. The following formulae are used to compute stature, but a nonogram is available for quick calculation (Chumlea et al., 1984; Chumlea et al., 1985):

$$\text{Men} = 64.19 - (0.04 \times \text{age}) + \left(0.02 \times \frac{\text{knee}}{\text{height}}\right)$$

$$\text{Women} = 84.88 - (0.24 \times \text{age}) + \left(1.83 \times \frac{\text{knee}}{\text{height}}\right)$$

Weight From Arm and Calf Circumferences and Subscapular Skinfold

Measures of arm and calf circumference and subscapular skinfold thickness can be used to estimate the body weight of an elderly person who is bedfast or chairfast or for whom a measure of weight cannot be obtained. As for estimating stature, there are sex-specific formulae for estimates of weight. In these equations, the units for arm and calf circumference and subscapular skinfold can be ignored, but the estimated weight is in kilograms. At present, a hand calculator is needed to help perform these computations.

$$\text{Men} = 1.92 \text{ (arm circ.)} + 1.44 \text{ (calf circ.)} + 0.25 \text{ (subscap. skinfold)} - 39.97$$

$$\text{Women} = 0.92 \text{ (arm circ.)} + 1.50 \text{ (calf circ.)} + 0.42 \text{ (subscap. skinfold)} - 26.19$$

Reference Data

Reference data for recumbent nutritional anthropometry for elderly persons 65 to 90 years of age are available (Chumlea et al., 1984; Chumlea et al., 1985). These reference data were obtained from 119 elderly white men and 150 elderly white women, so they are limited as a nationally representative sample. However, at corresponding ages, these reference data do not differ significantly from those reported by the National Center for Health Statistics (Chumlea et al., 1985). Because there are no reported systematic differences in values from corresponding standing and recumbent measurements (Chumlea & Roche, 1984), these reference data can be used for standing measurements taken from ambulatory elderly persons.

It is not known whether one set of nutritional anthropometric reference data can be used for elderly blacks and whites in the United States. Differences have been reported between younger white and black American adults in distributions of triceps and subscapular skinfolds and in the index of weight divided by stature squared (Cronk & Roche, 1982). Despite these differences, however, these reference data can be used effectively to monitor changes in the nutritional status of elderly persons, regardless of race.

References

Chumlea, W.C., & Roche, A.F. (1984). Nutritional anthropometric assessment of nonambulatory persons using recumbent techniques. *American Journal of Physical Anthropology*, **63**, 146.

Chumlea, W.C., Roche, A.F., & Mukherjee, D. (1984). *Nutritional assessment of the elderly through anthropometry*. Columbus, OH: Ross Laboratories.

Chumlea, W.C., Roche, A.F., & Steinbaugh, M.L. (1985a). Estimating stature from knee height for persons 60 to 90 years of age. *Journal of the American Geriatrics Society*, **33**, 116-120.

Chumlea, W.C., Roche, A.F., Steinbaugh, M.L., Mukherjee, D. (in press). Errors of measurement for methods of recumbent nutritional anthropometry in the elderly. *Journal of Nutrition for the Elderly*.

Chumlea, W.C., Steinbaugh, M.L., Roche, A.F., Mukherjee, D., & Gopalaswamy, N. (1985b). Nutritional anthropometric assessment in elderly persons 65 to 90 years of age. *Journal of Nutrition for the Elderly*, **4**, 39-51.

Cronk, C.E., & Roche, A.F. (1982) Race- and sex-specific reference data for triceps and subscapular skinfolds and weight/stature. *American Journal of Clinical Nutrition*, **35**, 347-354.

Part III

APPLICATIONS

Measurement of the human body has had considerable uses throughout history. In his authoritative book *A History of the Study of Human Growth*, Professor Tanner writes that the ancient Greeks, as well as sculptors and painters of the Renaissance, measured the human body to estimate body proportions and, thus, reproduce life-like images of varying sizes. Interest in absolute size developed later in the 17th and 18th centuries out of military concerns. The European armies preferred taller soldiers, and recruiting officers became anthropometrists. Interest in the scientific study of growth and in the relative importance of nature versus nurture in explaining human variation has been pronounced since the 19th century.

The study of human variation and its causes is the main thrust of the first two chapters. In chapter 9, Malina discusses the use of anthropometry in physical or biological anthropology and focuses on applications relevant to the study and understanding of human morphological variability. Bouchard pursues this theme from the perspective of genetics in chapter 10 as he presents a framework for identifying the relative contribution to anthropometric variation of genetic and environmental factors.

Johnston and Martorell write in chapter 11 about the use of anthropometry in large-scale surveys; they emphasize the use of measurements to produce reference data and/or to evaluate the health and nutritional status of populations. The next two chapters are also concerned with the assessment of nutritional status. These contain guidelines for the assessment of body size and composition in infants, children, and youth (chapter 12, Seefeldt & Harrison) and adults (chapter 13, Chumlea & Roche). Chapters 12 and 13 underscore the value of anthropometry relative to more direct measures of nutritional status. Among the advantages of anthropometry noted by Roche and Chumlea are inexpensiveness, relative simplicity of methods, noninvasiveness, and portability of equipment.

The use of anthropometry as proxies or indicators of a state, condition, or risk is continued in subsequent chapters. Himes and Frisancho (chapter 14) deal with body frame and review the use of bone, joint, and skeletal breadths and depths to characterize body build and physique. Lohman (chapter 15) explores the rationale and limitations of anthropometry to estimate body fatness and fat-free mass. The subject of fatness is addressed as well by Bray and Gray (chapter 16) who indicate that obesity poses special problems for the use of anthropometric techniques in estimating body fat. Bray and Gray note that the many predictive equations available from body-composition studies, such as those reviewed by Lohman, may not be applicable to the obese and that it is not always possible to follow recommended techniques in measuring the obese.

Heymsfield (chapter 17) deals with the extremes of energy and nutrient balance in the context of acute and chronic illness. His chapter demonstrates the usefulness and limitations of anthropometry for assessing changes in the nutritional status of patients. In chapter 18, Van Itallie provides the rationale and discusses the use of anthropometry to assess the risk of mortality from coronary heart disease. The use of anthropometry in epidemiological investigations of cancer is the subject of chapter 19. In this chapter, Micozzi argues that anthropometric variables can be used as indirect indicators of dietary practices and earlier nutritional status in the context of investigations of the causes of cancer.

Wilmore discusses the varied uses of an-

thropometry in sports medicine and athletics in chapter 20. In this field, the anthropometric variables of interest are those best related to function and performance.

As noted earlier, the 12 chapters do not contain an exhaustive discussion of all the uses of anthropometry. Rather, the chapters illustrate the many uses of anthropometry in research, clinical practice, and sports medicine.

Chapter 9

Physical Anthropology

Robert M. Malina

Physical or biological anthropology is concerned to a large extent with the study and understanding of human biological variability, including, of course, morphological variation. Anthropometry is a major tool in this study.

Much of our information on human morphological variation is derived from adults. This is unfortunate because studies of children and youth provide more information about the development of morphological variation and the factors that influence it. Studies of morphological variation, by their very nature, have a comparative focus in which variation within and among populations is the central theme. Questions of interest thus relate to which dimensions best differentiate among populations and whether these differences have a genetic or environmental explanation. Because anthropometric data are often collected in settings far removed from the conveniences of laboratories or clinics, an important concern is the suitability of anthropometric procedures and equipment to field conditions.

The terms *racial* and *ethnic* have significant social and perhaps political overtones. The term *racial* implies membership in groups in which there are substantial genetic similarities among individuals. Groups so defined vary genotypically and phenotypically. The term *ethnic*, though it is sometimes used as a substitute for *racial*, applies to cultural rather than genetic affinity (Damon, 1969). The two terms are often confused because biological and cultural homogeneity quite frequently overlap or coincide. With few exceptions, racial or ethnic affiliation in the American culture complex has historically been viewed in three contexts: (a) Native Americans, that is, Amerindians; (b) on the basis of color and surname, that is, American whites, American blacks, Hispanic Americans, and Japanese Americans; and (c) more recently, in terms of geographic origin, that is, Asian Americans. Although individuals are labeled as belonging to a particular racial or ethnic group, the considerable variation within each category must be recognized.

Population variation in anthropometric dimensions that may be ascribed to genetic differences occurs primarily in proportions and fat patterning. Population variation in overall body size is more difficult to attribute to race given the many environmental factors that can influence weight and stature during growth. Body proportions vary among racial/ethnic groups, although most data are limited to comparison of blacks and whites. Blacks have, on the average, shorter trunks, longer upper and lower extremities, and more slender hips (Eveleth & Tanner, 1976; Malina, 1973; Malina et al., 1974). Hence, for the same stature, blacks have relatively longer extremeties, and for the same biacromial breadth, blacks have relatively narrow bicristal breadths. Data for other racial/ethnic groups are more limited and refer primarily to relative leg length, that is, sitting height/stature ratio. These data indicate that Asiatic populations have relatively shorter lower extremities (Eveleth & Tanner, 1976; Kondo & Eto, 1975; Tanner et al., 1982).

Fat patterning refers to the relative distribution of subcutaneous fat on the body as opposed to absolute amounts of fat. The available evidence suggests that the major cause of variation in fat patterning is genetic rather than environmental. Variation in fat patterning relates primarily to the distribution of subcutaneous fat on the extremities and the trunk, although more recent efforts compare the ratio of lower to upper body subcutaneous fat. Whites, for example, tend to have relatively more fat on the extremities than on the trunk compared to blacks, who have relatively more fat on the trunk than on the extremities (Johnston et al., 1974; Malina, 1966; Malina et al., 1982). Compared to American whites, Mexican Americans (Malina et al., 1983; Mueller et al., 1982) and possibly American Indians tend to have relatively more fat on the trunk than on the extremities (Szathmary & Holt, 1983). Variation in fat patterning also has clinical relevance because an upper-body pattern of fat accumulation is apparently associated with Type II, adult-onset diabetes (see Mueller et al., 1984; Szathmary & Holt, 1983), and both Mexican Americans and American Indians have a high prevalence of adult-onset diabetes (Weiss et al., 1984).

Anthropometric data, particularly for children and youth, are useful for monitoring social and economic circumstances in society. Developmental processes are quite plastic and respond readily to environmental stress. It is in this context that many anthropometric surveys are done, for example, to monitor the growth status of children and youth as an indicator of the health and nutritional conditions (World Health Organization, 1976), or of social inequalities in a society (Bielicki & Welon, 1982). An extension of the above relates to the monitoring of anthropometric changes over time. Analysis of intergenerational changes or secular trends can reveal increases in size, reductions in size, or lack of change. All three situations have been documented in human populations (Malina, 1979; Roche, 1979).

A key issue in the use of anthropometry is the selection of measurements. This, of course, depends on the purpose of the study and on the questions under consideration. The measurements should be selected to provide specific information within the context of the study design. Hence, no single battery of measurements will meet the needs of every study. As a corollary, it makes no sense to take an extensive battery of measurements simply because one has the opportunity to measure.

Most variation in human morphology relates to the development of bone, muscle, and fat tissues, as well as the viscera. The suggested measurements focus on bone, muscle, and fat, although the viscera comprise a significant portion of the body mass. The suggested measurements also consider regional variation in morphology; hence, both trunk (upper and lower) and extremity (upper and lower) dimensions are indicated. The measurements are also selected on the basis of ease of site location and accessibility, although local cultural preferences may, at times, limit the accessibility of some sites for measurement (e.g., trunk skinfolds in adolescent girls).

1. Overall body size
   - Weight
   - Stature
2. Specific segment lengths
   - Sitting height
   - Stature minus sitting height provides an estimate of leg length (subischial length)
   - If a measure of upper-extremity length is required, directly measured acromiale-dactylion length is preferred over the projected length of the upper extremity
3. Skeletal breadths, indicators of skeletal robusticity
   - Extremity
     —Biepicondylar breadth of the humerus
     —Bicondylar breadth of the femur
   - Trunk
     —Biacromial breadth
     —Bricristal (biiliocristal) breadth
4. Limb circumferences, indicators of relative muscularity
   - Midarm circumference, relaxed
   - Medial calf circumference
   - Tensed midarm circumference, that is, with the biceps muscle maximally contracted, may be included if an estimate of the Heath-Carter anthropometric somatotype is desired (Carter, 1980)
5. Skinfold thicknesses, indicators of subcutaneous fatness
   - Extremity
     —Triceps
     —Medial calf
   - Trunk
     —Subscapular
     —Suprailiac, over the anterior superior iliac spine. This site is used in the Heath-Carter anthropometric somatotype. The suprailiac skinfold over the crest in the midaxillary line is used in some fat-prediction equations.

The suggested measurements provide information on overall body size, lengths of the upper and lower components of stature, and skeletal, muscular, and subcutaneous fat tissue development in different parts of the body. Obviously, other dimensions can be added depending on research objectives and study design. The suggested measurements can be used to derive a variety of indices: the sitting height/stature ratio, the ratio of bicristal to biacromial breadths, midarm circumference fat and muscle areas, and so on. The suggested dimensions also include those necessary for estimates of the Heath-Carter anthropometric somatotype (Carter, 1980), recognizing, of course, that the definition of somatotype by this method is not identical with the Sheldonian somatotype (see Wilmore's chapter in this volume for more discussion on the Heath-Carter technique).

In any suggested list of anthropometric dimensions, there are always special considerations. Three aspects deserve mention:

1. Head circumference is a useful indicator of the growth of the skull and, of course, its contents during infancy and early childhood.

2. If variation on craniofacial morphology is of importance, the following dimensions provide basic information:

   - Head length, glabella-opisthocranion
   - Head breadth, euryon-euryon
   - Bizygomatic breadth
   - Bigonial breadth

3. Given the recent concern for the usefulness of trunk girths as indicators of fat distribution in adults, it may be useful to collect information on two trunk circumferences:
   - Abdominal circumference
   - Hip circumference

The preceding is largely concerned with anthropometric dimensions that are useful in documenting morphological variation in the context of physical or biological anthropology. However, an additional component of physical anthropology concerns the use of anthropometric data in the design of furniture, clothing, equipment, and so on for children and adults. These objectives require a greater variety of dimensions, many of which are functional (see chapter 2 on Segment Lengths in this manual).

References

Bielicki, T., & Welon, Z. (1982). Growth data as indicators of social inequalities: The case of Poland. *Yearbook of Physical Anthropology*, **25**, 153-167.

Carter, J.E.L. (1980). *The Heath-Carter Somatotype Method*. San Diego, CA: San Diego State University Syllabus Service.

Damon, A. (1969). Race, ethnic group, and disease. *Social Biology*, **16**, 69-80.

Eveleth, P.B., & Tanner, J.M. (1976). *Worldwide variation in human growth*. Cambridge: Cambridge University Press.

Johnston, F.E., Hamill, P.V.V., & Lemeshow, S. (1974). *Skinfold thickness of youths 12-17 years, United States* (Vital and Health Statistics, Series 11, No. 132). Washington, DC: U.S. Government Printing Office.

Kondo, S., & Eto, M. (1975) Physical growth studies on Japanese-American children in comparison with native Japanese. In S.M. Horvath, S. Kondo, H. Matsui, & H. Yoshimura (Eds.), *Human adaptability: Vol. I. Comparative studies on human adaptability of Japanese, Caucasians and Japanese Americans* (pp. 13-45). Tokyo: University of Tokyo Press.

Malina, R.M. (1966). Patterns of development in skinfolds of Negro and white children. *Human Biology*, **38**, 89-103.

Malina, R.M. (1973). Biological substrata. In K.S. Miller & R.M. Dreger (Eds.), *Comparative studies of blacks and whites in the United States* (pp. 53-123). New York: Seminar Press.

Malina, R.M. (1979), Secular changes in growth, maturation, and physical performance. *Exercise and Sport Science Reviews*, **6**, 203-255.

Malina, R.M., Hamill, P.V.V., & Lemeshow, S. (1974). *Body dimensions and proportions, white and Negro children 6-11 years, United States* (Vital and Health Statistics, Series 11, No. 143). Washington, DC: U.S. Government Printing Office.

Malina, R.M., Little, B.B., Stern, M.P., Gaskill, S.P., & Hazuda, H.P. (1983). Ethnic and social class differences in selected anthropometric characteristics of Mexican American and Anglo adults: The San Antonio Heart Study. *Human Biology*, **55**, 867-883.

Malina, R.M., Mueller, W.H., Bouchard, C., Shoup, R.F., & Lariviere, G. (1982). Fatness and fat patterning among athletes at the Montreal Olympic Games, 1976. *Medicine and Science in Sports and Exercise,* **14**, 445-452.

Mueller, W.H., Joos, S.K., Hanis, C.L., Zavaleta, A.N., Eichner, J., & Schull, W.J. (1984). The Diabetes Alert Study: Growth, fatness, and fat patterning, adolescence through adulthood in Mexican Americans. *American Journal of Physical Anthropology,* **64**, 389-399.

Mueller, W.H., Shoup, R.F., & Malina, R.M. (1982). Fat patterning in athletes in relation to ethnic origin and sport. *Annals of Human Biology,* **9**, 371-376.

Roche, A.F. (1979). Secular trends in stature, weight, and maturation. *Monograph of the Society for Research and Child Development,* **44**(3-43), 3-27.

Szathmary, E.J.E., & Holt, N. (1983). Hyperglycemia in Dogrib Indians of the Northwest Terri-tories, Canada: Association with age and a centripetal distribution of body fat. *Human Biology,* **55**, 493-515.

Tanner, J.M., Hayashi, T., Preece, M.A., & Cameron, N. (1982). Increase in length of leg relative to trunk in Japanese children and adults from 1957 to 1977: Comparison with British and with Japanese-Americans. *Annals of Human Biology,* **9**, 411-423.

Weiss, K.M., Ferrell, R.E., & Hanis, C.L. (1984). A new world syndrome of metabolic diseases with a genetic and evolutionary basis. *Yearbook of Physical Anthropology,* **27**, 153-178.

World Health Organization. (1976). *New trends and approaches in the delivery of maternal and child care in health services* (WHO Technical Report Series, No. 600). Geneva: World Health Organization.

Chapter 10

Human Variation in Anthropometric Dimensions

Claude Bouchard

Understanding the causes of human variation is a continuing goal of research. Anthropometric traits vary within and between populations, and many studies have attempted to identify the relative contribution to variation of genetic and environmental factors.

A model integrating the major sources of human variation for a given anthropometric trait, say P, is useful in discussing the causes of interindividual differences in a systematic manner. One such model partitions the variation in P as follows (Bouchard, 1986; Bouchard & Malina, 1983):

$$P = G + E + G \times E + e.$$

In this equation, G represents the variation related to heredity or genetic factors, E stands for the effects associated with environmental conditions and lifestyle, $G \times E$ is the interaction effect between genetic factors and nongenetic influences, and e is the variation caused by random sources of error.

This simplified model assumes that age and sex of subjects do not contribute to individual differences. Of course, this is an assumption that is rarely met, unless one controls these effects by design or uses statistical procedures to remove these influences from the variance. In the study of human variation in anthropometric measurements one has, therefore, to be aware of the possibility that several complex agents are simultaneously operative. A discussion about the other assumptions associated with the use of this model can be found elsewhere (Bouchard & Malina, 1983).

The E Effect

The E component represents all sources of influence on the anthropometric dimension that are independent of genotype and that do not represent error in the system. It is generally assumed that the E effect is caused by variation in milieu, lifestyle, and environmental conditions. Thus, skeletal dimensions or skinfolds for a given age and sex class may exhibit considerable interindividual differences as a result of nutritional history and current status, past and current habitual energy expenditure associated with occupation and leisure activities, history of diseases and present health status, socioeconomic and general living conditions, altitude, climate, and undoubtedly many other factors. In other words, the E component is a composite of complex, often interrelated causes. It is, most of the time, quite difficult to assess the full extent of the E effect on a given anthropometric dimension because the potentially contributing factors are numerous and one can seldom control them all in a given study.

The G and $G \times E$ Effects

The G and $G \times E$ effects stand for all the causes of individual differences that are associated with inherited characteristics. The G effect for a given anthropometric phenotype can be considered as the average contribution of heredity in the population, irrespective of environmental conditions and variations in lifestyle. In other words, the G effect is a population parameter reflecting the extent of transmissible genetic variance from one generation to the next. G is a population parameter in that it represents the contribution of genetic variation to interindividual differences under average environmental conditions. The genetic variation for any individual will vary depending upon that person's unique characteristics and life history.

The estimate of the population parameter G for a given anthropometric trait requires a complex database. One would like to rely on data gathered on all types of two- and three-generation relatives including adoption data, twins reared together and apart, families of monozygotic twins and others. Moreover, large sample sizes would be desirable to derive reliable estimates of G and related parameters. Data currently available never meet these stringent conditions, and thus any estimates of G (or heritability) for anthropometric characteristics must be viewed with caution at present.

The situation becomes much more complex if the interaction term, $G \times E$, is large. Figure 1 illustrates the situation where G and E effects are additive and noninteractive; in this case, variations in P are linear over the range of E conditions. Figure 2 describes a situation that is probably closer to reality for most phenotypes (Bouchard, 1983, 1986; Poehlman et al., 1986; Prud'homme et al., 1984). In this case, variation is a function of not only G and E but the interaction $G \times E$ as well. Thus, changes in P associated with variation in E are not identical for all genotypes. Little has been written on the $G \times E$ effect for anthropometric measurements, but recent evidence from our laboratory in-

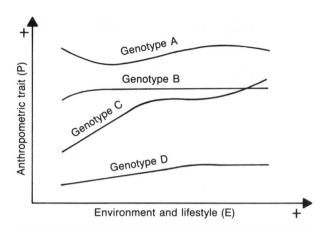

Figure 2 Variation in a given anthropometric measurement (P) when $e = 0$. In this case, $P = G + E = G \times E$.

dicates that there is a significant $G \times E$ effect for body weight and skinfold measurements when individuals are exposed to a positive energy balance over a period of a few weeks (Poehlman et al., 1986).

Variation Within and Between Populations

It is becoming increasingly recognized that most of genetic variation, as determined from antigenic and protein systems, is common to all human beings. Estimates are that only about 10% to 15% of human variation in single gene systems is specific to populations or races, whereas the remaining variation is shared by all humans regardless of race or population (Nei, 1982; Nei & Roychoudhury, 1974).

A wealth of data has accumulated on body dimensions of individuals of all races and ethnic groups. Even though there are often mean differences for anthropometric measurements among populations, the ranges of values overlap considerably.

Attention should be focused more on the within-population and between-populations heterogeneity to better describe the importance of race or human group differences in total human phenotype variance. In this context, it has been suggested that the between-population variance tends to be generally less than the within-population variance for skeletal dimensions of the body (Weiner, 1971).

In summary, when measurement unreliability and age and sex of the individuals are controlled

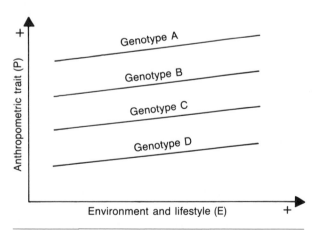

Figure 1 Variation in a given anthropometric measurement (P) when $G \times E = e = 0$. In this case, $P = G + E$.

for either statistically or experimentally, then human variation in a given anthropometric trait can be accounted for by three major components. Complex databases and elaborate experimental designs are needed to estimate the influence of each of these components of the model for any anthropometic trait. In addition, population differences and heterogeneity can be considered, but this should be undertaken only with sample sizes and appropriate controls over concomitant variables.

References

Bouchard, C. (1983). Human adaptability may have a genetic basis. In F. Landry (Ed.), *Health risk estimation, risk reduction and health promotion* (pp. 463-476). Ottawa: Canadian Public Health Association.

Bouchard, C. (1986). Genetics of aerobic power and capacity. In R.M. Malina & C. Bouchard (Eds.), *Sport and human genetics* (pp. 59-88). Champaign, IL: Human Kinetics.

Bouchard, C., & Malina, R.M. (1983). Genetics for the sport scientist: Selected methodological considerations. In R.L. Terjung (Ed.), *Exercise and sport sciences reviews* (pp. 275-305). Philadelphia: Franklin Institute.

Nei, M. (1982). Evolution of man races at the gene level. In B. Bonne-Tamir & T. Cohen (Eds.), *Human genetics: Part A. The unfolding genome* (pp. 167-181). New York: Alan R. Liss.

Nei, M., & Roychoudhury, A.K. (1974). Genetic variation within and between the three major races of man, Causasoids, Negroids, and Mongoloids. *American Journal of Human Genetics, 26*, 421-443.

Poehlman, E.T., Tremblay, A., Deprés, J.P., Fontaine, E., Pérusse, L., Thériault, G., & Bouchard, C. (1986). Genotype-controlled changes in body composition and fat morphology following overfeeding in twins. *American Journal of Clinical Nutrition, 43*, 723-731.

Poehlman, E.T., Tremblay, A., Fontaine, E., Després, J.P., Nadeau, A., Dussault, J., & Bouchard, C. (1986). Genotype dependence of the thermic effect of a meal and associated hormonal changes following short-term overfeeding. *Metabolism, 35*, 30-36.

Prud'homme, D., Bouchard, C., Leblanc, C., Landry, F., & Fontaine, E. (1984). Sensitivity of maximal aerobic power to training is genotype dependent. *Medicine and Science in Sports and Exercise, 16*, 489-493.

Weiner, J.S. (1971). *The natural history of man.* New York: Universe Books.

Chapter 11

Population Surveys

Francis E. Johnston and
Reynaldo Martorell

Large-scale anthropometric surveys are usually undertaken to produce reference data and/or to evaluate the health and nutritional status of populations. Properly done, such surveys produce extremely useful data sets that have applications far beyond their original, usually descriptive, purposes. However, such surveys also carry inherent constraints.

Chief among these constraints is the limited choice of anthropometric dimensions. One cannot hope to collect an extensive battery of anthropometric measurements on a sample of, perhaps, 15,000 or more subjects, measured in multiple locations during a 2 or 3 year period. This problem becomes even more acute if, as is usually the case, information on sociological, psychometric, medical, and other areas is being collected as well. The time allotted to the anthropometric component of the examination may not be enough to permit taking a large group of measurements. Advance planning and appropriate consultation are required so that the choice of measurements reflects the needs and interests of users of the survey results. The purpose of the survey must be stated explicitly, and data to be collected should, insofar as is possible, achieve that purpose. The addition of measurements to satisfy peripheral interests must be done judiciously and only after considering the value of the data relative to time and other resources required to collect, edit, and analyze them.

Interpretation and Use of Anthropometric Indicators

There is no single list of measurements that is appropriate for all large-scale surveys. Every measurement selected should provide useful information congruent with the purpose of the survey. However, the basic components of human biological variability should be kept in mind and, as a minimum, measures of stature or body length, body mass, and its two major compartments, adipose tissue and lean body mass and body breadths (e.g., bioacromial and bicristal breadths) should be included.

Anthropometric indicators generally exhibit high sensitivity (Habicht et al., 1979). That is, anthropometric indicators are often very responsive to environmental effects. Epidemiological investigators take advantage of this general property in assessing the health effects of numerous variables, including infections, nutrient deficiencies or excesses, and environmental factors such as high altitude, psychological stress, and airport noise. The very sensitivity of growth to numerous factors accounts for the fact that anthropometric indicators alone tell researchers little about the nature of the problems that are affecting growth. In order to identify these influencing factors, as noted earlier, surveys need to collect data on a wide range of variables.

Anthropometric data have varied uses in public health. An especially important application is to identify significant growth retardation in children (Martorell, 1985). Simple indicators based on weight-to-length comparisons and indices that use arm circumference are, for example, useful for identifying individuals at high risk for morbidity and mortality. Monitoring weight velocities with growth charts is even better because children at risk can be identified long before the point at which they become wasted (Morley, 1976). Other uses include the selection of zones or groups within countries that are likely to be malnourished, the evaluation of the impact of specific interventions, and the monitoring of secular changes in particular areas or countries.

The use of anthropometry in nutrition work in developing countries is not without its problems. For countries that are ethnically diverse, the question of genetic differences among ethnic groups is frequently raised in the interpretation of anthropometric data (Martorell, 1985). Reference standards from developed nations are used in many countries; the latest of these standards is the NCHS-Fels amalgamation of a large cross-sectional survey of the U.S. population (NCHS) with a longitudinal study of predominantly middle–class Ohio children (Hamill et al., 1979). The use of such reference data is questioned by some who consider that such standards exaggerate the prevalence of malnutrition through being confounded by genetic variables (Goldstein & Tanner, 1980). Others believe that poverty is the predominant factor explaining body-size differences among children of various ethnic groups and income levels and, as a result, hold the view that reference data from a well-nourished population from the United States are appropriate (Graitcer & Gentry, 1981).

Anthropometry is also useful for studies of chronic diseases endemic to developed countries, including cardiovascular disease, cancer, obesity, and diabetes (see relevant chapters in this section). In these studies, anthropometric variables are often viewed as long-term indicators of life patterns and as overall measures of health. Much research focuses on identifying the anthropometric characteristics most predictive of disease risk. Body size, frame, fat patterning, and body-composition measures are key aspects in this regard.

Description of Samples

The process followed in selecting the sample must be described in detail to facilitate data interpretation and comparisons to other studies. Data on the degree of subject participation in the study is essential for assessing bias. All possible characteristics that may be related to the outcomes of subjects who refuse to participate should be coded for later analysis.

The sample selected should be described adequately for all key, relevant factors. Although the description will vary from study to study, it should include date of examination, birthdate, age, sex, ethnic group, geographic location, and socioeconomic status. Age should be expressed in days up to the age of one month; thereafter decimals of years should be used, employing, if necessary, tables for their computation (Weiner & Lourie, 1981). Distribution statistics based on decimal ages should be reported for each group.

For studies of infants, gestational ages should be reported if there is a greater-than-expected number of preterm or postterm subjects. Studies should report whether the subjects selected belong to a specific group (e.g., term births). The method used to estimate gestational age should be described or referenced.

In the absence of known chronological ages, weight-for-recumbent length (stature) is useful until puberty, because it is almost age independent (Hamill et al., 1977; Van Wieringen, 1972). Arm circumference may also be used as a general index of nutritional status during the preschool period when chronological age is unknown because age changes in arm circumference are small during this period (Jelliffe, 1966; Johnson et al., 1981). Finally, chronological age may be estimated for groups from dental eruption data, but only if there are reference values from a similar population of known chronological ages (Hagg & Matsson, 1985). Whenever age is estimated, the method employed should be described fully.

Wherever possible, indicators of maturation level should be utilized and included in the report. As above, the method employed should be described clearly, along with measures of its reliability in the survey being conducted. Reviews of the methods available, including noninvasive approaches, have been published (Roche, 1980; Roche et al., 1983).

Quality Control

One of the major problems of anthropometric surveys derives from the fact that large-scale surveys usually involve a number of measurers and multiple teams. Because scheduling is tight and only limited time is available for the anthropometric component, the actual process of measurement must be expeditious. Because technicians may have been selected for other skills appropriate to the survey and usually have other kinds of data to collect, additional possibilities for error are introduced.

Quality control for large-scale anthropometric surveys should include four kinds of training and evaluation sessions, as follows:

1. Initial training sessions to achieve standardization to a trained measurer
2. A set of "dry runs" at the outset of the survey
3. Periodic session throughout the survey that involve repeated measurements of the same subjects
4. Periodic retraining sessions throughout the survey

The initial training sessions are conducted in a didactic manner. The technicians are told of the rationale for each measurement, what it indicates, and why it has been included. They learn measurement techniques and practice them while being observed and corrected as necessary. These sessions are repeated as needed.

The dry runs consist of carrying out all procedures with subjects who could have been part of the sample but whose data will not be included in the survey database. The purpose is to allow technicians to become comfortable with the protocol and proficient in taking measurements within the allotted time. Measurement techniques are evaluated and refined. Discussion sessions later will allow more general problems to be resolved.

Throughout the survey there should be periodic sessions reserved for the collection of data on measurement reliability. At these sessions, each subject is measured by at least two technicians, following the standard protocol without interruption for error correction or other discussion. In other words, conditions are identical to regular survey sessions. The analysis of these data permits the quantification of error and measurement reliability. When analyzed, the data will allow identification of technicians with unusually large systematic errors. If necessary, appropriate adjustments could then be made in the data editing or analysis phase.

Periodic training sessions should be held. In these sessions, technicians are observed by trainers as subjects are measured. Corrections in technique are made immediately, and problems that have arisen are discussed. This provides for ongoing quality control and helps keep systematic errors at a minimum.

It is essential that measurement reliability be determined in all surveys and that these estimates be published as a component of the method section. Assessments must be periodic because reliabilities may change during the course of the survey.

Finally, the procedures used for taking measurements and ensuring quality control must be written into a procedure manual. This manual not only provides a ready reference during the course of the survey, but it serves as an important record of survey procedures for those who will use the data.

References

Goldstein, H., & Tanner, J.M. (1980, March 15). Ecological considerations in the creation and the use of child growth standards. *The Lancet*, pp. 582-585.

Graitcer, P.L., & Gentry, E.M. (1981, August 8). Measuring children: One reference for all. *The Lancet*, pp. 297–299.

Habicht, J.-P., Yarbrough, C., & Martorell, R. (1979). Anthropometric field methods: Criteria for selection. In D.B. Jelliffe & E.F.P. Jelliffe (Eds.), *Nutrition and growth* (pp. 365-387). New York: Plenum.

Hagg, U., & Matsson, L. (1985). Dental maturity as an indicator of chronological age: The accuracy and precision of three methods. *European Journal of Orthodontics*, **7**, 25-34.

Hamill, P.V.V., Drizd, T.A., Johnson, C.L., Reed, R.B., & Roche, A.F. (1977). *NCHS growth curves for children (Department of Health Education, and Welfare Pub [PHS] 78-1650)*. Washington, DC: U.S. Government Printing Office.

Hamill, P.V.V., Drizd, T.A., Johnson, C.L., Reed, R.B., Roche, A.F., & Moore, W.M. (1979). Physical growth: NCHS percentiles. *American Journal of Clinical Nutrition*, **32**, 607-629.

Jelliffe, D.B. (1966). *The assessment of the nutritional status of the community (WHO Monographs Series 63)*. Geneva: World Health Organization.

Johnson, C.L., Fulwood, R., Abraham, S., & Bryner, J.D. (1981). *Basic data on anthropometric measurements and angular measurements of the hip and knee joints for selected groups 1-74 years of age, United States, 1971-1979 (Department of Health and Human Services Pub [PHS] 81-1669)*. Washington, DC: U.S. Government Printing Office.

Martorell, R. (1985). Child growth retardation: A discussion of its causes and its relationship to health. In Sir K. Blaxter & J.C. Waterlow (Eds.), *Nutrition adaptation in man*. London and Paris: John Libbey.

Morley, D. (1976). Nutritional surveillance of young children in developing countries. *International Journal of Epidemiology*, **5**, 51-55.

Roche, A.F. (1980). The measurement of skeletal maturation. In F.E. Johnston, A.F. Roche, & C. Susanne (Eds.), *Human physical growth and maturation: Methodologies and factors* (pp. 61-82). New York: Plenum.

Roche, A.F., Tyleshevski, F., & Rogers, E. (1983). Noninvasive measurements of physical maturity in children. *Research Quarterly on Sport and Exercise*, **54**, 364-371.

van Wieringen, J.C. (1972). *Secular changes of growth, 1964-1966 height and weight survey in the Netherlands in historical perspective*. Thesis, Leiden, The Netherlands.

Weiner, J.S., & Lourie, J.A. (1981). *Practical human biology*. New York: Academic Press.

Chapter 12

Infants, Children, and Youth

Vernon D. Seefeldt and
Gail G. Harrison

Literature pertaining to the assessment of body size and composition in infants, children, and youth contains a variety of opinions regarding the selection of anthropometric variables to describe and predict current and future status (Babson & Lubchenco, 1975; Cravioto & Delicardie, 1986; Harrison et al., 1964; Johnston, 1986; Roche & Falkner, 1975). The variety of methods that have been used to assess the growth status of children suggests that much ambivalence exists concerning which sites, techniques, and instruments will provide the most meaningful data (Brandt, 1980; Cameron, 1986; Garn & Shamir, 1958; Krogman, 1970; Marshall, 1966; Ross et al., 1980; Weiner & Lourie, 1981). The tendency to obtain a large number of measurements has been replaced by a practice of measuring only those dimensions likely to provide answers to specific questions.

Uses of Anthropometry

Anthropometric data have varied uses in research on infants, youth, and children:

- *Assessment of present condition or status of individuals or groups.* One of the most common uses of anthropometric data is to compare specific dimensions of individuals or groups to those of a group or standard. For example, anthropometric characteristics are the most commonly used indices of nutritional status for infants and children.
- *Description of changes over time.* Information about the rate of change in individuals or

populations is often more valuable than knowledge about current status. Longitudinal information is more appropriate than cross-sectional data for evaluating treatment effects on individuals or populations (e.g., WIC program).
- *Documentation of variation in samples or populations.* Knowledge about within- and between-population variation may enrich our knowledge about the process of normal growth and the relative importance of genetic and environmental factors.
- *Derivation of proxy measures.* Measures that are expensive, dangerous, difficult, or otherwise prohibitive may be estimated by one or more anthropometric indicators (e.g., obesity, body density).
- *Prediction.* Accurate prediction of some events in growth and maturation may be possible if the relevant growth process is orderly.

The selection of measures to include in a study depends on the purposes of the study. In making the selection, the following guidelines may prove useful:

- The variables selected should be valid indicators or useful descriptors of the aspects being studied.
- The dimensions to be measured should lend themselves to precise definition, and the resultant measurements should be reliable.
- The variables selected should show sufficient change during the phase of growth to be studied to warrant their inclusion in the battery.

- The measures chosen should not endanger or embarrass the subject.
- If an overall descriptive profile is desired, the measurement patterns should include the four components of body size and shape; namely lengths, breadths, circumferences, and skinfold thicknesses.

Recommended Anthropometric Dimensions

The recommended list of anthropometric dimensions (see Table 1) reflects the variety of uses reviewed above and is probably longer than would be necessary for any particular study. The list is divided according to the instrument used for measurement. Each subcategory is listed in the order recommended for ease of measurement. The time required for measurement is kept to a minimum if an observer does not have to switch instruments constantly and if the subject remains basically in the same position for a subset of measurements. Finally, a distinction is made between clinical research and more general research purposes.

Table 1 Recommended Battery of Measures for Studies of Infants, Children, and Youth

Scale Weight[a,b]	*Tape Measure* Chest circumference[a,b] Waist circumference
Sliding Calipers Biacromial breadth[b] Biiliac breadth[b] Elbow breadth Wrist breadth	Buttocks (hip) circumference[b] Calf circumference Arm circumference[a,b] Head circumference[a]
Anthropometer Sitting height[a] Stature[b] Lower extremity length Upper extremity length[b]	*Skinfold Calipers* Triceps skinfold[a,b.] Subscapular skinfold[a,b] Suprailiac skinfold[a,b] Abdominal skinfold[a,b] Medial calf skinfold
Infant Measuring Table Crown-rump length[a] Recumbent length[a]	

[a]Recommended for clinical studies of infants.
[b]Recommended for clinical studies in children and youth.

Methodological Considerations

Measurement techniques for older children and youth are similar to those for adults, but attention to measurement error deserves emphasis. Measurement error is likely to be higher in infants and young children because they are less likely to maintain a standard position.

Special situations are encountered in obtaining and interpreting anthropometric measurements on infants. These are related primarily to (a) the small size and variability in size of the infant—and thus of the measurement—in relation to measurement error; (b) the physical, anatomical, and behavioral immaturity of the infant that dictates special positioning and measurement techniques, and (c) the necessity for accurate assessment of age.

Age Determination

Although the specification of age is important for most anthropometric studies, its accuracy is especially critical for infants. Body size, shape, and composition change rapidly during infancy, and the relationships of these characteristics to age changes from birth onward. An error of a few weeks in the determination of post conceptional age can make a great deal of difference in the interpretation of anthropometric measures on a newborn. The relative age dependence of most measurements diminishes rapidly with increasing age; thus the same amount of error might introduce only minor bias into the interpretation of data on a 3-year-old and be completely insignificant for an adult.

Errors in *postnatal age* determination occur most often in field situations with poor vital or medical records and in cultures in which the anniversary of actual birth is not socially important and thus not specially remembered by the child's family. Method of ascertainment and degree of certainty of birth dates should always be described. *Gestational age estimation* is important in studies of anthropometric status at birth. Except in research facilities, hospital records are seldom accurate in this regard, and accurate assessment depends on documentation of the date of the mother's last menstrual period prior to pregnancy (usually by recall), on estimates of fetal size during gestation by sonogram and/or fundal height measures, and by clinical assessment of the maturity of the infant at birth. Anthropometric studies of newborns should always specify the method(s) of gestational age assessment used.

Anthropometric Measures

Weight is the most commonly used measure of anthropometric status in children and infants. Birthweights are commonly measured immediately after delivery, but where newborn weights are measured some hours or days later, the timing should be standardized or reported, because newborns commonly lose weight during the first few days and regain it at somewhat variable rates. The selection of equipment is important; beam scales are commonly used for infants, but electronic scales that can average several weights over a short period of time offer a significant advantage when the infant is moving.

Recumbent length is conventionally measured, rather than stature until age 24 months. Crown-rump length is usually measured as an upper-lower segment estimate approximately analogous to sitting height in older subjects. It requires the same equipment and care and cooperation by two observers as does the measurement of recumbent length. Measures of other segment lengths and of skeletal diameters in infants must usually be done in either the prone or supine position; positioning should always be described. Equipment must be selected for scale; for example, small sliding calipers prove easier to use for skeletal diameters in young infants than does an anthropometer. Circumferences must usually be measured in the recumbent or propped sitting position. The former is usually the more practical with very young infants.

Skinfold thicknesses are relatively easy to measure in infants and young children but nonetheless pose some special problems. The selection of calipers may depend partly on feasibility (e.g., Lange calipers may be desirable when measuring premature and ill newborns because of the difficulty of manipulating the larger Harpenden calipers inside the small space of an incubator). Because of shifts in body water in the immediate postnatal period, skinfold thicknesses should be measured 24 or more hours after birth. The relatively higher water content of subcutaneous fat in the newborn makes it advisable to leave the caliper in place longer than would be necessary in older children before the reading is taken. Some investigators have specified 60 s, whereas others have recorded thicknesses at 15 s, or when the reading stabilized, whichever was longer. Measurement error for skinfold thicknesses in infants has approximately the same relative magnitude as for older subjects (Branson et al., 1982; Vaucher et al., 1984).

References

Babson, S., & Lubchenco, L. (1975). Fetal growth, Section 1. In W. Frankenburg & B. Camp (Eds.), *Pediatric screening tests*. Springfield, IL: Charles C Thomas.

Branson, R.S., Vaucher, Y.E., Harrison, G.G., Vargas, M., & Thies, C. (1982). Inter- and intraobserver reliability of skinfold measurements in newborns. *Human Biology, 54*, 37-143.

Brandt, I. (1980). Postnatal growth of preterm and full-term infants. In F. Johnston, A. Roche, & C. Susanne (Eds.), *Human physical growth and maturation* (pp. 139-160). New York: Plenum Press.

Cameron, N. (1986). The methods of auxological anthropometry. In F. Falkner & J. Tanner (Eds.), *Human growth, a comprehensive treatise: Vol. 3. Methodology. Ecological, genetic and nutritional effects on growth* (2nd ed., pp. 3-46). New York and London: Plenum Press.

Cravioto, J., & Delicardie, E. (1986). Nutrition, mental development, and learning. In F. Falkner & J. Tanner (Eds.), *Human growth, a comprehensive treatise: Vol. 3. Methodology. Ecological, genetic and nutrition effects on growth* (2nd ed., pp. 501-536). New York and London: Plenum Press.

Garn, S., & Shamir, Z. (1958). *Methods for research in human growth* (pp. 35-57). Springfield, IL: Charles C Thomas.

Harrison, G., Weiner, J., Tanner, J., & Barnicot, N. (1964). The size and shape of the body. *Human biology: An introduction to human evolution, variation and growth* (pp. 197-216). New York: Oxford University Press.

Johnston, F. (1986). Somatic growth of the infant and preschool child. In F. Falkner & J. Tanner (Eds.), *Human growth, a comprehensive treatise: Vol. 2. Postnatal growth* (2nd ed., pp. 3-24). New York: Plenum Press.

Krogman, W. (1970). Growth of the face, trunk, and limbs in Philadelphia white and Negro children of elementary and high school age. *Monographs of the Society for Research in Child Development, 35*, 80.

Marshall, W. (1966). Basic anthropometric measurements. In J. Van Der Werff, Ten Bosch, & A. Haak (Eds.), *Somatic growth of the child* (pp. 1-5). Springfield, IL: Charles C Thomas.

Roche, A.F., & Falkner, F. (1975). Physical growth charts. In W.K. Frankenburg & B.W. Camp

(Eds.), *Pediatric screening tests*. Springfield, IL: Charles C Thomas.

Ross, W., Drinkwater, D., Whittingham, N., & Faulkner, R. (1980). Anthropometric prototypes: Ages six to eighteen years. In K. Berg & B. Eriksson (Eds.), *Children & exercise IX* (p. 312). Baltimore: University Park Press.

Vaucher, Y.E., Harrison, G.G., Udall, J.N., & Morrow, G., III. (1984). Skinfold thickness in North American infants 24–41 weeks gestation. *Human Biology*, **56**, 713-73

Weiner, J., & Lourie, J., (1981). *Practical human biology*. New York: Academic Press.

Chapter 13

Assessment of the Nutritional Status of Healthy and Handicapped Adults

William Cameron Chumlea and

Alex F. Roche

Anthropometry provides information about nutritional status from measures of body size and regional measures of subcutaneous adipose tissue thicknesses or cross-sectional muscle areas on the limbs. Measures of whole-body stores of nutrients require data collected from body densitometry, gamma radiation, isotope dilution, organ biopsy, radiography, or magnetic resonance imaging. These procedures are expensive, commonly unavailable, and frequently invasive. Anthropometry is inexpensive, relatively simple, noninvasive, and requires portable equipment. The common use of anthropometry to assess nutritional status should continue.

The recommended measurements are divided into those for healthy adults and those for handicapped adults. Techniques for taking the recommended measurements from healthy adults are presented in earlier sections of this manual, but techniques for taking the recommended measurements from handicapped adults are included in this chapter. Recommendations for assessing the nutritional status of other adults with specific diseases (acute illness, cancer, coronary heart disease, diabetes and obesity, etc.) or measurements relevant to frame size or fat patterning are made elsewhere in this manual.

Healthy Adults

A minimal list of recommended measurements is presented in Table 1. It is stressed that all the vari-

Table 1   List of Recommended Measurements

Healthy Adults	Handicapped Adults
Stature	Weight
Weight	Triceps skinfold
Triceps skinfolds	Subscapular skinfold
Subscapular skinfold	Arm circumference
Arm circumference	Calf circumference
Calf circumference	Knee height

ables in Table 1 be measured, because even self-reported values for weight and stature are not reliable. In addition, the measurements obtained from an individual must be compared with appropriate reference data if an interpretation of a nutritional assessment is to be complete. Sources of suitable reference data are provided in Table 2.

Percentiles or distribution statistics for weight and triceps skinfold thicknesses can provide guides to the levels of total body fat for individuals or groups. Weight and triceps skinfold thicknesses are equally highly correlated with total body fat (Roche et al., 1981), perhaps because the nonspecificity of weight is offset by the limited extent to which the triceps skinfold thickness represents the subcutaneous adipose tissue and the deep adipose tissue and the greater error of measurement for the triceps skinfold. The subscapular skinfold is included in the basic list of measurements for

Table 2   Reference Data for Recommended Measurements

Measurement	References
Stature	Abraham et al. (1979) Chumlea et al. (1984a)
Weight	Abraham et al. (1979) Chumlea et al. (1984a)
Weight/stature^2 (Men & Women)	Chumlea et al. (1984a) Abraham et al. (1983) Cronk & Roche (1983)
Weight/stature$^{1.5}$ (Women) Percent body fat from weight$^{1.2}$/stature$^{3.3}$ Triceps skinfold thickness	Abraham et al. (1983) Roche (available on request) Johnson et al. (1981) Chumlea et al. (1984a) Chumlea et al. (1985a)
Subscapular skinfold thickness	Chumlea et al. (1984a) Chumlea et al. (1985c) Cronk & Roche (1982)
Arm circumference	Johnson et al. (1981) Chumlea et al. (1985c)
Calf circumference	Webb (1978) Chumlea et al. (1985c)

the assessment of nutritional status, although it requires more undressing.

Arm-circumference and triceps skinfold thickness can be used to estimate cross-sectional areas of adipose tissue and of "muscle plus bone" in the arm. The formulae applied in the past to calculate these areas are inaccurate, particularly in regard to "muscle plus bone" area (Heymsfield et al., 1982), but the available reference data were derived using the earlier formulae (Frisancho, 1981). Arm adipose tissue area is only slightly more correlated with total body fat than is triceps skinfold thickness (Himes et al., 1980). Consequently, the calculation of arm adipose tissue area is not recommended as a basic procedure. "Muscle plus bone" area is useful as an index of fat-free mass if calculated using the formula of Frisancho (1981), or as an index of muscle mass if calculated using the revised formulae of Heymsfield et al. (1982).

Calf circumference is an important index of fat-free mass, particularly in the elderly (Chumlea et al., 1984a). Also, calf circumference is needed to estimate total body fat or fat-free mass from bioelectric impedance in women (Guo et al., in press).

Ratios can be constructed from pairs of anthropometric variables, or either total body fat, percentage of body fat or fat-free mass can be predicted from appropriate regression equations. Weight (W) and Stature (S) can be combined to form indices that are closely related to total body fat. The best known such index is the body mass index (W/S^2), which can be easily obtained from a nomogram (see Table 3). The W-S index maximally correlated with percentage of body fat (%BF) is the Fels index (W$^{1.2}$/S$^{3.3}$), at least for a white U.S. group (Abdel-Malek et al., 1985), and a nomogram provides direct estimates of %BF from W and S based on this relation. Although stature decreases with aging, present stature, instead of an estimate of stature for the individual as a young adult, is important if W-S indices are used to assess the nutritional status of an elderly person (Chumlea et al., 1985a).

Anthropometric variables can be used to predict total body fat or fat-free mass using regression equations, but they must be measured using the same techniques as those used to develop the equation. Measurements other than those listed in Table 1 may have to be taken. Also, published regression equations, particularly those for groups other than young white adults, need revision using recently published formulae to calculate body com-

Table 3 Indices, Formulae and Corresponding Nomograms Useful for Assessing the Nutritional Status of Adults

Index	Formula	Source of nomogram
Body mass index	$\dfrac{\text{Weight}}{\text{Stature}^2}$	Roche et al. (1981) Chumlea et al. (1984a)
Fels index	$\dfrac{\text{Weight}^{1.2}}{\text{Stature}^{3.3}}$	Abdel-malek et al. (1985)
Arm adipose tissue area	$\dfrac{\text{arm circ} \times \text{triceps skf/10}}{2} - \dfrac{\pi \ (\text{triceps skf/10})^2}{4}$	Gurney & Jelliffe (1973)
Muscle plus bone area	$\dfrac{\text{arm circ} - (\pi \times \text{triceps skf/10})^2}{4\pi}$	Gurney & Jelliffe (1973) Chumlea et al. (1984a)
Stature in the elderly	men = $64.19 - (0.04 \times \text{age}) + (2.02 \times \text{knee ht})$ women = $84.88 - (0.24 \times \text{age}) + (1.83 \times \text{knee ht})$	Chumlea et al. (1984a, 1985c)
Weight in the elderly	men = $(1.73 \times \text{arm circ}) + (0.98 \times \text{calf circ}) + (0.37 \times \text{subscap skf}) + (1.16 \times \text{knee ht}) - 81.69$ women = $(0.98 \times \text{arm circ}) + (1.27 \times \text{calf circ}) + (0.40 \times \text{subscap skf}) + (0.87 \times \text{knee ht}) - 62.35$	Chumlea et al. (available on request)

Note. circ = circumference, skf = skinfold, subscap = subscapular, ht = height.

position variables from body density (Lohman, 1986). More important, the validity of an index or prediction of body composition is assured only if relation between the measured or calculated variables and the outcome variable, for example, percentage of body fat, are established in a random subgroup of the sample to which an acceptable "direct" method, such as body densitometry, has been applied.

Handicapped Adults

If an adult is confined to a bed or a wheelchair, standard anthropometric techniques may not be practical or their attempted use may provide spurious information. As a result, the clinical management and treatment of such individuals may be hampered by lack of body measurements obtained with standard techniques. Nutritional anthropometry is still important for such individuals because extremes of fatness or leanness can lead to health problems in the elderly and be of prognostic significance (Kemm & Allcock, 1984; Mitchell & Lipschitz, 1982).

Methods of "recumbent anthropometry," developed for the elderly, remove the effects of mobility status that prevent accurate anthropometry using standard techniques (Chumlea et al., 1984b; Chumlea et al., 1985c). The recommended recumbent measurements are triceps and subscapular skinfolds, arm and calf circumferences, and knee height for estimating stature (see Table 1). Sources of reference data are presented in Table 2. Using recumbent techniques, accurate anthropometric data can be collected from nonambulatory elderly persons or from those who are ambulatory but too frail to stand for the time required for an examination (Chumlea et al., 1985b). These recumbent measurement techniques can be applied to handicapped children and young adults also (Chumlea & Roche, 1984), but the relations of these recumbent measures to nutritional status have not been established for these groups of individuals.

The position of the subject will vary depending on the recumbent measurements to be taken. Weight can be measured with portable bed scales or by placing the subject in a wheelchair scale. The subject is placed in a supine position for measurements of arm and calf circumference and knee height. Recumbent measurements of triceps and subscapular skinfold thicknesses are made with the subject lying on the right or left side. Persons confined to wheelchairs should also be measured in a recumbent position because measurements taken from a person sitting in wheelchair are prone to error (Chumlea et al., 1985b). The subject is placed in a recumbent position, but the basic techniques for these recumbent measurements, the sites where the measurements are taken, and the placement of the skinfold calipers or tape measure on the body are the same as when the corresponding standard techniques are applied to ambulatory persons (Chumlea et al., 1985c). There are no systematic differences in values from corresponding recumbent and standing measurements (Chumlea & Roche, 1984).

Arm circumference is measured recumbently at the midpoint of the upper arm, with the arm extended alongside the body and the palm facing upward with the subject supine. The tape is perpendicular to the long axis of the upper arm and held snug around the arm, but not compressing the tissue. For measuring calf circumference, the subject remains supine with the knee bent to a 90° angle. The tape is placed around the calf and moved proximally and distally perpendicular to the long axis of the calf until the maximum circumference is located. The tape is held snug around the calf but not tight enough to compress the tissue.

For measuring knee height, the supine subject bends the knee and ankle each to a 90° angle. One blade of a Mediform sliding caliper is placed under the heel of the foot, and the other blade is placed on the anterior surface of the thigh over the femoral condyles. The shaft of the caliper is held parallel to the long axis of the calf just posterior to the head of the fibula, and pressure is applied to compress the tissue.

Triceps skinfold is measured recumbently on the posterior aspect of the arm over the triceps muscle at the level of the marked midpoint. With the subject lying on the side, the arm to be measured rests along the trunk, palm down. An imaginary line connecting the acromial processes should be perpendicular to the surface of the bed and to the spine. With the subject still lying on the side, the subscapular skinfold is measured recumbently at the standard site in the usual way.

Recumbent measurement data can be used to derive additional quantitative nutritional indices

(see Table 3). An estimate of stature can be computed from knee height (Chumlea et al., 1985a), and an estimate of weight can be computed from arm and calf circumferences, subscapular skinfold thickness and knee height (Chumlea et al., unpublished). These estimates of stature and weight are needed to calculate indices such as weight-for-stature, weight/stature², and to apply equations for estimating basal energy expenditure in the nonambulatory elderly (Chumlea et al., 1986).

Reference data for recumbent nutritional anthropometry for elderly white persons 65 to 90 years of age are available (Chumlea et al., 1986; Chumlea et al., 1984b; Chumlea et al., 1985c). These recumbent reference data are not from a nationally representative sample, but they do not differ significantly from standing values reported by the National Center for Health Statistics at ages to 75 years (Chumlea et al., 1985c). It is not known whether one set of nutritional anthropometric reference data can be used for elderly blacks and whites in the United States. There are differences between younger white and black American adults in distributions of triceps and subscapular skinfolds and in W/S² (Cronk & Roche, 1982). Despite these differences, it is recommended that the available recumbent reference data be used to monitor changes in the nutritional status of elderly persons, regardless of race.

References

Abdel-Malek, A., Mukherjee, D., & Roche, A.F. (1985). A method of constructing an index of obesity. *Human Biology*, **57**, 415-430.

Abraham, S., Carroll, M.D., Najjar, M.F., & Fulwood, R. (1983). *Obese and overweight adults in the United States* (Data from the National Health Survey. Series 11, No. 230. Department of Health and Human Services Pub. No. [PHS] 83-1680). Washington, DC: U.S. Government Printing Office.

Abraham, S., Johnson, C.L., & Najjar, M.F. (1979). *Weight and height of adults, 18-74 years of age, United States, 1971-1974* (Vital and Health Statistics. Series 11, No. 211. Department of Health, Education and Welfare Pub. No. [PHS] 79-1695). Washington, DC: U.S. Government Printing Office.

Chumlea, W.C., & Roche, A.F. (1984). Nutritional anthropometric assessment of nonambulatory persons using recumbent techniques. *American Journal of Physical Anthropology*, **63**, 146.

Chumlea, W.C., Roche, A.F., & Mukherjee, D.

(1984a). Nutritional assessment of the elderly through anthropometry. Columbus, OH: Ross Laboratories.

Chumlea, W.C., Roche, A.F., & Mukherjee, D. (1986). Some anthropometric indices of body composition for elderly adults. *Journal of Gerontology*, **41**, 36–39.

Chumlea, W.C., Roche, A.F., & Steinbaugh, M.L. (1985a). Estimating stature from knee height for persons 60 to 90 years of age. *Journal of the American Geriatric Society*, **33**, 116-120.

Chumlea, W.C., Roche, A.F., Steinbaugh, M.L., & Mukherjee, D. (1985b). Errors of measurement for methods of recumbent nutritional anthropometry in the elderly. *Journal of Nutrition for the Elderly*, **5**, 3-11.

Chumlea, W.C., Roche, A.F., & Webb, P. (1984b). Body size, subcutaneous fatness and total body fat in older adults. *International Journal of Obesity*, **8**, 311–317.

Chumlea, W.C., Steinbaugh, M.L., Roche, A.F., Mukherjee, D., & Gopalaswamy, N. (1985c). Nutritional anthropometric assessment in elderly persons 65 to 90 years of age. *Journal of Nutrition for the Elderly*, **4**, 39–51.

Cronk, C.E., & Roche, A.F. (1982), Race- and sex-specific reference data for triceps and subscapular skinfolds and weight/stature². *American Journal of Clinical Nutrition*, **35**, 347–354.

Frisancho, A.R. (1981). New norms of upper limb fat and muscle areas for assessment of nutritional status. *American Journal of Clinical Nutrition*, **34**, 2540–2545.

Guo, S., Roche, A.F., Chumlea, W.C., Miles, D., & Pohlman, R.S. (in press). The use of bioelectric impedance in the prediction of body composition. *Human Biology*.

Gurney, J.M., & Jelliffe, D.B. (1973). Arm anthropometry in nutritional assessment: Nomogram for rapid calculation of muscle circumference and cross-sectional muscle and fat areas. *American Journal of Clinical Nutrition*, **26**, 912–915.

Heymsfield, S.B., McManus, C., Smith, J., Stevens, V., & Nixon, D.W. (1982). Anthropometric measurement of muscle mass: Revised equations for calculating bone-free arm muscle area. *American Journal of Clinical Nutrition*, **36**, 680–690.

Himes, J.H., Roche, A.F., & Webb, P. (1980). Fat areas as estimates of total body fat. *American Journal of Clinical Nutrition*, **33**, 2093–2100.

Johnson, C.L., Fulwood, R., Abraham, S., & Bryner, J.D. (1981). *Basic data on anthropometric measurements and angular measurements of the hip and knee joints for selected age groups 1-74 years of age: United States, 1971-1975* (Vital and Health Statistics, Series 1, No. 219, Department of Health and Human Services Pub. No. [PHS] 81-1669). Washington, DC: U.S. Government Printing Office.

Kemm, J.R., & Allcock, J. (1984). The distribution of supposed indicators of nutritional status in elderly patients. *Age and Aging*, **13**, 21-28.

Lohman, T.G. (1986). Applicability of body composition techniques and constants for children and youths. *Exercise and Sport Sciences Review*, **14**, 325-357.

Mitchell, C.O., & Lipschitz, D.A. (1982). Detection of protein caloric malnutrition in the elderly. *American Journal of Clinical Nutrition*, **35**, 398–406.

Roche, A.F., Siervogel, R.M., Chumlea, W.C., & Webb, P. (1981). Grading body fatness from limited anthropometric data. *American Journal of Clinical Nutrition*, **34**, 2831–2838.

Webb, P. (1978). *Anthropometric Source Book: Vol. II. A Handbook of Anthropometric Data* (NASA Reference Publication 1024). Washington, DC: Aeronautics and Space Administration.

Chapter 14

Estimating Frame Size

John H. Himes and
Roberto A. Frisancho

Frame size is more a concept than a specific measurement. Frame size is related to informal definitions of body build and physique, though it is primarily measured by means of skeletal dimensions, exclusive of stature and its segments. Frame size encompasses bone, joint, and skeletal breadths and depths that are representative of the supportive structure as a whole. There may be, however, appreciable independence among skeletal measurements (Skibinska, 1977). The popular phrase ''big boned'' describes a skeletal robustness included in the concept of frame size, but this and other easy descriptions may be difficult to quantify and validate. Because there is no single standard measure of frame size with which other measures can be compared, one can only estimate frame size and indirectly evaluate the appropriateness of the estimates based on the assumptions of a particular application.

Thus, the rationale for estimating frame size varies acccording to its general applications. Distributions of skeletal breadths are of interest in clothing and equipment design (Damon et al., 1966) because of the obvious requirements for accommodating body dimensions in static and dynamic situations. Skeletal breadths are important estimators of fat-free mass because the skeleton is a chief component of the fat-free mass, and are also predictors of muscle mass, the other major component of fat-free mass (Behnke, 1959).

It is generally recognized that body weight varies not only with stature and age but also that it is influenced by body width, bone thickness, muscularity, and body proportions. Therefore, an appropriate evaluation of individual variability in weight would include some estimate that reflects these factors. An estimate of frame size may be such a measurement. In considering obesity, a basic rationale for including an estimate of frame size is that the health consequences of a given high level of weight for stature are more severe for individuals with a relatively smaller skeletal frame and muscularity (fat-free mass) compared with individuals whose fat-free mass is relatively large. An implication here is that an estimate of frame size allows discrimination between those who are heavy because of large fat-free mass and those whose overweight is largely fat.

Several approaches have been used for estimating and using frame-size information. In 1959, the Metropolitan Life Insurance Company published ''ideal'' weight for categories of stature and frame size based on minimum subsequent mortality of insured adults in the United States and Canada. Frame size (small, medium, large) was based on self-appraisal, and no instructions or definitions of frame size were included. Simple measures proposed as estimates of frame size to be used when evaluating body weight include bony chest diameter measured from radiographs (Garn et al., 1983), wrist circumference (Grant, 1980), and elbow breadth, that is, bicondylar breadth of humerus (Frisancho & Flegel, 1983). Frisancho (1984) has provided reference data for categories of frame size, based on the 15th and 85th percentiles of elbow breadth by age groups from the first and second National Health and Nutrition Examination Surveys (NHANES I and II; see Table 1). Additionally, selected percentiles of weight, triceps skinfold, subscapular skinfold, and bone-free arm-muscle area by stature, sex, and frame size were included, based on the same data.

Table 1 Frame-Size Categories of Elbow Breadth (cm) of U.S. Men and Women

Age (years)	Small	Frame Size Medium	Large
Men			
18–24	⩽ 6.6	> 6.6 and < 7.7	⩾ 7.7
25–34	⩽ 6.7	> 6.7 and < 7.9	⩾ 7.9
35–44	⩽ 6.7	> 6.7 and < 8.0	⩾ 8.0
45–54	⩽ 6.7	> 6.7 and < 8.1	⩾ 8.1
55–64	⩽ 6.7	> 6.7 and < 8.1	⩾ 8.1
65–74	⩽ 6.7	> 6.7 and < 8.1	⩾ 8.1
Women			
18-24	⩽ 5.6	> 5.6 and < 6.5	⩾ 6.5
25-34	⩽ 5.7	> 5.7 and < 6.8	⩾ 6.8
35-44	⩽ 5.7	> 5.7 and < 7.1	⩾ 7.1
45-54	⩽ 5.7	> 5.7 and < 7.2	⩾ 7.2
55-64	⩽ 5.8	> 5.8 and < 7.2	⩾ 7.2
65-74	⩽ 5.8	> 5.8 and < 7.2	⩾ 7.2

Note. Adapted from Frisancho (1984)

When the Metropolitan Life Insurance Company updated its previous stature-weight tables in 1983, it specified elbow breadth as the estimate of frame size (Metropolitan Life Insurance Company, 1983). Weight-for-stature categories were based on minimum subsequent mortality of insured American adults, and elbow reference values were the 25th and 75th percentiles within stature categories derived from United States national data from NHANES I (see Table 2).

Table 2 Metropolitan Life Insurance Frame Size Categories of Elbow Breadth (cm) by Stature (cm)

Stature	Small	Frame Size Medium	Large
Men			
158–161	<6.4	6.4–7.2	>7.2
162–171	<6.7	6.7–7.4	>7.4
172–181	<6.9	6.9–7.6	>7.6
182–191	<7.1	7.1–7.8	>7.8
192–193	<7.4	7.4–8.1	>8.1
Women			
148–151	<5.6	5.6–6.4	>6.4
152–161	<5.8	5.8–6.5	>6.5
162–171	<5.9	5.9–6.6	>6.6
172–181	<6.1	6.1–6.8	>6.8
182–183	<6.2	6.2–6.9	>6.9

Note. Adapted from Metropolitan Life Insurance Company (1983); stature is given including 2.5-cm heels.

A more complex "HAT" frame size index has been proposed by Katch and Freedson (1982), based on the regression of the sum of biacromial and bitrochanteric breadths on stature. Frisancho (1985) has proposed a frame index of elbow-breadth $\times 10/\sqrt{\text{stature}}$ to accommodate disparities between elbow breadth and stature.

There are certain theoretical considerations when judging the appropriateness and applicability of frame-size estimators. When evaluating body weight, the primary interest is to identify those who are at increased risk of morbidity, dysfunction, or mortality. Inclusion of frame size in evaluation instruments should improve the identification of those at risk beyond that achieved without using frame size. Evidence to support this validation requirement, however, is lacking. Although the weight-for stature categories in the Metropolitan Life Insurance (1983) tables were based on minimum subsequent mortality during a period of from 4 to 22 years, accompanying frame-size categories based on elbow breadth were neither measured on the insured sample, nor specified according to mortality risk. Categories of bony chest breadth (BCB) and weight/BCB are positively associated with 16-year cardiovascular mortality in Scots (Garn et al., 1983), but it is unclear whether considering BCB improved identification of those at risk beyond weight alone or weight and stature. There is no evidence relating frame size to morbidity or dysfunction.

Given the lack of evidence relating frame estimates and body weight to the most important outcome measures (morbidity, dysfunction, mortality), one must rely on valid intermediate assumptions accompanying use of frame size and body weight to determine appropriateness of particular frame-size measures. These intermediate assumptions concern theoretical constraints and associations of estimates of frame size as they relate to stature, weight, fat-free mass, and fatness.

Measures of frame size should be highly correlated with body weight, particularly with fat-free mass. Bony chest breadth and elbow breadth categories separate distributions of body weight more than corresponding categories of stature (Frisancho & Flegel, 1983; Garn et al., 1983). Categories of Frisancho's elbow-stature frame index (1985) separate considerably the distribution of estimated arm muscle, which may be considered a correlate of body muscle mass. A similar association exists between categories of the HAT frame index and lean body weight (Katch & Freedson, 1982). Breadths of shoulder, elbow, wrist, hip, knee, and ankle each have significant correlations with densitometrically determined fat-free mass (Himes & Bouchard, 1985), as do sums of elbow, wrist, knee, and ankle breadths (Behnke, 1959).

If used in conjunction with stature or stature categories, estimates of frame size should correlate with fat-free mass independent of stature. Significant partial correlations from 0.3 to 0.5 have been reported for each of six body breadths with fat-free mass, while controlling for stature (Himes & Bouchard, 1985). Differences among the individual frame estimates in the degree to which they are related to body weight and fat-free mass appear to be small. Even so, some question whether the magnitudes of the associations between frame size and fat-free mass justify using frame size in weight-for-stature tables and indices (Rookus et al., 1985).

Estimates of frame size should have minimal associations with body fat so that variability in frame size reflects tissue variation. Furthermore, because fat-free mass is positively associated with body fat, estimates of frame size should have minimal associations with body fat beyond that which can be accounted for by associations with fat-free mass.

Elbow breadth was selected as an estimate of frame size over bitrochanteric breadth by Frisancho and Flegel (1983) because of relatively lower correlations with the sum of triceps and subscapular skinfolds. The elbow-stature frame index has similar low correlations with skinfold thicknesses as elbow breadth (Frisancho, 1985).

Table 3 presents first-order correlations of six body-frame estimates with percentage of total body fat and fat weight determined densitometrically for a sample of French Canadians, and corresponding partial correlations controlling for fat-free mass (Himes & Bouchard, 1985). Although none of the correlations with body fat are high, significant proportions of variation in whole-body fatness are shared with breadths of shoulder, elbow, hip, and knee. Wrist and ankle breadths have the lowest correlations approximating zero. Hence, by this criterion, wrist and ankle breadth are preferred estimates of frame size.

A disadvantage in recommending wrist or ankle breadths as frame-size estimates is that there are no good national reference data for these dimensions. At present, for using frame size in evaluating body weight and obesity in U.S. adults, one must recommend the elbow breadth-related reference data of the Metropolitan Life Insurance Company (1983) and of Frisancho (1984), with a caveat concerning their limitations. Beyond the theoretical concerns discussed, there are issues

Table 3 Correlations of Frame-Size Estimates With Body Fatness and Partial Correlations Controlling Fat-Free Mass

Frame Estimates	Percent fat		Fat weight	
	First order r	Partial r	First order r	Partial r
Men ($n = 225$)				
Shoulder	.22	.26	.35	.26
Elbow	.22	.25	.33	.24
Wrist	−.01	−.01	.11	−.02
Hip	.41	.47	.53	.48
Knee	.23	.30	.39	.30
Ankle	.07	.09	.19	.08
Women ($n = 212$)				
Shoulder	.14	.26	.30	.26
Elbow	.25	.38	.46	.41
Wrist	−.08	.00	.07	.00
Hip	.48	.62	.63	.62
Knee	.33	.50	.53	.52
Ankle	−.02	.08	.14	.07

Note. Adapted from Himes and Bouchard (1985); coefficients $\geq .14$ are significantly different from 0, $p \leq .05$.

relating to the applicability of these and all reference data to diverse ethnic groups that are beyond the purview of the present report.

Finally, it is important that estimates of frame size be measured. In a study of self-appraisal of frame size, Katch et al. (1982) found that 41% of a sample of young adults misclassified their frame category (small, medium, large) relative to the measured HAT estimate. The concern in misclassifying frame size in this context is that individuals also incorrectly determine frame-associated weight goals; these unrealistic goals may be associated with increased health risk. The more common estimates of frame size can be measured reliably (Himes & Bouchard, 1985), and the recommended equipment and methods are described elsewhere in this volume.

References

Behnke, A.R. (1959). The estimation of lean body weight from "skeletal" measurements. *Human Biology*, **32**, 295-315.

Damon, A., Stoudt, H.W., & McFarland, R.A. (1966). *The human body in equipment design*. Cambridge, MA: Harvard University Press.

Frisancho, A.R. (1984). New standard of weight and body composition by frame size and height for assessment of nutritional status of adults and the elderly. *American Journal of Clinical Nutrition,* **40,** 808-819.

Frisancho, A.R. (1985). *Standards of weight, fat, and muscle by frame size for assessment of nutritional status for adults and the elderly developed for use with the Frameter.* Ann Arbor, MI: Health Products.

Frisancho, A.R., & Flegel, P.N. (1983). Elbow breadth as a measure of frame size. *American Journal of Clinical Nutrition,* **37,** 311-314.

Garn, S.M., Pesick, S.D., & Hawthorne, V.M. (1983). The boney chest breadth as a frame size standard in nutritional assessment. *American Journal of Clinical Nutrition,* **37,** 315-318.

Grant, J.P. (1980). *Handbook of total parenteral nutrition.* Philadelphia: W.B. Saunders.

Himes, J.H., & Bouchard, C. (1985). Do the new Metropolitan Life Insurance weight-height tables correctly assess body frame and body fat relationships? *American Journal of Public Health,* **75,** 1076-1079.

Katch, V.L., & Freedson, P.S. (1982). Body size and shape: Derivation of the "HAT" frame size model. *American Journal of Clinical Nutrition,* **36,** 669-675.

Katch, V.L., Freedson, P.S., Katch, F.I., & Smith, L. (1982). Body frame: Validity of self-appraisal. *American Journal of Clinical Nutrition,* **36,** 676-679.

Metropolitan Life Insurance Company. (1959). New weight standards for men and women. *Statistical Bulletin,* **40,** 1-4.

Metropolitan Life Insurance Company. (1983). Metropolitan height and weight tables. *Statistical Bulletin,* **64,** 2-9.

Rookus, M.A., Burema, J., Duerenburg, P., & van der Weil-Wetzels, W.A.M. (1985). The impact of adjustment of a weight-height index (W/H²) for frame size on prediction of body fatness. *British Journal of Nutrition,* **54,** 335-342.

Skibinska, A. (1977). A factor analysis of skeletal measurements in Warsaw students. *Annals of Human Biology,* **4,** 73-78.

Chapter 15

Anthropometry and Body Composition

Timothy G. Lohman

The use of skinfolds, circumferences, and skeletal breadths to estimate body fatness is well established. Both theoretical and empirical evidence supports the utility of this approach in many populations. This chapter briefly explores the rationale and limitations of anthropometry to estimated body fatness and fat-free body mass, prediction equations, and prediction errors and selection of sites for future body-composition studies.

Skinfolds

Skinfold thicknesses are related to total body fatness through their association with total subcutaneous fat. Where the ratio of a given set of skinfolds is closely related to the total subcutaneous fat and where the subcutaneous fat is closely related to other fat depots, for example, abdominal fat and intermuscular fat, the relation between skinfolds and total body fatness should be fairly close. For many samples, the association between skinfolds and body fatness is moderate to moderately high, with 50 to 80% percent of the variance in the criterion measure of fatness accounted for and with standard errors of estimate between 3 and 4% (Lohman, 1982). This relationship has been established in children (Harsha et al., 1978; Mukherjee & Roche, 1984; Pařízková, 1961) and adults (Durnin & Womersley, 1974; Jackson & Pollock, 1984; Sloan, 1967; Sloan et al., 1962). Both sedentary and active populations have been studied, and many equations have been developed

for describing the relation between anthropometry and body composition. Cross-validation studies have also been done on a number of their equations, and from these studies the linear equations of Sloan (Sloan, 1967; Sloan et al., 1962), the logarithmic equation of Durnin and Womersley (1974), and the curvilinear equations of Jackson and Pollock (1984) have been found to apply to the adult male and female population (see Table 1). In general, the Sloan equations yield lower percentage of fat values for a given sample, and the Durnin and Womersley equation yields higher values. In addition to the conversion of skinfolds to percentage of fat, they can be used as they are in comparison with national norms, which are available for selected sites (triceps and subscapular for all ages).

Circumferences and Skeletal Breadths

Various combinations of circumferences and skeletal breadths have been used to estimate body fatness and fat-free body weight (FFB) in number of populations. Theoretical and empirical validity for this approach is described by Behnke and Wilmore (1974) and Katch and Katch (1980). Circumferences are affected by fat mass, muscle mass, and bone size, and thus have some limitations in accurately predicting the fatness of the FFB. However, a combination of three to five circumferences has been shown to yield results similar to skinfolds in

Table 1   Selected Skinfold Sites Widely Used in the Adult Male and Female Populations

	Sloan et al. (1967)		Durnin & Womersley (1974)	Jackson & Pollock (1974)	
	Female	Male	Female and male	Female	Male
Skinfold sites	Triceps Suprailiac	Subscapular Thigh	Biceps Triceps Subscapular Suprailiac	Triceps Suprailiac Abdominal Thigh	Triceps Subscapular Chest Abdominal Thigh
Skinfold equation	Linear		Log of sum of 4	Sum of 3 or 4 (linear and quadratic components)	

predicting body fatness. The combination of skeletal breadths, along with circumferences, decreases the prediction error, especially when FFB mass is used as the criterion variable. Skeletal breadths alone yield somewhat larger prediction errors than circumferences or skinfolds. Skinfolds in combination with circumferences and skeletal breadths further decrease the prediction error and may offer the optimal approach to estimation of body composition from anthropometry if a considerable number of dimensions can be measured on the sample under study. However, no one set of dimensions can be put forward as ideal at this stage. Circumferences often found related to body fatness and FFB mass include arm circumferences, waist circumference, abdominal circumference, and thigh circumference. However, few equations have been extensively cross-validated on other samples to test their generalizibility.

Development of Prediction Equations

Many different statistical procedures are used to develop prediction equations based on anthropometric dimensions. First, a criterion method of estimating percentage of fat or FFB must be selected. If the criterion method is not a perfect measure of body fatness, as is usually the case, for example, body density, then part of the variation unaccounted for by anthropometry should be attributed to the criterion method. To select which anthropometric dimensions are best associated with body composition, forward and backwards stepwise elimination regression analyses are commonly used. These and other approaches have recently been discussed by Mukherjee and Roche (1984), and several limitations have been presented. The

cross-validation procedures to test for the generalizability of equations developed have been reviewed by Lohman (1981) and carefully applied by Sinning and Wilson (1984) and Sinning et al. (1985).

Prediction Errors

The estimation of percentage of fat and FFB (kg) from anthropometry needs to be established in many populations under standardized conditions. Previous research has failed to follow a uniform measurement protocol in validation and cross-validation studies, so that an optimal set of anthropometric predictors cannot be advanced at this stage. Typical prediction errors for percentage of fat from various equations are between 3 and 4% (Lohman, 1982), and these are partly due to the imperfect relation of anthropometric variables to body composition and partly due to the errors in estimating composition from the criterion variable, for example, body density, body water, and body potassium (Lohman, 1981). If we extend this error analysis to a hypothetical situation where a criterion variable is used that measures body fatness without error, then we can calculate a theoretical error for prediction of body fatness from anthropometry for a given population. As an example, let us assume that the prediction error of estimating body fatness in the young adult population is 3.5% from anthropometry, using body density as the criterion variable. Furthermore, let us assume that the error in the density method for this population is 2.5% for estimating percentage of fat (Lohman, 1981). Assuming the errors are independent between methods, we can subtract out the density error from the total error and thus estimate the hypothetical error in the anthropometric approach, using an error-free criterion method as follows:

$$\begin{aligned} \text{Theoretical error} &= \sqrt{\left(\frac{\text{total}}{\text{error}}\right)^2 - \left(\frac{\text{criterion}}{\text{method error}}\right)^2} \\ &= \sqrt{(3.5)^2 - (2.5)^2} \\ &= 2.52\%. \end{aligned}$$

Thus the theoretical error from anthropometry for predicting body fatness may be as low as 2.5% in this young adult population. The actual error will become better established as more accurate criterion methods for estimating body fatness are developed.

Measurement Issues

In examining 13 skinfold sites for their reliability of measurement as well as for their correlation in body composition indices, Roche et al. (1985) indicated that studies support five sites as good predictors of body composition, four of which are also reliably measured (see Table 2).

Table 2 Selected Skinfold Sites for Body Composition Studies

Site	Index of body composition	Reliability of measurement
Subscapular	x	x
Chest	x	
Abdomen	x	x
Triceps	x	x
Thigh	x	
Calf[a]	?	x

[a]Calf skinfold site has been included in only a few body composition studies but shows promise as a good indicator of fatness.

Measurement errors came about because of variation in fat-fold compressibility, the variation of site location, and variation in measurement technique. In addition, it has been shown that measurement error is a function of thickness of skinfolds (Pollock et al., 1986). This error between investigators was found to be about 10% of the skinfold thickness from 10 to 40 mm. The variation in location of skinfold for a stated site is well illustrated with the suprailiac location. Because it has been measured at various locations and because it varies in thickness considerably among locations, it presents real limitations for general use in body-composition prediction equations.

Population Specific Equations

The finding that certain anthropometric equations apply only to populations from which they were derived has lead to the concept that anthropometric equations are highly specific to a given population. Here population specific is defined as equations derived from a given population that do not apply to other populations because of biological factors that influence the relation of anthropometry to total body fatness. In addition to these biological factors, we know there are investigation differences that affect the equations developed. Thus, investigation-specific equations are characteristic of the sample under study and do not apply to other samples because of methodological factors that influence the relation of anthropometry to body fatness. Such methodological factors include sampling procedures (most body-composition studies involved nonrandom samples), sample size, variables selected in a given study, measurement description and procedures used, criterion variable selected for estimating percentage of fat, and statistical analysis procedures used to develop the prediction equations. Recommended statistical approaches have been described by Lohman (1981) and Mukherjee and Roche (1984). The difficulty of separating investigation effects from biological effects is illustrated in the cross-validation studies of Sinning and Wilson (1984) and Sinning et al. (1985), where modification of the Jackson-Pollock equations is suggested to more closely predict percentage of fat in the athletic population. Because body density is used as the criterion method and because the athletic population may differ from the nonathletic population in the density of the fat-free body, we cannot determine whether the skinfold to total body fatness relation is different or if the criterion method to total body fatness relationship, for example body density to body fatness, is different. The use of multicomponent body-composition analysis along with anthropometry is needed in such a population along with other populations, such as children, youth and the aging, to develop more accurate anthropometric equations in diverse populations (Lohman, 1986).

Recommended Minimal Set of Anthropometric Dimensions

For future body-composition studies where prediction equations are to be developed between anthropometry and some criterion measure of body composition, the following four skinfolds, three circumferences, and two skeletal breadths are recommended as a set of nine anthropometric dimensions to be included in all research studies (see Table 3). The skinfolds and circumferences were recommended on the basis of correlations with other measures of body fatness, good reliability, and representation of trunk and limb subcutaneous fat. Skeletal breadths were selected to obtain commonly used indices of frame size.

Table 3 Minimal Set of Anthropometric Dimension for Future Body-Composition Studies

Skinfolds	Circumferences	Skeletal breadths
Triceps	Upper arm	Wrist or elbow
Subscapular	Waist	Ankle or knee
Paraumbilical	Thigh (mid)	Biiliac or crest
Calf (medial)		

Additional anthropometric dimensions are recommended in body-composition studies, but these will vary greatly with the purpose of the study. For example, with the validation of bioelectric resistance as a measure of body composition, it may be helpful to measure specific segment lengths, widths, and circumferences because of theoretical effects of segment volume on tissue resistance to an electrical current. Though the resistance of the body to a given current is related to the composition of the conductor as well as length of conductor, the cross-sectional area may also affect the resistance and thus the estimates of body composition. Thus, a much larger set of dimensions would be appropriate, along with the recommended set of nine dimensions. The widespread use of such a common set of anthropometric dimensions by each investigator should facilitate cross validation of proposed equations and enable the development of a more optimal anthropometric approach for body-composition assessment.

Summary

The use of anthropometry for body-composition assessment is reviewed, with an emphasis on prediction error, measurement error, and the present limitations and approaches using anthropometric equations. A proposed set of nine anthropometric dimensions is given for future use in research studies designed to enhance the prediction of fat content from anthropometry. Such an approach offers promise of reducing the investigation-specific influences on the development of new equations and of enhancing the development of a general anthropometric approach to be used in many populations.

References

Behnke, A.R., & Wilmore, J.H. (1974). *Evaluation and regulation of body build and composition.* Englewood Cliffs, NJ: Prentice Hall.

Durnin, J.V.G.A., & Womersley, J. (1974). Body fat assessed from total body density and its estimation from skinfold thickness: Measurements on 481 men and women aged 16 to 72 years. *British Journal of Nutrition,* **32,** 77–97.

Harsha, D.W., Frerichs, R.R., & Berenson, G.S. (1978). Densitometry and anthropometry of black and white children. *Human Biology,* **50,** 261–280.

Jackson, A.S., & Pollock, M.L. (1984). Practical assessment of body composition. *Physiology and Sports Medicine,* **13,** 76–82.

Katch, F.I., & Katch, V.L. (1980). Measurement and prediction errors in body composition assessment and the search for the perfect equation. *Research Quarterly of Exercise and Sport,* **51,** 249–260.

Lohman, T.G. (1981). Skinfolds and body density and their relation to body fatness: A review. *Human Biology,* **53,** 81–225.

Lohman, T.G. (1982). Body composition methodology in sports medicine. *Physiology and Sports Medicine,* **10,** 46-58.

Lohman, T.G. (1986). Applicability of body composition techniques and constants for children and youth. *Exercise and Sport Sciences Review,* **14**, 325–358.

Lohman, T.G., Pollock, M.L., Slaughter, M.H., Brandon, L.J., & Boileau, R.A. (1984). Methodological factors and the prediction of body fat in female athletes. *Medicine and Science in Sports and Exercise,* **16**, 92–96.

Mukherjee, D., & Roche, A.F. (1984). The estimation of percent body fat, body density and total body fat by maximum R^2 regression equations. *Human Biology,* **56**, 79–109.

Pařižková, J. (1961). Total body fat and skinfold thickness in children. *Metabolism,* **10**, 794–809.

Pollock, M.L., Jackson, A.J., & Graves, J.E. (1986). Analysis of measurement error related to skinfold site, quantity of skinfold, fat and sex. *Medicine and Science in Sport and Exercise,* **18**, S32.

Roche, A.F., Abdel-Malek, A.K., & Mukherjee, D. (1985). New approaches to clinical assessment of adipose tissue. In *Body composition assessments in youth and adults (Report of the Sixth Ross Conference on Medical Research).* Columbus, OH: Ross Laboratories.

Sinning, W.E., & Wilson, J.R. (1984). Validity of "generalized" equations for body composition analysis in women athletes. *Research Quarterly on Sport and Exercise,* **55**, 153–160.

Sinning, W.E., Dolny, D.G., Little, K.D., Cunningham, L.N., Racaniello, A., Siconolfi, S.F., & Sholes, J.L. (1985). Validity of "generalized" equations for body composition analysis in male athletes. *Medicine and Science in Sports and Exercise,* **17**, 124–130.

Sloan, A.W. (1967). Estimation of body fat in young men. *Journal of Applied Physiology,* **23**, 311–315.

Sloan, A.W., Burt, J.J., & Blyth, C.S. (1962). Estimation of body fat in young women. *Journal of Applied Physiology,* **17**, 967–970.

Chapter 16

Anthropometric Measurements in the Obese

George A. Bray and
David S. Gray

Obesity poses special problems and challenges for the use of anthropometric techniques in estimating body fat. First, most of the standard equations were developed with only a handful of substantially obese individuals. Thus, it is often unclear whether the equations are valid for this group. Second, the obese individual has more body fat beneath the skin, and it is not always possible to follow the "recommended" techniques of measurement. These problems and the recommendations that come from reviewing this area are discussed below.

Skinfolds

Because subcutaneous fat may represent up to 50% of total body fat, the measurement of skinfold thickness can provide a useful technique for evaluating body fat. Because the thickness of two layers of skin is only about 1.8 mm (Edwards, 1955), most of the thickness of a fold of skin represents subcutaneous fat. The technical problems with the use of skinfolds in the measurement of fatness are discussed elsewhere in this handbook. The special problems associated with measuring skinfolds in obesity include site selection and adequacy of instrumentation. The problem of site selection is more problematic in obese subjects than in normal-weight subjects because bony landmarks are more difficult to identify. The location of the site at

which a measurement is to be made is thus done with less precision. Such problems are compounded by the fact that in several sites the measurement of skinfold thickness in obese subjects is frequently impossible due to one of two reasons: (a) It is not possible to pull a skinfold away from underlying tissues with skin sides that are parallel to one another; or (b) if possible, the thickness between the parallel skin sides is larger than the opening of the currently available commercial calipers.

To assess interobserver variability in measurements, three to eight members of a clinic team made a series of measurements of the biceps and triceps skinfolds in four lean and four obese subjects (see Table 1; Bray et al., 1978). As expected, the biceps and triceps skinfolds were significantly thicker in the obese than in the lean subjects. In general, variability in measurement was considerably larger among the obese subjects. Table 2 shows the measurements of skinfolds in a group of 117 obese subjects enrolled in an outpatient weight-loss program who were measured two times, one week apart by the same observer with the same calipers (Bray et al., 1978). Subscapular and suprailiac skinfolds thicknesses were measurable in only two thirds of the subjects, compared with biceps and triceps, which could be measured in essentially all. The abdominal skinfold, on the other hand, could only be measured in 16 subjects. The percentage difference between the two measurements is shown in the right-hand column.

Table 1   Variation in Skinfold Measurement in 4 Obese and 4 Lean Subjects[a]

Subject	Biceps	Triceps
Lean		
1	7.6 ± 15.6 (8)	12.0 ± 10.7
2	3.2 ± 2.8 (8)	5.5 ± 2.0
3	9.7 ± 6.7 (8)	22.3 ± 14.4
4	10.8 ± 12.7 (8)	14.5 ± 9.3
Obese		
5	27.7 ± 11.0 (4)	50.0 ± 20.8
6	32.0 ± 35.8 (5)	45.2 ± 22.1
7	30.0 ± 12.0 (3)	46.7 ± 9.9
8	34.6 ± 30.3 (3)	46.7 ± 12.5

Note. Data from Bray et al., 1978. [a]Data are means and *SD* in millimeters. Measurements were performed by 3 to 8 members of the clinic team. Numbers in parentheses indicate the number of team members who performed the measurements on each subject and are the same for biceps and triceps skinfolds.

The differences ranged from 11.0 to 21.6% with standard errors of 1.2 to 4.1 % for these skinfold measurements. These observations, although on a small sample of obese subjects, indicate the severe limitations associated with the use of skinfold measurements in assessing obesity.

Several investigators have developed equations using measurements of skinfolds at various sites to estimate body fat (see Table 3). One group has even developed a nomogram for this purpose (Sloan & de V. Weir, 1970). Because these formulas are in general based on multiple linear regression analysis, they tend to be population specific.

They work very well for the population samples from which they were derived but generalize poorly to others (Johnston, 1982). A review of the literature shows that very few obese subjects have been included in the databases for these equations. Table 3 lists the mean body weights plus two standard deviations of subjects included in studies relating anthropometric measurements to body density. The low weight values indicate that few obese subjects were included in these studies, a fact that makes the use of these formulas in obese subjects questionable—apart from any concern over the feasibility, accuracy, or reliability of the measurements required for the predictions. It is also clear that skinfolds in relation to predictions of obesity vary with age as well as with race and sex.

There has been no demonstration that currently used formulas for prediction of body fat from body density are valid in obese people. Validity has been based, among other factors, on cadaver analysis (Brozek, 1963). A review of the cadaver-analysis data shows that the largest human body analyzed to date had a body-mass index of 31.4 kg/m², which is just at the borderline for diagnosis of obesity. Most of the rest were relatively lean (Clarys et al., 1984).

Circumferences

The use of trunk and limb circumferences provides an additional approach to measuring obesity. The definitions for each of the appropriate measurement sites are included elsewhere in this monograph. In the studies of Steinkamp et al. (1965) the circumference at the iliac crest had a correlation co-

Table 2   Differences in Repeated Skinfold Measurements Performed by One Observer

Skinfolds	Number of possible observations[a]	Percentage difference[b]
Triceps	115	21.6 ± 1.7
Biceps	116	20.4 ± 1.9
Subscapular	80	11.9 ± 1.2
Suprailiac	82	13.5 ± 1.2
Abdominal	16	11.0 ± 4.1

Note. Data from Bray et al., 1978. [a]Repeated measures were made on 116 obese subjects 1 week apart by one individual. Number of possible observations indicates the number of data pairs available for comparison. Data are missing when the skinfolds were too large to accommodate the calipers. [b] Data are means ± *SEM.*

Table 3 Body Weights of Subjects in Studies Relating Anthropometric Measurements to Body Density

Study	Number of subjects		Mean + 2 SD body weight (kg)[a]		Comments
	Male	Female	Male	Female	
Allen et al.(1956)	87	—	—	—	9 greater than 40% fat
Pascale et al. (1956)	88	—	90	—	
Young et al. (1961)	—	94	—	72	
Pařižková (1961)	123	118	—	—	Children
Sloan et al. (1962)	—	50	—	67	
Steinkamp et al. (1965)	416	438	99	81	
Sloan (1967)	50	—	—	—	Maximum wt. 85.7 kg
Durnin & Rahaman (1967)	60	45	90	74	
Wilmore & Behnke (1970)	—	128	—	73	
Hermansen & von Döbeln (1971)	19	19	88	71	
Pařižková & Buzkova (1971)	101	—	88	—	
Forsyth & Sinning (1973)	50	—	95	—	
Katch & McArdle (1973)	53	69	89	75	
Durnin & Wormersley (1974)	209	272	94–104	80–101	Five age groups
Jackson & Pollock (1978)	308	—	98	—	
	95	—	101	—	
Katch et al. (1979)	50	1357	—	—	
Jackson, et al. (1980)	—	249	—	72	
	—	82	—	72	
Boileau et al. (1981)	86	—	48	—	
	97	—	44	—	10-year-old boys
Mukhergee & Roche (1984)	140	135	104	84	
Slaughter et al. (1984)	317	—	—	—	
Thorland et al. (1984)	141	133	90	70	

[a]In order to indicate the extent of obesity in these data bases, the weight corresponding to 2 SD above the mean is given for each population sample.

efficient with body fat that ranged between .815 and .938. It has been shown that in normal weight subjects, skinfold measurements are better correlated with body density than circumferences (Boileau et al., 1981; Sloan et al., 1962), but this has not been evaluated in obese subjects. Weltman and Katch (1975) proposed a prediction equation for body volume from several circumferences. Body volume, which is felt to be more theoretically related to circumference measurements, could then be used to calculate body density and percentage of fat.

We have found that the interobserver variability in circumference measurements for obese and lean subjects is smaller than for skinfolds. Table 4 shows circumference measurements on 4 lean and 4 obese subjects by three to eight clinic team members (Bray et al., 1978). The waist, chest, and midarm circumferences were all larger, as expected in the obese subjects. Coefficients of variation were, in general, smaller than observed with skinfold measurements. When differences were assessed on a group of 117 obese subjects measured on two occasions, 1 week apart by the same individual (see Table 5), the measurements of the circumferences (including midarm, chest, waist, iliac, and thigh) showed percentage differences of 1.90 to 2.85, with standard errors of 0.16 to 0.32 (Bray, et al., 1978). The circumferences were measurable in all subjects in contrast to the inability to measure skinfolds in many of the obese patients. Thus, circumferences are preferable to skinfolds in obesity because they are obtainable in all subjects and have lower intra- and interobserver variabilities.

Table 4 Variation in Circumference Measurements in 4 Obese and 4 Lean Subjects[a]

Subject	Waist	Chest	Midarm
Lean			
1	35.2 ± 2.8 (8)	41.2 ± 0.8	13.9 ± 0.3
2	29.7 ± 2.3 (8)	33.2 ± 1.1	11.0 ± 0.1
3	40.2 ± 1.1 (8)	43.8 ± 4.2	14.7 ± 0.8
4	30.9 ± 2.0 (8)	40.5 ± 1.4	13.3 ± 0.6
Obese			
5	47.2 ± 3.8 (4)	48.3 ± 4.6	17.5 ± 0.2
6	45.4 ± 3.4 (5)	46.0 ± 1.3	17.7 ± 0.9
7	42.8 ± 2.8 (3)	42.3 ± 1.0	17.5 ± 0.9
8	48.0 ± 5.2 (3)	45.8 ± 2.3	16.0 ± 0.2

Note. Data from Bray et al., 1978. [a]Data are means and *SD* in centimeters. Measurements were performed by three to eight members of the clinic team. Numbers in parenthesis indicate the number of team members who performed the measurements on each subject and are the same for all three circumferences.

Table 5 Differences in Repeated Circumference Measurements Performed by One Observer

Circumference	Number of possible observations[a]	Percent difference[b]
Midarm	117	2.10 ± 0.19
Chest	116	1.90 ± 0.16
Waist	117	2.14 ± 0.17
Iliac	117	2.40 ± 0.32
Thigh	117	2.85 ± 0.28

Note. Data from Bray et al., 1978. [a]Repeated measures were made on 117 obese subjects 1 week apart by one individual. Number of possible observations indicates the number of data pairs available for comparison. [b]Data are means ± *SEM*.

Body-Fat Distribution

In addition to predicting body density, anthropometric measurements may be used to define the distribution of body fat. Mueller and Stallones (1981) separated the variances in skinfold measurements into two principle components based on the degree of intercorrelation between them: (a) total body fat and (b) body-fat distribution. They suggested that a leg skinfold (e.g., calf) and a truncal skinfold (e.g., suprailiac, lateral chest, or abdomen) would best define the trunk-extremity distribution of body fat. The importance of body-fat distribution has been demonstrated by two independent laboratories. Kissebah et al. (1982) and Krotkiewski et al. (1983) have used measurements of the circumference of the waist divided by the circumference of the hips to provide a quantitative measurement of regional fat distribution. Although each investigator has used slightly different definitions for these locations, their conclusions in terms of risk assessment are the same. Individuals with larger waist-to-hip circumference ratios, be they male or female, are at higher risk from the major diseases associated with obesity than individuals with a lower waist-to-hips ratio. In evaluating the genetic factors of distribution of fat, Bouchard et al. (1985) found that the ratio of trunk to extremity fat folds was under more genetic control than either site alone.

Conclusions

Based on this brief review of available information, measurements of circumferences are to be preferred to skinfolds in the obese for three reasons: (a) the interobserver variability is less; (b) the intraobserver variability is less; and (c) the measurement is obtainable in all individuals. However, more work needs to be done to examine the relative variability and correlation of body circumferences and skinfolds with body density. For the time being, it is best to include both circumferences and skinfold thicknesses in the assessment of obese patients. When skinfolds or circumferences are measured on obese subjects, it is important to include limb and truncal measurements to define body-fat distribution as well as to estimate total body fat. At least two skinfolds thicknesses and/or circumferences should be measured in both central and peripheral locations. Suggested measurements are as follows: skinfolds thicknesses—triceps, biceps, calf, subscapular, and suprailiac; circumferences—midarm, calf, waist, and hips.

References

Allen, T.H., Peng, M.T., Chen, D.P., Huang, T.F., Chang, C., & Fang, H.S. (1956). Prediction of total adiposity from skinfolds and the curvilinear relationship between external and internal adiposity. *Metabolism, 5*, 346-352.

Boileau, R.A., Wilmore, J.H., Lohman, T.G., Slaughter, M.H., & Riner, W.F. (1981). Estimation of body density from skinfold thicknesses, body circumferences and skeletal widths in boys aged 8 to 11 years: Comparison of two samples. *Human Biology, 53*, 575-592.

Bouchard, C., Savard, R., Després, J.P., Tremblay, A., & Leblanc, C.J. (1985). Body composition in adopted and biological siblings. *Human Biology, 57*, 61-75.

Bray, G.A., Greenway, F.L., Molitch, M.E., Dahms, W.T., Atkinson, R.L., & Hamilton, K. (1978). Use of anthropometric measures to assess weight loss. *American Journal of Clinical Nutrition, 31*, 769-773.

Brožek, J., Grande, F., Anderson, J.T., & Keys, A. (1963). Densitometric analysis of body composition: Revision of some qualitative assumptions. *Journal of the Annals of the New York Academy of Sciences, 110*, 113-140.

Clarys, J.P., Martin, A.D., & Drinkwater, D.T. (1984). Gross tissue weights in the human body by cadaver dissection. *Human Biology, 56*, 459-473.

Durnin, J.V.G.A., & Rahaman, M.M. (1967). The assessment of the amount of fat in the human body from measurements of skinfold thickness. *British Journal of Nutrition, 21*, 681-689.

Durnin, J.V.G.A., & Womersley, J. (1974). Body fat assessed from total body density and its estimation from skinfold thickness: Measurements on 481 men and women aged from 16 to 72 years. *British Journal of Nutrition, 32*, 77-97.

Edwards, D.A.W., Hammond, W.H., Healy, M.J.R., Tanner, J.M., & Whitehouse, R.H. (1955). Design and accuracy of calipers for measuring subcutaneous tissue thickness. *British Journal of Nutrition, 9*, 133-143.

Forsyth, H.L., & Sinning, W.E. (1973). The anthropometric estimation of body density and lean body weight of male athletes. *Medicine and Science in Sports, 5*, 174-180.

Hermansen, L., & von Döbeln, W. (1971). Body fat and skinfold measurements. *Journal of Clinical and Laboratory Investigations, 27*, 315-319.

Jackson, A.S., & Pollock, M.L. (1978). Generalized equations for predicting body density of men. *British Journal of Nutrition, 40*, 497-504.

Jackson, A.S., Pollock, M.L., & Ward, A. (1980). Generalized equations for predicting body density of women. *Medicine and Science in Sports and Exercise, 12*, 175-182.

Johnston, F.E. (1982). Relationships between body composition and anthropometry. *Human Biology, 54*, 221-245.

Katch, F.I., Behnke, A.R., & Katch, V.L. (1979). Estimation of body fat from skinfolds and surface area. *Human Biology, 51*, 411-424.

Katch, F.I., & McArdle, W.D. (1973). Prediction of body density from simple anthropometric measurements in college-age men and women. *Human Biology, 45*, 445-454.

Kissebah, A.H., Videlingum, N., Murray, R., Evans, D.J., Hartz, R.J., Kalkhoff, R.K., & Adams, P.W. (1982). Relation of body fat distribution to metabolic complications of obesity. *Journal of Clinical and Endocrinological Metabolism, 54*, 254-260.

Krotkiewski, M., Bjorntorp, P., Sjostrom, S., & Smith, U. (1983). Impact of obesity on metabolism in men and women. *Journal of Clinical Investigation, 72*, 1150-1162.

Mueller, W.H., & Stallones, L. (1981). Anatomical distribution of subcutaneous fat: Skinfold site choice and construction of indices. *Human Biology, 53*, 321-335.

Mukhurjee, D., & Roche, A.F. (1984). The estimation of percent body fat, body density, and total body fat by maximum R^2 regression equations. *Human Biology, 56,* 79–109.

Pařiźková, J. (1961). Total body fat and skinfold thickness in children. *Metabolism, 10,* 794–807.

Pařiźková, J., & Buzkova, P. (1971). Relationship between skinfold thickness measured by Harpenden caliper and densitometric analysis of total body fat in men. *Human Biology, 43,* 16–21.

Pascale, L.R., Grossman, M.I., Sloane, H.S., & Frankel, T. (1956). Correlations between thicknesses of skinfolds and body density in 88 soldiers. *Human Biology, 28,* 165–176.

Slaughter, M.H., Lohman, T.G., Boileau, R.A., Stillman, R.J., VanLoan, M., Horswill, C.A., & Wilmore, J.H. (1984). Influence of maturation on relationship of skinfolds to body density: A cross-sectional study. *Human Biology, 56,* 681–689.

Sloan, A.W. (1967). Estimation of body fat in young men. *Journal of Applied Physiology, 23,* 311-315.

Sloan, A.W., Burt, J.J., & Blyth, C.S. (1962). Estimation of body fat in young women. *Journal of Applied Physiology, 17,* 967–970.

Sloan, A.W., & de V. Weir, J.B. (1970). Nomograms for prediction of body density and total body fat from skinfold measurements. *Journal of Applied Physiology, 28,* 221–222.

Steinkamp, R.C., Cohen, N.L., Siri, W.E., Sargent, T.W., & Walsh, H.E. (1965). Measures of body fat and related factors in normal adults: I & II. *Journal of Chronic Disease, 18,* 1279–1289, 1291–1307.

Thorland, W.G., Johnson, G.O., Tharp, G.D., Housh, T.J., & Cisar, C.J. (1984). Estimation of body density in adolescent athletes. *Human Biology, 56,* 439–448.

Weltman, A., & Katch, V. (1975). Preferential use of casing (girth) measures for estimating body volume and density. *Journal of Applied Physiology, 38,* 560–563.

Wilmore, J.H., & Behnke, A.R. (1970). An anthropometric estimation of body density and lean body weight in young women. *American Journal of Clinical Nutrition, 23,* 267–274.

Young, C.M., Martin, M.E.K., Chihan, M., McCarthy, M., Manniello, M.J., Harmuth, E.H., & Fryer, J.H. (1961). Body composition of young women. *Journal of American the Dietetic Association, 38,* 332–340.

Chapter 17

Anthropometric Measurements in Acute and Chronic Illness

Steven B. Heymsfield

Once the skeletal epiphyses close, the human frame retains relatively fixed dimensions. Contrastingly, the soft tissues can undergo substantial remodeling. The chemical composition of nonosseous tissue consists primarily of water, triglyceride, protein, and glycogen. Collectively, the nonaqueous organic components of soft tissue are sources of energy.

In the healthy adult, energy ingested in the diet balances energy losses as heat and in excreta; therefore energy balance remains zero, and body composition remains constant. On the other hand, soft tissues increase in mass during periods of positive energy balance. Channeling the excess fuel into triglyceride results in expansion of the adipose tissue mass while biosynthesis of protein and glycogen enlarge the fat-free soft tissues. Chronically positive energy balance results in weight gain and obesity.

The reverse situation results during periods of negative energy balance. Soft tissue fuels are utilized in energy production, and body weight decreases. As the wasting process evolves, the functional decrements created by protein depletion result in the group of clinical syndromes referred to as *protein-energy malnutrition* (Heymsfield et al., 1979).

The adult human frame can thus support a wide range of soft tissue mass and energy supply. This process is depicted schematically in Figure 1. Point A is an arbitrarily established body weight and energy content range consistent with "health"; energy, protein (i.e., nitrogen), and water balance are zero. Positive balance leads to soft-tissue

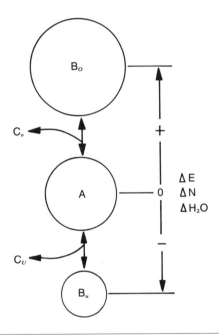

Figure 1 Relation between energy, protein (nitrogen), and water balance (ΔE, ΔN, ΔH_2O and body mass). Points B_u and B_o represent the minimum and maximum soft-tissue mass consistent with survival for a given skeletal mass, respectively. Point A is the range of body composition of an arbitrarily defined reference group. Points C_u and C_o are the complications associated with over- and undernutrition, respectively (from Heymsfield & Williams, in press).

growth and weight gain up to a hypothetical maximum obese Point B_o. Negative balance likewise leads to tissue wasting and a minimun undernourished soft tissue mass Point B_u. The biological energy content supported by a given adult human frame can thus range between Points B_u and B_o. As one moves between Point A and Points B_u and B_o, the risk of a morbid event rises. These complications of undernutrition and obesity are depicted in the figure as Points C_u and C_o, respectively.

The aims of anthropometric nutritional assessment in the acute or chronically ill patient are related directly to the scheme presented in Figure 1:

- To establish a subject's protein-energy content relative to the normal range
- To determine if and at what rate protein-energy balance changes over time during observation or with nutritional therapy
- To estimate the risk of potential complications of undernutrition or obesity

Strengths and Limitations of Anthropometry

Anthropometry provides a simple and practical method of rapidly accomplishing these three goals (Bishop et al., 1981; Heymsfield et al., 1984). By combining the results of measured body weight, girths, circumferences, and skinfold thicknesses, the clinician can establish the amount and rate of change over time in protein-energy content of the patient. Moreover, a growing body of literature provides the background information necessary to establish a subject's risk of complications under specified conditions (Frisancho, 1974; Heymsfield & Casper, in press).

Although the strength of anthropometry is its practicality, a variety of errors offset the method's accuracy. The sources of these errors are now briefly reviewed with a specific focus on the acute and chronically ill patient.

Observer Error.   Interobserver and intraobserver errors are an important source of variability. This topic is discussed in detail elsewhere in this book (see Mueller & Martorell, this volume). Proper training, the use of a single observer, and marking the measurement site with indelible ink minimizes observer errors (Bishop et al., 1981; Heymsfield et al., 1984).

Instrument Errors.   The use of inexpensive or free instruments provided by pharmaceutical companies is commonplace in the hospital setting. The reliability of these measuring devices needs to be established prior to their widespread application. Even expensive instruments such as commercially available skinfold calipers may become unreliable with long-term use or damage. Periodic checking of all instruments is essential.

Errors Related to Changes in the Composition or Physical Properties of a Patient's Tissues.   Age-related tissue changes, fluctuations in hydration with the menstrual cycle, and other factors can introduce error in the anthropometric measurement of healthy subjects. Additional factors must be considered with the onset of disease. The relation between a tissue's size or mass and the tissue's protein energy content can be altered by a relative expansion of total body water during weight loss, hyperalimentation with high-sodium fluids, congestive heart failure, liver disease, and numerous other medical conditions. The size of a muscle (e.g., circumference) and the muscle's protein content, although usually directly related in health, can be altered by intermyofibrillar edema or fat and rapid changes in intramyofibrillar glycogen. Although there are many more examples, the fundamental premise that tissue size and composition have a fixed relation to each other is often an invalid assumption in diseased patients.

Inappropriate Use of the Anthropometric Data.
The two major considerations in this category are the inaccuracies that result from extrapolation of the anthropometric measurement to a larger body space and the application of inaccurate prediction equations. Two examples will serve to underscore the importance of these types of error. First, a common practice is to measure one skinfold thickness (e.g., triceps) and assume that this dimension is proportional to the absolute amount and rate of change in total body fat (Bishop et al., 1981; Heymsfield et al., 1984). Obviously individual differences in fat distribution and the differing rates of fat loss or replacement among anatomical sites with alterations in energy balance limit the accuracy of this assumption. The second example concerns the application of prediction equations for deriving fat-free body mass from anthropometric measurements. The accuracy of these equations in severely ill patients, especially those with altered body habitus and composition (e.g., ascites), is unknown.

Clinical Application of Anthropometry

With the aforementioned strengths and limitations of the clinical application of anthropometry kept in mind, what uses should be considered in the individual hospitalized patient? The answers to these questions can be organized according to the three goals of clinical anthropometry stated earlier.

Goal 1:

Baseline assessment of energy-protein status relative to a reference population (an earlier review examined the strengths and limitations of clinical anthropometric techniques; Heymsfield et al., 1984). The aim in this section is to make general recommendations.

When selected measuring techniques are applied to appropriate patients (that is, excluding those with the medical complications mentioned earlier), anthropometry supplies an estimate of the patient's position between points B_u and B_o, as presented in Figure 1. Although limited information is available on the anthropometric features of subjects at these two points, the practical approach is to compare the patient's measurement to that of a healthy reference group. The development of appropriate reference values is an ongoing process, and there are now several good sources of this information that apply to most patients (Bishop et

al., 1981; Frisancho, 1974). The gaps in current reference data are for the infrequently used anthropometric dimensions, the elderly, and ethnic minorities.

The usual approach is to measure and/or calculate one or more indices of total body energy content (e.g., one skinfold thickness, calculated total body fat, calculated fat-free body mass) and protein mass (e.g., fat-free body mass, arm muscle area). The result is then used as an absolute value (e.g., total body energy stores in kcal) or expressed as a percentile or percentage relative to the reference group. Overall, in carefully performed studies most of the anthropometric indices used clinically are highly correlated with the corresponding body compartment measured by classic research techniques (see Figure 2). Of course, the prediction interval will vary depending on the particular anthropometric measurement. Although this variability is of concern, a key point to consider is that the biological range of soft-tissue energy supply is very wide (Point $B_u = 4 \times 10^4$ kcal to Point $B_o = 4 \times 10^6$ kcal), and anthropometric techniques are reasonably effective in establishing a patient's baseline status relative to these two extremes and the normal range.

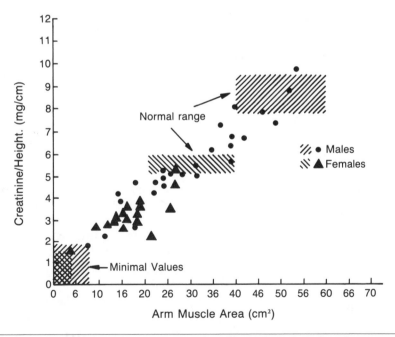

Figure 2 Correlation between muscle indices creatinine/height (ordinate) and anthropometric arm-muscle area (abscissa) in healthy and chronically undernourished subjects. Each point represents the average of three consecutive study days on metabolic ward. The subjects ingested a meat-free diet during the study period. The normal ranges are based upon healthy men and women ($n = 50$ each) evaluated in our laboratory. The minimal values represent boundaries below which adults show limited survival. The close correlation between total body-muscle mass as represented by urinary creatinine and arm-muscle area is evident from the figure (from Heymsfield & Casper, in press).

Goal 2: Protein-Energy Balance

Occasional anthropometric measurements during the course of a nutrition-support program provide useful documentation of changes in body composition. This information can be discussed at teaching rounds and used for later patient follow-up. However, anthropometric data collected in the acute-care setting are not a substitute for more accurate measurements of protein (nitrogen) and energy balance.

The limitations of short-term anthropometric monitoring of nitrogen balance (Δ N) are evident in Figure 3. The subjects were either undernourished patients or normal volunteers who participated in 1-week metabolic balance studies (Heymsfield &

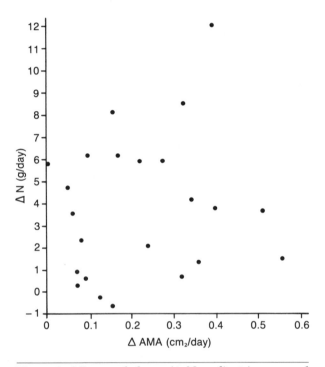

Figure 3 Nitrogen balance (Δ N, ordinate) measured on a metabolic ward versus change in arm-muscle area (Δ AMA, abscissa) in subjects undergoing 1-week balance studies (from Heymsfield & Casper, in press).

Casper, in press). Nitrogen balance was calculated as intake minus urinary and fecal losses; corrections were applied for integumental losses (7 mg/kg) and for changes in total body urea N. The correlation between Δ N and the change in arm muscle area (Δ AMA) was not statistically significant.

In contrast to a short-term hospitalization, anthropometry is a useful technique for establishing protein-energy balance over long time periods. An example is the severely underweight subject with

short bowel syndrome who is renourished by home parenteral feeding over months or years (Heymsfield et al., 1983).

Goal 3: Predicting Complications of Under- or Overnutrition

The complications of over- and undernutrition can be divided into two general categories. The first category relates to an inadequate or excess mass of tissue fuels. Sustained undernutrition results in negative energy balance, exhaustion of metabolic fuels, and death (Point B_u, Figure 1). Some rough estimates of Points B_u are as follows (Heymsfield & Williams, in press; Heymsfield et al., 1984): The maximal weight loss in total starvation is about 30% of initial body weight; in chronic semistarvation body weight can decrease to about 50 to 60% of ideal; and in chronic semistarvation subjects at or near Point B_u have 1 to 3 kg of total body fat and 4 to 6 kg of skeletal muscle (Heymsfield et al., 1984). Thus, several anthropometric approximations of Point B_u in total starvation and chronic semistarvation are available.

With chronic positive energy balance and massive fat accumulation, the host will ultimately succumb (Point B_o), due to respiratory and cardiac failure. Maximal recorded body weights in subjects of average height range between 300 and 400 kg.

The second category of complication is a morbid event related directly to under- and overnutrition (Points C_u and C_o). With undernutrition, examples include infections, sepsis, wound dehiscence, and arrhythmias. For overnutrition, the complications include high blood pressure, coronary artery disease, gallstones, hypoxia, pulmonary hypertension, and congestive heart failure. Several recent studies have attempted to predict complications of undernutrition from anthropometric dimensions and other standard nutritional assessment indices (Buzby & Mullen, 1984; Mullen et al., 1979). Although anthropometric dimensions in some cases have predictive value, their usefulness in this regard is currently undergoing critical analysis. Similarly, anthropometric indices have predictive value in obesity-related complications.

Unique Applications of Anthropometry

Several unique aspects of anthropometry are worthy of mention. The first relates to the subject with massive dependent edema; body weight in these individuals consists of a disproportionately large amount of extracellular fluid. Body weight is therefore no longer a measure of energy supply and protein content. However, the upper extremities, neck, and head are usually only minimally affected by the relative excess of total body water. Thus, specific regional anthropometric measurements (e.g., midarm fat and muscle indices) in these patients represent an alternative to body weight as a means of estimating total body energy supply and protein content. Although occult edema might affect upper body tissues, the errors involved are most likely relatively small.

Another similar example is the increase in body weight caused by massive tumor growth. Our group occasionally evaluates patients with 8- to 10-kg tumors. Severe undernutrition is often not apparent from the measured body weight because the decrease in fat and muscle tissue mass corresponds to gain in tumor bulk. In this setting, the selective use of anthropometric measurements can provide estimates of nonmalignant tissue mass.

There are two additional important clinical applications of anthropometry. The first is related to the ease with which anthropometric measuring techniques can provide quantitative estimates of regional tissue mass. The pattern of regional fat and muscle distribution correlates with a variety of physiological and biochemical indices of interest to the practicing physician (Krotkiewski et al., 1983). The second additional application of anthropometry is in the prediction of energy expenditure. The fasting-resting oxygen consumption and maximal oxygen consumption during exercise are both related to fat-free body mass, muscle mass, and total body fat (Heymsfield et al., 1986). These components of body weight can be derived by anthropometric techniques and the patient's energy requirements calculated accordingly.

Conclusion

Anthropometric techniques are now widely used in hospitalized patients. Areas needing critical attention include the following: instrument development and validation; preparation of reference data for the elderly, recumbent patients, and the less-commonly-used anthropometric dimensions; and establishing the validity of specific anthropometric techniques in diseased patients. Finally, the potential exists for developing imaginative, clinical applications of anthropometry.

References

Bishop, C.W., Bowen, P.E., & Ritchey, S.J. (1981). Norms for nutritional assessment of American adults by upper arm anthropometry. *American Journal of Clinical Nutrition*, **34**, 2530-2539.

Buzby, G.P., & Mullen, J.L. (1984). Analysis of nutritional assessment indices—Prognostic equations and cluster analyses. In R.A. Wright & S.B. Heymsfield (Eds.), *Nutritional assessment of the adult hospitalized patient* (pp. 141-155). Boston: Blackwell Scientific Publications.

Frisancho, A.R. (1974). Triceps skinfold and upper arm muscle size norms for assessment of nutritional status. *American Journal of Clinical Nutrition*, **27**, 1052-1058.

Heymsfield, S.B., Bethel, R., & Ansley, J. (1979). Enteral hyperalimentation: An alternative to central venous hyperalimentation. *Annals of Internal Medicine*, **90**, 63-71.

Heymsfield, S.B., & Casper, K. *Anthropometric assessment of the adult hospitalized patient*. Manuscript submitted for publication.

Heymsfield, S.B., Erbland, M., Casper, K., Grossman, G., Roongpisuthipong, C., Hoff, J., & Head, A. (1986). Enteral nutritional support: Metabolic, cardiovascular and pulmonary interrelations. *Chest Clinics of North America*, **7**, 41-67.

Heymsfield, S.B., McManus, C., & Seitz, S. (1984). Anthropometric assessment of adult protein-energy malnutrition. In R.A. Wright & S.B. Heymsfield (Eds.), *Nutritional assessment of the adult hospitalized patient* (pp. 27-82). Boston: Blackwell Scientific Publications, Inc.

Heymsfield, S.B., Smith-Andrews, J.L., & Hersh, T. (1983). Home nasoenteric feeding malabsorption and weight loss refectory to conventional therapy. *Annals of Internal Medicine*, **98**, 168-170.

Heymsfield, S.B., & Williams, P.J. (in press). Nutritional assessment by clinical and biochemical methods. In M.E. Shils & V.R. Young (Eds.), *Modern nutrition in health and disease*. Philadelphia: Lea & Febiger.

Krotkiewski, M., Björntorp, P., Sjöström, L., & Smith, U. (1983). Impact of obesity on metabolism in men and women. *Journal of Clinical Investigation*, **72**, 1150-1162.

Mueller, H.M., & Martorell, R. (1988). Reliability and accuracy of measurement. In T.G. Lohman, A.F. Roche, & R. Martorell (Eds.), *Anthropometric standardization reference manual* (pp. 83-86). Champaign, IL: Human Kinetics.

Mullen, J.L., Buzby, G.P., Waldman, M.T., Gert-
ner, M.H., Hobbs, C.L., & Rosato, E.F. (1979).
Prediction of operative morbidity and mortality by preoperative nutritional assessment.
Surgical Forum, 30, 80–82.

Chapter 18

Topography of Body Fat: Relationship to Risk of Cardiovascular and Other Diseases

Theodore B. Van Itallie

Epidemiologic and clinical studies have disclosed that a number of anthropometrically measurable attributes of the human body can be related to risk of developing metabolic disorders and various illnesses. These attributes include stature, relative weight (i.e., relative to some set of weight standards), muscularity, frame size, various weight/height indices, waist circumference (girth) in relation to chest or hip circumference, skinfold thicknesses at various sites, and the overall pattern of distribution of subcutaneous fat. The relationship of relative weight and of the body mass index (BMI) to morbidity and mortality ratios has been extensively reviewed elsewhere (*Build Study 1979*, 1980; Burton et al., 1985; Hubert et al., 1983; Van Itallie, 1985; Waaler, 1984) and will not be further considered in this survey. Instead, this paper will primarily examine evidence linking skinfold thicknesses at various sites, as well as overall pattern of subcutaneous fat distribution, to the risk of developing cardiovascular and other diseases.

The Framingham Heart Study: Independent Contributions of Various Indices

The fourth biennial examination of the Framingham cohort was conducted on 2,420 women and 1,934 men, aged 34 to 68, between 1954 and 1958. Measurements at that examination included height, weight, circumferences of waist, upper and lower arms and wrists, and thicknesses of subscapular, triceps, abdominal and quadriceps skinfolds (Stokes et al., 1985). The circumference of the hips was not measured. The correlations of these "indices of obesity" with systolic blood pressure (SBP), serum total cholesterol and blood sugar were not high; however, they were all significant because of the large number of observations. In general, the closest association was with SBP. For 22-year coronary heart disease (CHD) incidence, the strongest independent obesity index was that of the subscapular skinfold (SSF) thickness measurement. In men, both SSF and serum total cholesterol contributed more than age to the risk of CHD. In the Framingham Study, obesity did not rank as high for total cardiovascular disease (CVD) as for CHD, suggesting that obesity is a weaker independent risk factor for stroke and other manifestations of CVD than it is for CHD.

SSF predicted 22-year CHD incidence best for women below age 50 and for men aged 50 to 59. Waist circumference and the four skinfold measurements were found to be generally more predictive of CHD for men than for women and for the young than the old. Skinfold measurements of the upper trunk and arms (SSF and triceps skinfold [TSF]) generally predicted CHD better than did those measured at the waist or over the quadriceps.

Subscapular Versus Triceps Skinfolds: Relation to Risk of Hypertension

Blair et al. (1984) used data from the first National Health and Nutrition Examination Survey 1971-74 (NHANES I) to examine the relationship between blood pressure and the distribution of subcutaneous fat in 5,506 survey participants, aged 30 to 59. They employed TSF and SSF as approximations of peripherally and centrally located subcutaneous fat. The effects of race, sex and age on the obesity-blood pressure relationship were analyzed and it was found that SSF was the better predictor of both systolic and diastolic blood pressure in each race-sex group. The amount of variation in blood pressure accounted for by SSF, alone or together with age, was not large. At the most, age and SSF explained 22% of the variance in the SBP of white females.

Overall, the results of this study (Blair et al., 1984) indicate that the blood pressure of middle-aged Americans is more directly associated with centrally than peripherally deposited fat.

Muscle Mass and Body Frame Size: Relation to Body Weight, Fatness and CHD

Data from NHANES I have shown that Americans aged 20 to 74 who are overweight but not obese *or* overweight *and* obese have both a larger body frame size (inferred from elbow breadth) and a larger muscle mass (inferred from arm muscle diameter) than nonoverweight Americans of the same height and within the same age range (Van Itallie & Abraham, 1985). These findings suggest that an increased body frame size may be a risk factor for obesity or that obesity (perhaps the form developing during childhood) somehow favors an increase in frame size.

Earlier authors (Rissanen, 1975; Robinson, 1941) have called attention to the relationship between increased muscularity (found in the mesomorph) and an increased susceptibility to premature coronary heart disease. Robinson and Brucer (1940) examined the relationship of body build to hypertension and concluded that build was a more important predisposing factor than fatness.

Pattern of Subcutaneous Fat Distribution and Risk of Cardiovacular Disease and Death

Abdominal Girth Relative to Circumference of the Expanded Chest.

In 1914, a report was published of mortality among insured lives showing, among other things, the effect on mortality ratio of an abdominal girth greater than that of the expanded chest (Medico-Actuarial Mortality Investigation, 1914). Within this category, four groups were identified in terms of inches of abdominal excess: A. 0-1; B. 1.25-2; C. 2.25-3; D. over 3. A further division was then made of weight groups 0 to 5 representing the percentages of departure from the average weight at age 37.

In some of the weight groups, namely 1, 3 and 5, there was a clear trend in the direction of increasing mortality with increasing excess of girth of abdomen over chest. It was determined that, if weight groups 2 to 5 were combined, the mortality ratios were 105% for girth groups A and B and 109% for groups C and D. Thus, it was concluded that the relative mortality of those with large abdominal girth was greater than the already heavy mortality found to exist among the general body of those of corresponding weight.

Waist-to-Hip Circumference Ratio in Relation to Ischemic Heart Disease and Stroke

Larsson et al. (1984) recently reported the results of a prospective study of risk factors for ischemic heart disease (IHD). The subjects were 792 Swedish men born in 1913 and first examined in 1967. Thirteen years later the baseline anthropometric findings were reviewed in relation to the number of men who had subsequently developed IHD, stroke, or who died from all causes. None of the initial indices of obesity (BMI, sum of three skinfolds thickness measurements, waist or hip-circumference) showed a significant correlation with any of the three end-points under consideration. However, the waist-to-hip circumference ratio (WHR) showed a significant association with the occurrence of stroke ($p = .002$) and IHD ($p = .04$). The risk ratio for the highest vs. lowest quintile for WHR was 1.7 for death, 2.5 for IHD and 5.9 for stroke. A high WHR carried a particularly high risk for stroke, as evidenced by a risk ratio of 11.5 when subjects in the 95th percentile and above were compared with those in the lowest quintile. No strokes occured in men who were at the 10th percentile or below.

In a separate communication, Lapidus et al. (1984) reported on the relation of subcutaneous fat distribution to risk of cardiovascular disease and death of 1,462 Swedish women aged 38 to 60 They found a significant positive association in their subjects between WHR and the 12-year incidence of myocardial infarction, angina pectoris, stroke, and death. Of all the anthropometric variables studied, WHR correlated best with myocardial infarction, angina pectoris, stroke, and death.

Waist-to-Hip Circumference Ratio in Relation to Diabetes, Hypertension, Gallbladder Disease and Menstrual Abnormalities

In 1984, Hartz et al. reported on their evaluation of the distribution of subcutaneous fat as a risk factor for disease, using girth and height and weight measurements in 21,065 women aged 40 to 59 years and 11,791 women 20 to 39 years of age. All of the women were enrolled in TOPS (a national self-help weight reduction organization). They found that the WHR was significantly associated with diabetes, hypertension, and gallbladder disease in women aged 40 to 59, and with menstrual abnormalities in women aged 20 to 39. Relatively, fat around the waist (as compared to hips) was associated with higher disease prevalence, even among women with a comparable total body fat content.

Relation of Body Fat Distribution to Metabolic Complications of Obesity

Kissebah et al. (1982) have reported studies indicating that in women, the sites of fat predominance provide a valuable prognostic marker for glucose intolerance, hyperinsulinemia, and hypertriglyceridemia. Thus, plasma glucose and insulin levels during oral glucose loading were significantly higher in women with predominantly upper body segment (UBS) obesity than in women with lower body segment (LBS) obesity. Of 16 women with UBS obesity, 10 had diabetic glucose tolerance curves; in contrast, none of the women with LBS obesity was diabetic. Fasting plasma triglyceride levels were also significantly higher in women with UBS obesity.

Women with UBS obesity had abdominal subcutaneous adipose tissue consisting of enlarged fat cells (ca. 0.58 nl/cell) while women with LBS obesity showed normal-sized abdominal (ca. 0.28 nl/cell) and thigh adipocytes (ca. 0.30 nl/cell). Abdominal fat cell size correlated significantly with postprandial glucose and insulin levels. Thigh adipocyte volume did not correlate with metabolic complications; moreover, these adipocytes showed reduced lipolysis upon epinephrine stimulation.

Other results obtained by Evans et al. (1984) have disclosed that WHR correlates with insulin resistance. Also, increasing WHR was accompanied by progressively rising fasting plasma insulin levels and, after glucose challenge, by increasing glucose and insulin areas. Obesity level was similarly correlated with these metabolic indices. However, multiple regression analysis revealed that the effects of body fat topography were independent of, and additive to, those of obesity level.

Android and Gynoid Forms of Obesity

In 1947, Vague called attention to the significance for health status of the fact that, in obese men and women, subcutaneous fat distribution is usually quite different. The male (android) type of obesity is characterized by the predominance of obesity in the upper half of the body: nape, neck, cheeks, shoulders and upper half of the abdomen. In contrast, the female (gynoid) form of obesity, most commonly found in women, predominates in the lower half of the body (hips, buttocks, thighs and lower half of the abdomen). As Vague has emphasized, the importance of making a distinction between these two forms of obesity lies in the fact that android obesity, whether it occurs in men or women, is associated with an increased risk of developing diabetes mellitus (noninsulin dependent), atherosclerosis and hyperuricemia. In contrast, gynoid obesity can cause mechanical and psychological problems but does not appear to be associated with metabolic complications. Although android obesity is not uncommon in women and gynoid obesity is not uncommon in men, large-scale population surveys have not been carried out to determine the prevalence of these two types of obesity in both men and women. Data on the distribution of WHRs in 54 year old Swedish men (*n* =792) are shown in Figure 1.

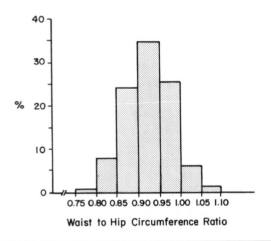

Figure 1 Percentage distribution of waist-to-hip circumference ratios at baseline in 54-year-old men. From "Abdominal Adipose Tissue Distribution, Obesity, and Risk of Cardiovascular Disease and Death" by B. Larsson et al., 1984. Reprinted by permission.

According to Kissebah et al. (1985) men tend to increase waist girth by increasing their intra-abdominal fat depot whereas women preferentially deposit abdominal fat subcutaneously. However, Ashwell et al. (1985) have used computed tomography to demonstrate that women with a high WHR also have a male pattern of intra-abdominal fat location.

Kissebah et al. (1985) have proposed that an imbalance in androgenic/estrogenic activity plays an important role in the localization of fat in the upper and/or lower body (see Figure 2). As indices of androgenic activity they used percentage free testosterone (% FT) in plasma and also sex hormone binding globulin (SHBG), which is extremely sensitive to changes in androgen/estrogen balance. They found that degree of androgenic activity in obese subjects correlated with abdominal but not with thigh adipocyte volume. It was reasoned that an increase in androgen/estrogen activity could result in a redistribution of body fat with enlargement of abdominal adipocytes, and a

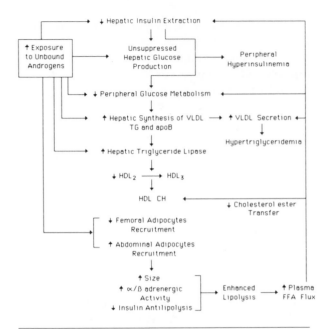

Figure 2 Working hypothesis summarizing possible direct and indirect sites of interaction between the increase in androgenic activity and the metabolic profile in upper body obesity. From *Metabolic Complications of Human Obesities* (p. 31-38) by J. Vague et al., 1985. Reprinted by permission.

decrease in SHBG—a profile like that observed in women with upper body fat predominance.

Discussion and Recommendations

Because great interest has focused on the WHR in recent years it may be helpful to consider briefly how this ration is measured in various studies. The Gothenburg group (Larsson et al., 1984; Lapidus et al., 1984) measured the waist circumference of men to the nearest centimeter at the level of the umbilicus with the subject standing and breathing normally. In women, waist circumference is measured midway between the lower rib margin and the iliac crest. Hip circumference in men is measured to the nearest centimeter at the level of the liliac crest, presumably at the anterior superior iliac spine. In women, hip circumference is measured at the widest point between hip and buttock. The Milwaukee group (Evans et al., 1984) measures "minimal" waist circumference and "maximal" hip girth, also with the subject standing. It would seem that, in very obese subjects, measurement of waist circumference at the umbilicus may be compromised if the abdomen becomes pendulous; also, in such subjects palpation of the iliac crest may be difficult. In the abscence of knowledge about which of the various measurement techniques best predicts metabolic disorder or morbidity risk, it is recommended that the maximum circumference of the buttocks be recorded as representing "hip circumference." The waist circumference should be taken at the "natural waist" (smallest waist circumference). If there is no natural waist, this measurement should be made at the level of the umbilicus.

Table 1, compiled by Kissebah et al. (1985), shows that WHR is as effective in predicting the glucose-insulin profile as more complicated indices such as Vague's brachio-femoral adipo-muscular ratio (B/F AMR) (Vague, 1986).

From the data reported by Larsson et al. (1984) it would appear that the highest risk of developing stroke or IHD occurs in men with a WHR of 0.90 or higher. Kissebah's studies of metabolic disorders in women indicate that a WHR greater than 0.85 is associated with an accelerated increase in insulin resistance (Evans et al., 1984). In the Paris prospective study (Ducimetiere et al., 1985), the risk of stroke and IHD among men increased

steeply when the WHR rose above 1.0 and in women when it rose above 0.8. There was a tendency for mildly obese men with a high WHR to show the highest risk of developing stroke and IHD.

Because the pattern of fat distribution has emerged as an important predictor of the health hazards of obesity, it has become urgent for those interested in anthropometry to evaluate the various methods used to assess body fat topography and to determine which ones are likely to predict risk of illness with the greatest sensitivity and specificity. A number of authors cited in the present review have characterized the ratio of waist-to-hip circumferences (WHR) as being a particularly convenient and specific method for measuring sites of body fat predominance. Accordingly, it is recommended that this ratio be determined whenever an anthropometric examination is undertaken.

The studies examined in this brief review indicate that the TSF and SSF thicknesses are better predictors of ischemic heart disease than skinfold thicknesses measured at the waist or at sites on the lower body segment (Blair et al., 1984). Hence, it is recommended the TSF and SSF thickness measurements be made during anthropometric examinations, regardless of the other skinfold measurements obtained.

Bjorntorp (1985) has pointed out that there are two theories to explain the weak association between obesity and precipitation of IHD.

First, a primary factor both causes obesity and precipitates IHD (or some other illness) as a secondary phenomenon. Second, the association with cardiovascular disease (or other illness) is found only in a subgroup of persons with obesity; this effect would then be diluted in large populations after a long period of observation. (p. 994-995)

Bjorntorp suggests that the second theory is the probable explanation. Future prospective studies will need to obtain a sufficient array of anthropometric measures to ensure that these and other plausible theories can be adequately tested.

Table 1 Correlations of the Metabolic Profile to Measures of Body Fat Localization in Premenopausal Women

Measures of body fat localization	Glucose	Insulin
Waist: Hip Girth Ratio	0.50*	0.53*
Skinfold Thickness:		
Subscapular	0.52*	0.66*
Iliac crest	0.47*	0.32
Biceps	0.16*	0.28
Triceps	0.17	0.33
Medial thigh	0.10	0.12
Lateral thigh	0.10	0.12
Vague's Diabetogenic Fat Mass Index	0.37*	0.48*
Brachial/Femoral Adipose Muscular Ratio (by Cat Scan)	0.46*	0.51*
Intra/Extra–Abdominal Fat Mass Ratio	0.79*	0.81*

*$p < .05$. *Note*. From *Metabolic Complications of Human Obesities* (p.115-130) by J. Vague et al., 1985. Reprinted by permission.

References

Ashwell, M., Cole, T.J., & Dixon, A.K. (1985). Obesity: New insight into the anthropometric classification of fat distribution shown by computed tomography. *British Medical Journal,* **290,** 1692–1694.

Blair, D., Habicht, J.-P., Sims, E.A.H., Sylvester, D., & Abraham, S. (1984). Evidence for an increased risk for hypertension with centrally located body fat and the effect of race and sex on this risk. *American Journal of Epidemiology,* **119,** 526–540.

Bjorntorp, P. (1985). Regional patterns of fat distribution. *Annals of International Medicine,* **103,** 994–995.

Build Study 1979. (1980). Chicago: Society of Actuaries and Association of Life Insurance Medical Directors of America.

Burton, B.T., Foster, W.R., Hirsch, J., & Van Itallie, T.B. (1985). Health implications of obesity: An NIH consensus development conference. *International Journal of Obesity,* **9,** 155–169.

Ducimetiere, P., Richard, J., Cambien, F., Avons, P., & Jacqueson, A. (1985). Relationships between adiposity measurements and the incidence of coronary heart disease in a middle-aged male population—The Paris Prospective Study I. In J. Vague, P. Bjorntorp, B. Guy-Grand, M. Rebuffé-Scrive, & P. Vague (Eds.), *Metabolic complications of human obesities* (pp. 31–38). Amsterdam: Elsevier.

Evans, D.J., Hoffmann, R.G., Kalkoff, R.K., & Kissebah, A.H. (1984). Relationship of body fat topography to insulin sensitivity and metabolic profiles in premenopausal women. *Metabolism,* **33,** 68–75.

Evans, D.J., Murray, R., & Kissebah, A.H. (1984). Relationship between skeletal muscle insulin resistance, insulin-mediated glucose disposal, and insulin binding: Effects of obesity and body fat topography. *Journal of Clinical Investigation,* **74,** 1515–1525.

Hartz, A.J., Rupley, D.C., & Rimm, A.A. (1984). The association of girth measurements with disease in 32,856 women. *American Journal of Epidemiology,* **119,** 71–80.

Hubert, H.B., Feinleib, M., McNamara, P.M., & Castelli, W.P. (1983). Obesity as an independent risk factor for cardiovascular disease: A 26-year follow-up of participants in the Framingham Heart Study. *Circulation,* **67,** 968–977.

Kissebah, A.H., Evans, D.J., Peiris, A., & Wilson, C.R. (1985). Endocrine characteristics in regional obesities: Role of sex steroids. In J. Vague, P. Bjorntorp, B. Guy-Grand, M.,

Rebuffé-Scrive, & P. Vague (Eds.), *Metabolic complications of human obesities* (pp. 115–130). Amsterdam: Elsevier.

Kissebah, A.H., Vydelingum, N., Murray, R., Evans, D.J., Hartz, A.J., Kalkhoff, R.K., & Adams, P.W. (1982). Relation of body fat distribution to metabolic complications of obesity. *Journal of Clinical Endrocrinology and Metabolism,* **54,** 254–260.

Lapidus, L., Bengtsson, C., Larsson, B., Pennert, K., Rybo, E., & Sjostrom, L. (1984). Distribution of adipose tissue and risk of cardiovascular disease and death: A 12-year follow-up of participants in the population study of women in Gothenburg, Sweden. *British Medical Journal,* **289,** 1257–1261.

Larsson, B., Svardsudd, K., Welin, L., Wilhelmsen, L., Bjorntorp, P., & Tibblin, G. (1984). Abdominal adipose tissue distribution, obesity, and risk of cardiovascular disease and death: 13-year follow-up of participants in the study of men born in 1913. *British Medical Journal,* **288,** 1401–1404.

Medico-Actuarial Mortality Investigation, 1914. Vol. IV, Part I (pp. 19–23). New York: The Association of Life Insurance Medical Directors and The Actuarial Society of America.

Rissanen, V. (1975). Coronary and aortic atherosclerosis in relation to body-build factors. *Annals of Clinical Research,* **7,** 402–411.

Robinson, S.C. (1941). Hypertension in relation to height: Its variation with body build and obesity. *Journal of Laboratory and Clinical Medicine,* **26,** 930–49.

Robinson, S.C., & Brucer, M. (1940). Body build and hypertension. *Archives of International Medicine,* **66,** 393–417.

Stokes, J., III, Garrison, R.J., & Kannel, W. B. (1985). The independent contributions of various indices of obesity to the 22-year incidence of coronary heart disease. In J. Vague, P. Bjorntorp, B. Guy-Grand, M. Rebuffé-Scrive, & P. Vague (Eds.), *Metabolic complications of human obesities* (pp. 49–57). Amsterdam: Elsevier.

Vague, J. (1947). La differenciation sexuelle, facteur determinant des formes de l'obesite [The sexual difference, determinant factor of the forms of obesity]. *Presse Med,* **55,** 339–340.

Vague, J. (1956). The degree of masculine differentiation of obesities: A factor determining predisposition to diabetes, antherosclerosis, gout and uric calculus disease. *American Journal of Clinical Nutrition,* **4,** 20–34.

Vague, J., Bjorntorp, P., Guy-Grand, B., Rebuffé-Serive, M., & Vague, P. (Eds.) (1985). *Metabolic Complications of Human Obesities*. Amsterdam: Elsevier.

Van Itallie, T.B. (1985). Health implications of overweight and obesity in the United States. *Annals of Internal Medicine*, **103**, 983–988.

Van Itallie, T.B., & Abraham, S. (1985). Some hazards of obesity and its treatment. In J. Hirsch & T.B. Van Itallie (Eds.), *Recent advances in obesity research IV* (pp. 1-19). London: John Libbey.

Waaler, H.T. (1984). Height, weight and mortality: The Norwegian experience. *Acta Medica Scandinavica* (Suppl. 679), 1-56.

Chapter 19

Cancer

Marc S. Micozzi

While death rates from coronary heart disease and stroke decrease, cancer remains an important public health priority. In order to have a positive effect on prevention of cancer and facilitate survival of cancer patients, cancer research has expanded into new areas directly related to aspects of human biology, such as human diet and nutrition. Diet is now considered to be a major risk factor for cancer, accounting for 35% (with a possible range of 10 to 70%) of attributable risk in human populations (Doll & Peto, 1981).

The potential of anthropometry in cancer research lies in its application as an indirect means of nutritional assessment, including early nutritional assessment. Given the difficulties associated with other means of dietary assessment and validation (Block, 1982), anthropometry may add a useful dimension to investigation of the relations between diet and cancer.

Epidemiologic Evidence on Diet and Cancer

Human epidemiologic and animal experimental evidence has suggested that excess intake of macronutrients (fat, protein, total calories) and relative deficiencies of certain micronutrients (carotenoids, selenium) may be associated with increased incidence and decreased survival of some site-specific cancers in different populations. The overall pattern of scientific evidence, including studies on migrants (Buell & Dunn, 1965) has further suggested that dietary patterns in early life may be important to the long-term risk of cancer (Miller, 1977).

Because cancer is currently thought to be a multistage process with a long latent period, early nutritional patterns that influence childhood growth and development may also influence the adult risk of cancer. Theoretically, enduring indicators of growth that can be measured in adults (e.g., stature, sitting height, frame size, lean body mass) may be reflective of early nutritional patterns that place individuals at increased risk of cancer. Anthropometric variables that may also be related to adult nutritional patterns (e.g., total body fat, percentage of body fat) are also associated with the risk of certain cancers in defined groups (Miller et al., 1978).

Given that growth is partially a function of dietary intake (Johnston, 1981), cross-cultural correlations among different populations between cancer rates (adjusted for differences in longevity) and various anthropometric measurements at different points during childhood may provide additional information about the impact of diet, especially overnutrition, on cancer. There are significant associations between cancer mortality rates and mean age-specific stature, weight, biacromial diameter, and other anthropometric dimensions (Micozzi, 1986a, 1986b).

Different anthropometric dimensions may integrate indices of linear growth, frame size, and lean body mass with indices of body fat. Childhood nutritional patterns may be reflected in any or all of these indices in adults (Garn et al., 1982; Himes & Roche, 1986; Roche, 1984). Additional information may be obtained by comparing the correlations of different age-specific anthropometric measurements in childhood with adult cancer rates such as for prostatic and pancreatic cancer rates in males (two prominent glandular cancers). Cross-national correlations among age-specific weight, arm, and chest circumferences in childhood (which indicate frame size and lean body mass, together with body fatness) are significantly greater than for triceps skinfold thickness (which indicates fatness). The same relationships hold true for pancreatic and ovarian cancer as for breast cancer in women (Micozzi, 1985, 1986b). Therefore, the discrimination of cancer risk by various anthropometric indicators of growth will vary with the specific dimensions measured.

Like most techniques of nutritional assessment used in cancer epidemiology, anthropometry is indirect. No single measurement (at the present time) can be taken as truly representative of total nutritional experience over a lifetime, the dimensions of the entire body, or overall cancer risk.

Criteria for the Selection of Anthropometric Techniques

The selection of anthropometric sites and techniques can be optimized to produce relevant data of acceptable quality for testing explicit diet and cancer hypotheses within the constraints of cancer epidemiology. Several factors enter into the appropriate selection of different anthropometric dimensions for cancer epidemiology studies in general, whether prospective or retrospective. The anthropometric technique should be justified by both theoretical and applied concerns. It should allow prediction of a parameter that is theoretically relevant to hypothesized relations among nutrition, body size, and cancer. Thus, anthropometric

data collected to test a specific hypothesis will be more appropriate and useful than data collected in surveys.

The anthropometric technique must generally be applied in a field or clinical situation, taking into consideration (a) the *accessibility* of the measurement site, (b) its *correlation* with other body dimensions, (c) its *comparability* to dimensions measured in other studies, and (d) its *reliability*. These considerations are summarized for selected skinfold measurements in Table 1. In case-control studies of cancer, the side of measurement should always be the side that is not involved by disease, due to the possible pathophysiologic effects of disease, surgery, and treatment.

Both the reliability and the biologic meaning of anthropometric dimensions should be assessed. Height and weight can generally be measured reliably (Abdel-Malek et al., 1985, Roche, 1984) but may have less biologic meaning or utility for a given analysis than do other more specific anthropometric dimensions that are generally, however, measured less reliably. The accuracy of skinfold measurements may be a particular problem. For example, in estimation of body fatness in the U.S. National Health and Nutrition Examination Surveys I and II, the arm circumference measurement is more highly correlated than the triceps skinfold measurement with measures of excess weight. This observation may result not because arm circumference is more biologically meaningful than triceps skinfold, but because it is more reliable (Micozzi et al., 1986). Adequate training and equipment can maximize the reliability and biologic utility of anthropometric dimensions measured in cancer epidemiology studies.

Table 1   Applied Considerations for Selection of Skinfold Measurements in Cancer Epidemiologic Studies

Skinfold site	Accessibility[a]	Correlation	Usage
Triceps	Excellent	Upper extremity fatness	Popular
Subscapular	Reasonable	Upper trunk	Popular
Midaxillary	Reasonable	Upper trunk	Less common
Suprailiac	Difficult	Pelvic fat	Common
Medial Calf	Somewhat difficult	Lower body	Less common

[a]Accessibility code—Excellent: minimal undressing, relatively brief time required for measurement, minimal technical difficulty, and/or minimal discomfort for observer or subject; Difficult: maximum undressing, relatively long time required for measurement, relatively difficult technically, and/or uncomfortable for observer or subject.

Sample Size

Anthropometry has considerable advantages for application to epidemiologic research where sample size is large. Epidemiologic analyses must be obtained on a large sample size in order to adequately test hypotheses about diet and cancer (Wynder & Bross, 1961), generally due to constraints on the degree of dietary variability observable within human populations and the small relative risks associated with dietary factors.

Standards of Practice

Different standards of practice may be applied to the uses of anthropometry in cancer research, as opposed to human growth studies. In longitudinal growth studies, *changes* in anthropometric measurements are the unit of study, and the required level of measurement precision is high. In cancer epidemiology, cross-sectional data on large populations are collected in the field under conditions that result in large random errors. For this reason, researchers often opt to divide the range into categories (e.g., quantiles) to at least identify extreme groups, which are the ones of greatest interest to epidemiologists anyway.

Due to the interest in groups at extremes of the distribution, the equipment, techniques, equations, and body mass indices must be carefully selected and their appropriateness for these sub-populations established. Thus, as recommended in other contexts (Abdel-Malek et al., 1985; Roche, 1984), standardization of all indirect techniques against a more direct technique should be carried out in a representative sample of the study population.

Conclusion

Anthropometry is an important method for biomedical research, which may be used to test current hypotheses on the relation between human diet and cancer, identify individuals and populations at increased risk of cancer, and help answer questions about the adaptiveness of growth and body size in humans. As the relations between nutrition and anthropometric dimensions become better understood, there will be increasing applications for anthropometry in the explicit statement and testing of hypotheses on the associations between nutrition and cancer.

References

Abdel-Malek, A.K., Mukherjee, D., & Roche, A.F. (1985). A method of construction a method of obesity. *Human Biology,* **57** 415-430.

Block, G. (1982). A review of validations of dietary assessment methods. *American Journal of Epidemiology,* **115,** 492–505.

Buell, P., & Dunn, J. (1965). Cancer mortality of Japanese Isei and Nisei of California. *Cancer,* **18,** 656–664.

Doll, R., & Peto, R. (1981). The causes of cancer: Quantitative estimates of avoidable risks of cancer in the United States today. *Journal of the National Cancer Institute,* **66,** 1191–1308.

Garn, S.M., Ryan, A.S., & Higgins, M.W. (1982). Implications of fatness and leanness. *American Journal of Physical Anthropology,* **57,** 191.

Himes, J.H., & Roche, A.F. (1986). Subcutaneous fatness and stature: Relationship from infancy to adulthood. *Human Biology,* **58,** 737-750.

Johnston, F.E. (1981). Physical growth and development and nutritional status: Epidemiological considerations. *Federation Proceedings,* **40,** 2583–2587.

Micozzi, M.S. (1986a). *Childhood nutrition, growth, and development: Relation to the long-term risk of breast cancer in human populations.* Unpublished doctoral dissertation, University of Pennsylvania, Philadelphia.

Micozzi, M.S. (1986b). Cross-national correlations of food consumption, childhood growth, and cancer rates. *American Journal of Physical Anthropology,* **69,** 240 (abstract).

Micozzi, M.S. (in press). Cross-cultural correlations of childhood growth patterns and adult breast cancer. *American Journal of Physical Anthropology.*

Micozzi, M.S., Albanes, D., Jones, D.Y., & Chumlea, W.C. (1986). Correlations of body mass indices with weight, stature, and body composition in men and women in NHANES I and II. *American Journal of Clinical Nutrition,* **44,** 725-731.

Micozzi, M.S., & Schatzkin, A.G. (1985). International correlation of anthropometric variables and adolescent growth patterns with breast cancer incidence. *American Journal of Physical Anthropology,* **66,** 206-207 (abstract).

Miller, A.B. (1977). Role of nutrition in the etiology of breast cancer. *Cancer,* **39**, 2704–2708.

Miller, A.B., Kelly, A., Choi, N.W., Matthews, V., Morgan, R.W., Munan, L., Burch, J.D., Feather, J., Howe, G.R., & Jain, M. (1978). A study of diet and breast cancer. *American Journal of Epidemiology,* **107**, 499-509.

Roche, A.F. (1984). Anthropometric methods: New and old, what they tell us. *International Journal of Obesity,* **8**, 509–523.

Wynder, E.L., & Bross, I.I. (1961). A study of etiological factors in cancer of the esophagus. *Cancer,* **14**, 389–413.

Chapter 20

Sports Medicine

Jack H. Wilmore

Sports medicine has evolved over the past half century primarily from the disciplines of medicine, physical education, and physiology. Presently, according to the American College of Sports Medicine, sports medicine includes more than 40 medical and nonmedical specialties, including the areas of exercise physiology, biomechanics, cardiovascular and pulmonary rehabilitation, orthopedics, podiatry, athletic training, physical therapy, and physical fitness. Consequently, the uses of anthropometric measurements in the field of sports medicine have been quite diverse and varied. This brief review will focus on how anthropometry has been used in the various areas of sports medicine in the past and how it might be of value in the future.

Body Composition

One of the most important aspects of preparing an athlete for competition is the establishment of an optimal weight for peak performance. There is little question that performance in various motor and sport skills is highly correlated with lean body mass and relative body fat (Boileau & Lohman, 1977). For most sports, a high lean body mass and a low relative body fat is considered optimal for maximizing performance. For those sports where a high lean body mass is not an advantage, for examply, distance running, there is a clear advantage to maintaining a low relative body fat (Wilmore, 1983).

Body physique assessments of athletes were made by means of anthropometry and somatotyping as early as the 1920s (Carter, 1982). The concept of body composition assessment in sports

medicine dates back to the original study of Welham and Behnke in 1942 when they determined the body density of members of the Washington Redskins professional football team. This study clearly differentiated between the terms overweight and overfat, that is, obesity. Seventeen of 25 players were at a weight that would have been considered unfit for military service and above that necessary to qualify for first-class life insurance. However, body density values demonstrated that only two of these athletes were above 20% body fat. Furthermore, 19 of these 25 athletes were below 14% body fat. Values ranging from 6 to 18 % body fat are considered acceptable in football by today's standards, dependent upon the player's position (Wilmore, 1983).

Body composition is most accurately determined by laboratory techniques, including hydrostatic weighing, dilution techniques for determining total body water, Potassium-40 radiography, inert gas dilution, and total body electrical conductivity. However, bringing subjects into the laboratory is not always practical. Consequently, field methods for assessing body composition are often used. Numerous equations have been derived for estimating body density, body volume, lean body weight, fat weight, and relative fat from one or more anthropometric measurement sites, using skinfolds, breadths, girths, or a combination of these three. Although arguments have been made for the use of population-specific equations for athletes in each of the various sports, the more recent generalized equations of Jackson and Pollock (1978) and Jackson et al. (1980) appear to provide reasonable estimates of the body composition of athletes in specific sports (Sinning & Wilson, 1984; Sinning et al., 1985).

Performance

The establishment of an optimal weight for athletes to maximize their performance potential is important. In the past, the major emphasis was on establishing minimal weights to which athletes were requested or required to reduce. For a number of reasons, too often athletes were assigned weights that were well below a physiological optimum. Consequently, there is growing concern for athletes who become too lean and develop eating and/or weight disorders such as bulimia and anorexia nervosa. As a result, it is imperative that many athletes be provided with an upper and lower optimal weight range recognizing both individual differences and methodological error in the assessment of body composition. It must be recognized that once weight drops below a certain critical level, which will be different for each individual, performance and health will be comprised. Secondary amenorrhea is a possible consequence of low body weight and body fat (Shangold, 1985), and secondary amenorrhea in distance runners has been closely linked to serious bone mineral disturbances (Drinkwater et al., 1984). Thus, it would seem important to establish a certain minimal weight for selected athletes below which an athlete would not be allowed to train or compete. Of particular concern are jockeys, wrestlers, runners, gymnasts, ballet dancers, and female athletes in general who have a preoccupation with low body weight. The potential use of anthropometry in the establishment of minimal weights should be investigated.

At the other extreme, there is probably a maximal weight that athletes need to consider. In contrast to minimal weight, maximal weight would be the greatest weight an athlete could attain without hindering performance or health. In such sports as football and basketball size does impart a significant advantage to the athlete, and weight gains are often prescribed. Thus, it would be important to maximize lean weight gains and minimize gains in body fat. What is the maximal amount of lean weight that an athlete can attain without the use of drugs? This important question has not been answered, or even adequately addressed, by researchers. It is quite possible that the ability to gain lean weight is related to the skeletal frame size of the individual; thus anthopometry may be an important key to estimating the potential for lean weight gains.

Much of the discussion to this point has focused on the use of anthropometry in the assessment of body composition, optimal weight, minimal weight, and maximal weight. Anthropometric measurements as ends in themselves have considerable use in the general field of sports medicine. Height, as one example, is a particularly important guide to the placement of basketball players into specific positions, whether by self-selection or by dictate of the coach.

Biomechanics

Segment lengths and/or limb lengths have been demonstrated to greatly affect the performance of the athlete. The length of the arm and forearm dictate the ultimate mechanical advantage to be gained by these levers and the associated muscles, thus affecting the force and speed of movement and the speed of objects propelled by these lever systems (Atwater, 1979). In running, stride length and stride rate are the determinants of running velocity, and leg length has been demonstrated to be directly and proportionally related to stride length, although this relationship is not perfect (Williams, 1985). Anthropometric measurements have also been used in the prediction of segmental moments of inertia (Hinrichs, 1985), as well as mass and density properties of various body segments and the body as a whole (Winter, 1979).

Body Physique and Proportionality

As mentioned above, determination of the body type or physique of athletes dates back to the early 1930s. Although the use of the classic Sheldon system for somatotyping served well in the initial studies of athletes, the complexity of this system led investigators to use simplified techniques that determined somatotype on the basis of anthropometric measurements. The most widely used of the more recent somatotype techniques is that of Heath and Carter introduced in 1967 (Carter, 1982). The Heath-Carter technique uses height, weight, skinfolds (triceps, subscapular, suprailiac, and medial calf), girths (flexed biceps and calf), and breadths (elbow and knee, or humerus and femur). The determination of one's somatotypes is relatively simple, as is illustrated in Figure 1. The somatotypes of athletes in numerous sports have been obtained over the years, including a large data base from Olympic athletes assessed at each

HEATH-CARTER SOMATOTYPE RATING FORM

NAME _____   AGE _____   SEX: M F   NO: _____

OCCUPATION _____   ETHNIC GROUP _____   DATE _____

PROJECT: _____   MEASURED BY: _____

TOTAL SKINFOLDS (mm)

Skinfolds (mm):
Triceps =
Subscapular =
Supraliac =
TOTAL SKINFOLDS = ☐
Calf =

	½	1	1½	2	2½	3	3½	4	4½	5	5½	6	6½	7	7½	8	8½	9	9½	10	10½	11	11½	12
Upper Limit	10.9	14.9	18.9	22.9	26.9	31.2	35.8	40.7	46.2	52.2	58.7	65.7	73.2	81.2	89.7	98.9	108.9	119.7	131.2	143.7	157.2	171.9	187.9	204.0
Mid-point	9.0	13.0	17.0	21.0	25.0	29.0	33.5	38.0	43.5	49.0	55.5	62.0	69.5	77.0	85.5	94.0	104.0	114.0	125.5	137.0	150.5	164.0	180.0	196.0
Lower Limit	7.0	11.0	15.0	19.0	23.0	27.0	31.3	35.9	40.8	46.3	52.3	58.8	65.8	73.3	81.3	89.8	99.0	109.0	119.8	131.3	143.6	157.3	172.0	188.0
FIRST COMPONENT	½	1	1½	2	2½	3	3½	4	4½	5	5½	6	6½	7	7½	8	8½	9	9½	10	10½	11	11½	12

Height (in.) = ☐	55.0	56.5	58.0	59.5	61.0	62.5	64.0	65.5	67.0	68.5	70.0	71.5	73.0	74.5	76.0	77.5	79.0	80.5	82.0	83.5	85.0	86.5	88.0	89.5
Bone: Humerus (cm) = ☐	5.19	5.34	5.49	5.64	5.78	5.93	6.07	6.22	6.37	6.51	6.65	6.80	6.95	7.09	7.24	7.38	7.53	7.67	7.82	7.97	8.11	8.25	8.40	8.55
Femur (cm) = ☐	7.41	7.62	7.83	8.04	8.24	8.45	8.66	8.87	9.08	9.28	9.49	9.70	9.91	10.12	10.33	10.53	10.74	10.95	11.16	11.37	11.58	11.79	12.00	12.21
Muscle: Biceps (cm) -(triceps skinfold) = ☐	23.7	24.4	25.0	25.7	26.3	27.0	27.7	28.3	29.0	29.7	30.3	31.0	31.6	32.2	33.0	33.6	34.3	35.0	35.6	36.3	37.1	37.8	38.5	39.3
Calf -(calf skinfold) = ☐	27.7	28.5	29.3	30.1	30.8	31.6	32.4	33.2	33.9	34.7	35.5	36.3	37.1	37.8	38.6	39.4	40.2	41.0	41.8	42.6	43.4	44.2	45.0	45.8
SECOND COMPONENT	½	1	1½	2	2½	3	3½	4	4½	5	5½	6	6½	7	7½	8	8½	9						

		½	1	1½	2	2½	3	3½	4	4½	5	5½	6	6½	7	7½	8	8½	9
Weight (lb.) = ☐	Upper limit	11.99	12.32	12.53	12.74	12.95	13.15	13.36	13.56	13.77	13.98	14.19	14.39	14.59	14.80	15.01	15.22	15.42	15.63
Ht./∛Wt. = ☐	and Mid-point	12.16	12.43	12.64	12.85	13.05	13.26	13.46	13.67	13.88	14.01	14.29	14.50	14.70	14.91	15.12	15.33	15.53
	below Lower limit	12.00	12.33	12.54	12.75	12.96	13.16	13.37	13.59	13.78	13.99	14.20	14.40	14.60	14.81	15.02	15.23	15.43
THIRD COMPONENT	½	1	1½	2	2½	3	3½	4	4½	5	5½	6	6½	7	7½	8	8½	9

	FIRST COMPONENT	SECOND COMPONENT	THIRD COMPONENT
Anthropometric Somatotype			
Anthropometric plus Photoscopic Somatotype			

BY: _____

RATER: _____

Figure 1. The Heath-Carter somatotyping form.

of the Olympiads from 1960 to the present. The data obtained to date demonstrate that athletes within a given sport, position, or event cluster within a relatively small area when plotted on a somatochart (Carter, 1982).

Body proportionality is another area that has received considerable interest within the field of sports medicine. The somatogram, developed by Behnke (Behnke & Wilmore, 1974), is illustrated in Figure 2. The purpose of the somatogram is to provide a visual appraisal of the symmetry of an individual with respect to a reference group. In Figure 2, the somatogram of a weight lifter is presented, illustrating rather substantial deviation from group symmetry for the chest, biceps, and forearm girths. Behnke and Wilmore (1974) have

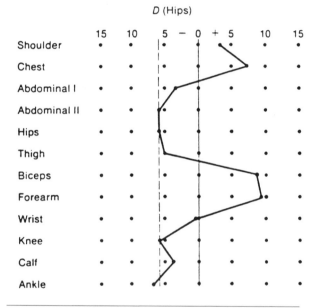

CIRCUMFERENCE   PERCENTAGE DEVIATION FROM D

Figure 2   Somatogram of a weight lifter.

proposed the estimation of "excess muscle" on the basis of extrapolations from the somatogram, a concept that could have considerable practical application. The somatogram has not been widely used, but the potential applications are considerable. Furthermore, it is possible to plot right and left sides for symmetry. This would be particularly useful when tracking injured athletes during their rehabilitation.

Research

Considerable research in the field of sports medicine has used anthropometry. For example,

changes in muscle girth with strength training have been used as noninvasive indices of muscle hypertrophy. Pre- and posttraining measurements of skinfold thicknesses have been used to estimate changes in body composition with general training, and the efficacy of "spot reduction" with specific types of training. In a recent research report, anthropometric dimensions were obtained from photographs to determine alterations in breast morphology consequent to an exercise program that purportedly was designed to increase breast size by a considerable amount (Wilmore et al., 1985). A similar study used a series of girth and skinfold measurements to evaluate the claims of two exercise devices (Wilmore et al., 1985). Slim-Skins, a pair of plastic pants that attach to a vacuum cleaner, according to the manufacturer, result in losses of 13 to 15 inches from the waist, abdomen, hips, and thighs following 3 days of use during an 8- to 10- min exercise period and a 15-min recovery period. The second device, the Astro-Trimmer, a rubber-surfaced belt placed around the waist, claimed similar results from short-term use. Precise anthropometric measurements taken immediately before and after each of the above interventions failed to support the claims of the manufacturers.

Standardization Anthropometric Measurement Test Battery

Because the field of sports medicine is so broad and far-reaching, it is difficult, if not impossible, to project a standardized anthropometric measurement test battery that would be appropriate for all purposes. It appears that any test battery would have to be devised individually according to the purpose for taking the measurements. In fact, it may be necessary under certain conditions to use measurement sites that have not been appropriately standardized due to the unique nature of the study. The measurements taken from the breast photographs mentioned earlier illustrate this point. Standardized measurement sites were not available, and new sites had to be selected, measurement procedures standardized, and reproducibility investigated. For most purposes, however, the measurement sites that have been standardized in this publication will be adequate. In the future it may be possible to establish a sport-specific standardized test battery for use with a given sport, or a more generalized battery that could be used by almost all sports.

References

Atwater, A.E. (1979). Biomechanics of overarm throwing movements and of throwing injuries. *Exercise and Sport Science Review, 7,* 43–85.

Behnke, A.R., & Wilmore, J.H. (1974). *Evaluation and regulation of body build and composition.* Englewood Cliffs, NJ: Prentice-Hall.

Boileau, R.A., & Lohman, T.G. (1977). The measurement of human physique and its effect on physical performance. *Orthopedic Clinics North America, 8,* 563–581.

Carter, J.E.L. (Ed.). (1982). *Physical structure of Olympic athletes: Part I. Medicine and sport* (Vol. 16). New York: S. Karger.

Drinkwater, B.L., Nilson, K., Chestnut, C.H., III, Bremner, W.J., Shainholtz, S., & Southworth, M.B. (1984). Bone mineral content of amenorreic and eumenorrheic athletes. *New England Journal of Medicine, 311,* 277–281.

Hinrichs, R.N. (1985). Regression equations to predict segmental moments of inertia from anthropometric measurements: An extension of the data of Chandler et al. *Journal of Biomechanics, 18,* 621–624.

Jackson, A.S., & Pollock, M.L. (1978). Generalized equations for predicting body density of men. *British Journal of Nutrition, 40,* 497–504.

Jackson, A.S., Pollock, M.L., & Ward, A. (1980). Generalized equations for predicting body density of women. *Medicine and Science in Sports and Exercise, 12,* 175–182.

Shangold, M.M. (1985). Causes, evaluation, and management of athletic oligo-/amenorrhea. *Medical Clinics of North America, 69,* 83–95.

Sinning, W.E., Dolny, D.G., Little, K.D., Cunningham, L.N., Racaniello, A., Siconolfi, S.F., & Sholes, J.L. (1985). Validity of "generalized" equations for body composition analysis in male athletes. *Medicine and Science in Sports and Exercise, 17,* 124–130.

Sinning, W.E, & Wilson, J.R. (1984). Validity of "generalized" equations for body composition analysis in women athletes. *Research Quarterly for Exercise and Sport, 55,* 153–160.

Welham, W.C., & Behnke, A.R., Jr. (1942). The specific gravity of healthy men. *JAMA, 118,* 498–501.

Williams, K. (1985). Biomechanics of running. *Exercise and Sport Science Review, 13,* 389–441.

Wilmore, J.H. (1983). Body composition in sport and exercise: Directions for future research. *Medicine and Science in Sport and Exercise, 15,* 21–31.

Wilmore, J.H., Atwater, A.E., Mazwell, B.D., Wilmore, D.L., Constable, S.H., & Buono, M.J. (1985). Alterations in breast morphology consequent to a 21-day bust developer program. *Medicine and Science in Sport and Exercise, 17,* 106–112.

Wilmore, J.H., Atwater, A.E., Mazwell, B.D., Wilmore, D.L., Constable, S.H., & Buono, M.J. (1985). Alterations in body size and composition consequent to Astro-Trimmer and Slim-Skins training programs. *Research Quarterly and for Exercise and Sport, 56,* 90–92.

Winter, D.A. (1979). *Biomechanics of human motion.* New York: Wiley.

Appendix A

List of Equipment and Suppliers

Equipment

Stadiometers, Scales, Miscellaneous

Holtain, Ltd.
Pfister Import-Export, Inc.

Harpenden Stadiometer
Portable
Pocket
Raven Equipment, Ltd.
Stanley-Mabo, Ltd.
CMS Weighing Equipment, Ltd.

Holtain Electronic Stadiometer
Holtain, Ltd.

Blueprints for the production of stadiometers
Center for Disease Control

Anthropometers

Harpenden Anthropometer
Pfister Import-Export, Inc.
Holtain, Ltd.

GPM (Martin type) Anthropometer
Pfister Import-Export, Inc.
Owl Instruments, Inc.

Recumbent Length/Sitting Height Measurement Equipment

Infant Heightometer
Hultafors AB
Infanitometer Instrumentation Corporation

Baby Length Measurer
Appropriate Health Resources and Technologies
Action Group (AHRTAC)

Harpenden Sitting Height Table
Harpenden Neonatometer

Harpenden Infantometer
Holtain Electronic Infantometer
Harpenden Supine Measuring Table
Holtain, Ltd.

Weighing Scales

Designs for making scales locally
Hesperian Foundation
AHRTAC
Continental Scale Corporation
CMS Weighing Equipment, Ltd.
Detecto Scales, Inc.
Salter International Measurement, Ltd.
Marsden Weighing Machine Group, Ltd.

Dial scales for field work
CMS Weighing Equipment, Ltd.
(Model 235-PBW)
Salter International Measurement, Ltd.
(Model 235)
John Chatillon and Sons
Rasmussen, Webb & Company

Electronic Scales:
Toledo scale
Infant Scale: "Baby weight"
Model 1365
Children/Adult Scales: "Weight plate"
a. Pediatric 12" x 12" plate, 150 lb. capacity
Model 2300
b. Adult 18" x 18" plate, 300 lb. capacity
Model 2300

Calipers

Sliding Calipers (Large)
Mediform sliding caliper (80 mm)

Sliding Calipers (Small)
Sliding Caliper (Martin Type)

Sliding Caliper (Holtain, 14 cm)
Sliding Caliper (Poech Type)
  Pfister Import-Export, Inc.

Spreading Calipers
Spreading Caliper (Martin Type) 0–300 mm
Spreading Caliper (Martin Type) 0–600 mm
  Pfister Import-Export, Inc.

Anthropometric Tapes

Disposable paper tape for newly-born infants
  Medline Industries

Retractable, Fiberglass Measuring Tape
  Buffalo Medical Specialties
  (available through local distributors)
  e.g. Burlingame Surgical Supply Co.

Retractable, Flexible Steel Tape
  Keuffel and Esser Co. (200 cm No. 860358)
  (available through local distributors)
  e.g. San Diego Blueprint

Scoville-Dritz Fiberglass Measuring Tape
  (available through local distributors)
  e.g. Quinton Instruments

Inser-Tape, Ross Insertion Tape
  Ross Laboratories

Linen Measuring Tape
  Pfister Import-Export, Inc.

Gulick Measuring Tape
  Country Technology, Inc.

Anthropometric Tape Measure (150 cm No. 67022)
  Country Technology, Inc.

Skinfold Calipers

Harpenden Skinfold Calipers
  H.E. Morse Co.
  British Indicators, Ltd.

Lange Skinfold Calipers
  Cambridge Scientific Industries
  Pfister Import-Export, Inc.
  J.A. Preston Corp.
  Owl Industries, Ltd.

Lafayette Skinfold Calipers
  Lafayette Instrument Co.

Slim Guide Skinfold Caliper
  Creative Health Products
  Rosscraft, Ltd.
  Country Technology, Inc.

Skyndex Electronic Body Fat Calculator—
  System I and II
  Cramer Products
  Human Performance Systems, Inc.

Fat-O-Meter Skinfold Caliper
  Health & Education Services
  Miller & Sons Assoc., Inc.

Fat Control Caliper
  Fat Control, Inc.

Adipometer Skinfold Caliper
  Ross Laboratories

McGaw Skinfold Caliper
  McGaw Laboratories

Holtain/Tanner/Whitehouse Skinfold Caliper
  and Holtain Slim-Kit Caliper
  Holtain, Ltd.
  Pfister Import-Export, Inc.

Miscellaneous by Supplier

Pfister Import-Export, Inc.
  Harpenden Vernier Caliper
  Survey Set—contains: Anthropometer, Skinfold
    Caliper, 2 Steel Tapes, Somatotype Turntable,
    Manual
  Base Plate for Anthropometer
  Curved Cross Bars
  Small Instrument Bag (Martin Type) contains:
    Sliding Caliper, Spreading Caliper, Steel
    Measuring Tape
  Large Instrument Bag (Martin Type) contains:
    Anthropometer, Recurved Measuring
    Branches, Sliding Caliper, Spreading
    Caliper, Steel Measuring Tape

Addresses of Suppliers

AHRTAC
85 Marlebone High Street
London, W1M 3DE, UK

British Indicators, Ltd.
Sutton Road
St. Albans, Herts., UK

Burlingame Surgical Supply Co.
1515 4th Avenue
San Diego, CA 92101
Phone: (619) 231-0187

Cambridge Scientific Industries
P.O. Box 265
Cambridge, MD 21613
Phone: (800) 638-9566
      (301) 228-5111

Center for Disease Control
Division of Nutrition
1600 Clifton Road
Atlanta, GA 30333

CMS Weighing Equipment, Ltd.
18 Camden High Street
London, NWI OJH, UK

Continental Scale Corporation
7400 West 100th Place
Bridgeview, IL 60455
Phone: (312) 598-9100

Country Technology, Inc.
P.O. Box 87
Gays Mills, WI 54631
Phone: (608) 735-4718

Cramer Products
P.O. Box 1001
Gardner, KS 66030
Phone: (913) 884-7511

Creative Health Products
5148 Saddle Ridge Road
Plymouth, MI 48170
Phone: (313) 453-5309
      (313) 455-0177

Detecto Scales, Inc.
Detecto International
103-00 Foster Avenue
Brooklyn, NY 11236

Fat Control, Inc.
P.O. Box 10117
Towson, MD 21204

H.E. Morse Co.
455 Douglas Avenue
Holland, MI 49423
Phone (616) 396-4604

Health & Education Services
Division of Novel Products
80 Fairbanks, Unit 12
Addison, IL 60101
Phone: (312) 628-1787

Hesperian Foundation
P.O. Box 1692
Palo Alto, CA 94302

Holtain, Ltd.
Crosswell, Crymmych, Dyfed
Wales

Hultafors AB
S-517 01 Bollebygd
Sweden

Human Performance Systems, Inc.
P.O. Drawer 1324
Fayetteville, AR 72701
Phone: (501) 521-3180

Infanitometer Instrumentation Corporation
Elimeankatv-22-24
SF-00510
Helsinki, No. 51
Finland

J.A. Preston Corp.
71 Fifth Avenue
New York, NY 10003

John Chatillon and Sons
83-30 Kew Gardens Road
Kew Gardens, NY 11415

Lafayette Instrument Co.
P.O. Box 5729
Lafayette, IN 47903
Phone: (317) 423-1505

McGaw Laboratories
Division of American Hospital Supply
Irvine, CA 92714

Marsden Weighing Machine Group, Ltd.
388 Harrow Road
London WG-2HV, UK

Mediform sliding caliper
5150 S.W. Griffith Drive
Beaverton, OR 97005
Phone: (800) 633-3676
      (503) 643-1670

Medline Industries
1825 Shermer Road
Northbrook, IL 60062
Phone: (800) 323-5886

Miller & Sons Assoc., Inc.
New Rochelle, NY 10801

Owl Industries, Ltd.
177 Idema Road
Markham, Ontario L3R 1A9
Canada

Pfister Import-Export, Inc.
450 Barell Avenue
Carlstadt, NJ 07072
Phone: (201) 939-4606

Quinton Instruments
2121 Terry Avenue
Seattle, WA 98121
Phone: (800) 426-0538
      (206) 223-7373

Rasmussen, Webb & Company
First Floor
12116 Laystall Street
London ECIR-4UB, UK

Raven Equipment, Ltd.
Little Easton
Dunmow, Essex, CM6 2ES, UK

Ross Laboratories
625 Cleveland Avenue
Columbus, OH 43216

Rosscraft, Ltd.
14732 16-A Avenue
Surrey, B.C. V4A 5M7
Canada
Phone: (604) 531-5049

Salter International Measurement, Ltd.
George Street
West Bromwich, Staffs, UK

San Diego Blueprint
4696 Ruffner Road
San Diego, CA 92111
Phone: (619) 565-4696

Toledo Scale
431 Ohio Pike
Suite 302, Way Cross Office Park
Toledo, OH
Phone: (513) 528-2300

Appendix B

Contributors' Mailing Addresses

Claude Bouchard, PhD
  Physical Activity Sciences Laboratory
  PEPS, Laval University
  Ste. Foy, Quebec City
  Canada, G1K 7P4

George A. Bray, MD
  Section of Diabetes and Clinical Nutrition
  University of Southern California
  2025 Zonal Avenue
  Los Angeles, CA 90033

Elsworth Buskirk, PhD
  Laboratory of Human Performance
  Penn State University
  119 Noll Lab
  University Park, PA 16802

C. Wayne Callaway, MD
  Director, Center for Clinical Nutrition
  George Washington University Medical Center
  2150 Penn Avenue N
  Washington, DC 20037

J.E. Lindsay Carter, PhD
  Department of Physical Education
  San Diego State University
  San Diego, CA 92182

William Cameron Chumlea, PhD
  Division of Human Biology
  Wright State University
  1005 Xenia Avenue
  Yellow Springs, OH 45387-1693

Roberto A. Frisancho, PhD
  Center for Human Growth and Development
  University of Michigan
  1111 East Catherine Street
  Ann Arbor, MI 48109

Claire Gordon, PhD
  Life Support Systems Division
  U.S. Army Natick Research and Development
    Center
  Natick, MA 01760

David S. Gray, MD
  Section of Diabetes and Clinical Nutrition
  University of Southern California
  2025 Zonal Avenue
  Los Angeles, CA 90033

Gail G. Harrison, PhD
  Department of Family and Community
    Medicine
  University of Arizona
  Tucson, AZ 85721

Keith C. Hendy, PhD
  DCIEM
  P.O. Box 2000
  Downsview, Ontario
  Canada, M3M 3BG

Steven B. Heymsfield, MD
  Department of Medicine
  St. Luke's Roosevelt Hospital Center
  Amsterdam Avenue & 114th Street
  New York, NY 10025

John H. Himes, PhD, MPH
  School of Public Health
  University of Minnesota
  Box 197, Mayo Memorial Building
  420 Delaware Street SE
  Minneapolis, MN 55455

Francis E. Johnston, PhD
  Department of Anthropology
  University of Pennsylvania
  33rd and Spruce Street
  Philadelphia, PA 19104

Timothy G. Lohman, PhD
Department of Exercise and Sport Sciences
University of Arizona
Ina E. Gittings Building
Tucson, AZ 85721

Robert M. Malina, PhD
Department of Anthropology
University of Texas
Austin, TX 78712-1086

Alan D. Martin, PhD
Medical Imaging Department
University Hospital
University of Saskatchewan
Saskatoon, Canada S7N 0X0

Reynaldo Martorell, PhD
Food Research Institute
Stanford University
Stanford, CA 94305

Fernando Mendoza, MD, MPH
Children's Hospital at Stanford
520 Willow Road
Palo Alto, CA 94304

Marc S. Micozzi, MD, PhD
Associate Director
Armed Forces Institute of Pathology
Walter Reid Medical Center
6825 16th Street NW
Washington, DC 20307

Carol D. Mitchell, PhD, RD
Department of Home Economics
Douglass/Cook Campus
Rutgers University
New Brunswick, NJ 08503

William H. Mueller, PhD
School of Public Health
University of Texas
P.O. Box 20186
Houston, TX 77225

Ivan G. Pawson, PhD
Koret Center for Human Nutrition
Room 4101
San Francisco General Hospital
1001 Potrero Avenue
San Francisco, CA 94110

Michael L. Pollock, PhD
College of Medicine Box J-277
Division of Cardiology and Physiology
University of Florida
Gainesville, FL 32610

Alex F. Roche, MD
School of Medicine
Wright State University
1004 Xenia Avenue
Yellow Springs, OH 45387-1695

Vernon D. Seefeldt, PhD
Department of Physical Education
Room 213, I.M. Sports Circle
Michigan State University
East Lansing, MI 48824

Jack H. Wilmore, PhD
Department of Physical and Health Education
222 Bellmont Hall
University of Texas at Austin
Austin, TX 78712

Theodore B. Van Itallie, MD
Department of Medicine
St. Luke's Roosevelt Hospital Center
Amsterdam Avenue & 114th Street
New York, NY 10025

Author Index

Subject Index

GN
51
A627 WITHDRAWN
1988 From Library Collection

103202

DATE DUE

WITHDRAWN
From Library Collection

Ireton Library
Marymount University
Arlington, VA 22207